Traders at Work

How the World's Most Successful Traders Make Their Living in the Markets

Tim Bourquin

Nicholas Mango

Traders at Work: How the World's Most Successful Traders Make Their Living in the Markets

Copyright © 2013 by Tim Bourquin and Nicholas Mango

ISBN-13 (pbk): 978-1-4302-4443-1

ISBN-13 (electronic): 978-1-4302-4444-8

President and Publisher: Paul Manning
Lead Editor: Morgan Ertel
Editorial Board: Steve Anglin, Mark Beckner, Ewan Buckingham, Gary Cornell,
    Louise Corrigan, Morgan Ertel, Jonathan Gennick, Jonathan Hassell,
    Robert Hutchinson, Michelle Lowman, James Markham, Matthew Moodie,
    Jeff Olson, Jeffrey Pepper, Douglas Pundick, Ben Renow-Clarke, Dominic
    Shakeshaft, Gwenan Spearing, Matt Wade, Tom Welsh
Coordinating Editor: Rita Fernando
Copy Editor: Kim Burton-Weisman
Compositor: SPi Global
Indexer: SPi Global
Cover Designer: Anna Ishchenko

Distributed to the book trade worldwide by Springer Science+Business Media New York, 233 Spring Street, 6th Floor, New York, NY 10013. Phone 1-800-SPRINGER, fax (201) 348-4505, e-mail orders-ny@springer-sbm.com, or visit www.springeronline.com. Apress Media, LLC is a California LLC and the sole member (owner) is Springer Science + Business Media Finance Inc (SSBM Finance Inc). SSBM Finance Inc is a Delaware corporation.

For information on translations, please e-mail rights@apress.com, or visit www.apress.com.

Apress and friends of ED books may be purchased in bulk for academic, corporate, or promotional use. eBook versions and licenses are also available for most titles. For more information, reference our Special Bulk Sales–eBook Licensing web page at www.apress.com/bulk-sales.

Any source code or other supplementary materials referenced by the author in this text is available to readers at www.apress.com. For detailed information about how to locate your book's source code, go to www.apress.com/source-code/.

For Courtney. You're my dream baby.

—Tim Bourquin

For Mom and Dad. You always believed,
even if I didn't. Love always.

—Nicholas Mango

Contents

Foreword

They were heady days, the late 1990s; the bull market was roaring, and everyone wanted to quit their day jobs to become day traders. Anyone could do it, and it seemed the easy way to riches. Why work when you can trade? Little did they realize, however, that trading was a business—and a tough business at that. Tim Bourquin knew the realities of trading and wanted to help, so he and his partner, Jim Sugarman, founded the Online Trading Expo (now Traders Expo). The Expo is a place where traders can come together, exchange ideas, meet vendors and suppliers, uncover new tools and techniques, and learn and improve their craft.

It has been a long time since those days of bull market glory. The S&P 500 has barely changed from its peak value in 1998, even though 14 years have passed. The entire idea of buy and hold has been discredited, leaving a generation of investors looking for the 10 percent annual gains they were supposedly "entitled" to bitterly disappointed. For more than a decade, it has been crystal clear that trading is not an impossibility or a luxury; it is a necessity if you want to make money in the financial markets. The whole buy-and-hold concept was a joke to begin with. There simply is no free lunch. Investing and trading are work—hard work that pays well.

Tim and co-author Nick have access to a lot of traders, including some of the very best, and this book contains the collected experience of a group of traders they both have come to know over the years. There are a lot of ideas here for the curious mind to explore, and a resource like this book can prove to be invaluable if you discover but a single idea that helps improve your process. Some of the ideas presented may seem contradictory, which is as it should be, for there is no single way to trade. The process is different for each trader, and each trader must find his or her own way.

As you might expect, I am often asked how to trade with Bollinger Bands. I usually reply with examples, some from my own process, some from the trading processes of others, some that I use, and some that I know to be valuable, even though I may not be using them. Why the diversity? Because it is hard to know what will click with any given investor or trader. Sometimes the "students" know more than the "teacher." In fact, the feedback I get from Bollinger Band users is often as valuable as—and occasionally better than—the advice. The reason for this is clear: others have thought about things that I haven't, which is the reason I read books like this.

One thing you can always be sure of is that no matter how specifically or clearly a given approach is taught, the person who receives it will take it home, mull it over, and modify it to suit his or her needs. That means that if one were to teach a trading approach to 100 traders, the result would likely be more than 100 different approaches traded by less than 100 different traders, not a single approach traded by 100 traders. Why more than 100 approaches? Because many variations will be tried. Why less than 100 traders? Because, as the old saw suggests, you can lead a horse to water, but you can't make it drink.

My experience suggests that the final results will be more consistent when the advice given is less specific. This is because there are general solutions to many trading problems that simply work well, and very general advice will cause traders to home in on those solutions, whereas very specific advice will cause traders to seek variation. Another reflection of that phenomenon is that, over the years, my team and I have developed many web sites for traders and investors. Often the sections of the sites that I think are most interesting and useful—"The Edge" on www.BBands.com, for example—are not the sections that our users are interested in. Indeed, our users often find ways of utilizing the sites that we had not expected or even thought of.

Therein lies the answer to one of those questions that comes up again and again: If one discloses a profitable trading method, won't it be quickly arbitraged out of existence? There are actually two answers to that seemingly simple question. First, if the method, tool, or approach draws its strength from a basic and fundamental market mechanism, it will likely prove to be durable until the market itself morphs. Second, if what is taught is a data-mined artifact from a specific market or time, it will not last; it will fail, and it will do so most likely sooner, rather than later. Therein lies a lesson: simple approaches that rely on basic market mechanisms, like volatility or mean reversion, are more likely to be useful and robust than their complex, often curve-fitted brethren.

So, what is a trader to do? First, be true to yourself. Stay within your comfort zone, and only push the envelope very gradually. Second, study the history of technical analysis. The old masters were very knowledgeable, and you can learn a great deal from a close reading of market history. Third, study a little math; not a lot, just some algebra and very basic statistics. You're going to be working with numbers, so get friendly with them. Fourth, learn a little bit of programming; Python is a good place to start. Most trading platforms today allow you to customize their functionality with very high-level languages that are easy to use. A little bit of programming knowledge can make your life as a trader much easier. Fifth, be disciplined. Sixth, pay a lot of attention to position sizing. Seventh, leverage is not your friend. Finally, make it fun. You will most likely be doing it a lot, so it had better feel good.

To sum it up: Trade with discipline, not too much, and mostly with technical analysis.

—John Bollinger, CFA, CMT
www.BollingerBands.com

About the Authors

Tim Bourquin is the co-founder of both the Online Trading Expo (now Traders Expo) and the Forex Trading Expo. While a police officer with the Los Angeles Police Department, Bourquin was trading the stock and currency markets by morning and arresting criminals by night. When he went looking for a convention for traders to learn more about how other traders were approaching the markets, he couldn't find one. So, in 1999, along with a business partner, Bourquin started an annual convention and tradeshow for online traders and investors. Those events, which are held each year in New York, Las Vegas, and Los Angeles, continue to be the premier conventions for active retail traders.

After speaking with countless traders throughout the past 14 years, Bourquin realized that the best way to learn how to make money trading was to ask those who were already doing it every day. Bourquin set out to find the best in the business and ask them exactly how they made their money. Some people talked to him and others refused, but through persistence, he slowly was able to interview hundreds of traders about the strategies they employ, the software they use, and how they became confident in the markets. In 2006, Bourquin founded TraderInterviews.com, an online media site featuring those frank discussions.

Nicholas Mango is a freelance writer and editor whose work in the active trading community spans more than seven years and numerous web portals and major media outlets. As a former Division I collegiate athlete, Mango experienced firsthand the need to continually learn and develop skills, the pressure to consistently perform at a high level, and the many highs and lows encountered along the way. While working his first Traders Expo in 2006, it became clear that traders endure a similar journey while facing an adversary that is equally alluring and potentially even more unforgiving: the financial markets.

There began a strong commitment to helping traders find clarity and the answers that could form the basis for long-lasting and prosperous careers in the markets. Mango has since worked with hundreds of professional traders and industry experts to publish their most reliable, clearly stated, and actionable methods and strategies for trading a variety of markets and time frames.

Acknowledgments

I wish to thank all of the interviewees in the following chapters who graciously and patiently allowed me to ask both "dumb" and complicated questions about how they make their living in the markets. Your willingness to talk about your craft will undoubtedly help thousands of struggling traders who are trying to find their edge. Thanks to Morgan Ertel from Apress, whose patience, encouragement, and motivational nudging brought this book to press when it looked like it would never be finished. And finally, I want to thank my co-author, Nicholas Mango, who took on the difficult task of turning rough transcripts into polished sentences. The only reason you are holding this book in your hand today is because Nick said, "Sure, sounds like fun!" Thank you, my friend.

—Tim Bourquin

For me, this book represents the realization of a lifelong dream, and I owe sincere gratitude to all who made it possible, starting with each of the traders, whose open, fearless participation produced timeless insights that we hope will entertain, inspire, and educate all who read them. Thanks to the team at Apress, including Morgan Ertel and Rita Fernando, for your patience, persistence, and enthusiasm throughout all stages of this project. Also, thanks to my loving and supportive parents, my grandfather, and all my friends. May this book finally quell your suspicions that I sit around and play on the computer all day, every day! Finally, my most heartfelt thanks to my friend and co-author, Tim Bourquin, whose passion for education and devoted leadership has not just shaped my career; it has touched my life.

—Nicholas Mango

Todd Gordon

Todd Gordon *is a founding partner and director of research and trading at Aspen Trading Group, as well as a principal in the money management company Floyd, Gordon & Partners. Formerly, he served a dual role as the senior technical strategist at FOREX.com as well as senior trader for GAIN Capital Asset Management, the parent company of FOREX.com.*

Gordon was one of six traders at GAIN Capital Asset Management responsible for trading capital in excess of $10 million. He is a regular contributor on the CNBC shows Fast Money *and* Money in Motion *and he has provided his expert analysis of the global market on Bloomberg, BNN (Business News Network), and Dow Jones Online, among others.*

While attending St. Lawrence University in upstate New York, Gordon competed on their Division I alpine ski team, racing against future Olympians, and he continues to enjoy hitting the slopes in the winter. He lives by the mantra "plan your trade, trade your plan."

Tim Bourquin: I heard trading was your first job right out of college. Where did you go to school?

Todd Gordon: I went to St. Lawrence University in upstate New York for my first two years. I was an economics major and business minor and at that point, I hadn't quite found my passion. My focus in college was downhill ski racing. St. Lawrence was a Division I ski school, so I fought to make the team and got to rub elbows with some future Olympians who were also on the team. Honestly, in college I was almost entirely focused on improving my slalom turn and that was about it. So after racing there for two years, I told myself it was time to focus on work and what I wanted to do as a career. I could see that my living wasn't going to be made on the ski slopes. So I switched from St. Lawrence to Albany State and finished my degree there. I didn't give up competitive skiing entirely, though. Albany State had a Division 3 ski team, so

I continued to race, but I began to focus more on my business and economics degrees. It was during those last two years that I began to seriously consider a career as a trader.

Bourquin: Did you know much about what it took to have a career as a trader at that time? Did you think you might work on Wall Street?

Gordon: I had an E-Trade account all the way through St. Lawrence and then my next two years at Albany, and it was more of just a hobby, day trading stocks just as the term "day trading" began appearing in the news. Back then, I was just throwing darts at a wall with my trades. I followed a chat room back then by a guy named "Tokyo Joe." He was the biggest sensation and had thousands of traders in his chat room every day while the market was open. He'd put up a stock pick and everyone would just go buy it without really knowing why. It was a crazy time.

Bourquin: Didn't he get indicted or something?

Gordon: Yeah, he wound up being a crook when his whole scheme was uncovered, but he would pump stocks in his chat room and everyone would go chase the stocks. Turns out he had bought those stocks a few days before and would literally start selling minutes after he recommended that everyone in the chat room buy the stock. His stock picks, and the number of members he had who would act on them, could really move the market quickly. I remember one trade I made was in the symbol GEEK. I think it was Internet America, and I think I made $10 per share in like 10 minutes.

Of course, there were a ton of other trades that went badly and I was stopped out all the time. I certainly loved the game of trading, but ultimately I knew that following a chat room blindly without any understanding of what's going on or why I was making certain trading decisions wasn't sustainable over the long run. You may make money here and there if you're lucky, but constructing your own strategy based on objective measures is the only way to make trading a full-time gig.

So that's when I began my quest to really learn how to trade on my own without having to rely on some chat room host to spit out buy and sell recommendations. One of the first books I read in college was Alexander Elder's *Trading for a Living* [Wiley, 1993]. I knew I wanted to trade for a living, so I figured that was the perfect book to start with! It was the first time I learned about reading charts and technical analysis, and all of a sudden I was learning how to draw a simple trend line on a chart. I began drawing trend lines all over and that's when I started to formulate some kind of plan about which stocks I was going to buy or sell. Those simple trend lines were the beginning of an objective way to look at the market and understand where good trades might be entered.

The funny thing was, while I was learning about economics, which I thought back then was going to be essentially useless in the trading world, I was starting to understand how to do basic technical analysis and applied it to every stock I was considering. When I saw how stocks behaved and bounced off these trend lines as support and resistance, that's when I got bitten by the trading bug completely, and I just knew it was what I wanted to do as a career.

It turned out my economics degree wasn't totally useless. I actually think it helps me understand the markets in a deeper way, especially now that I trade the currency markets. That broad understanding of how world economies work has been important to my success.

Bourquin: What kind of software and tools were you using back then?

Gordon: It's funny, because I can't even imagine trying to trade on that same system today. I was day trading with a web-based account and an E-Trade account very early on in that company's life. The interface and tools are nothing like they are today. I think I had five grand in the account. I was day trading on a ridiculously slow dial-up internet connection. But the competitor in me really got into it, and I was determined to be good at it, regardless of the crappy tools I was using. I remember I was on AOL dial-up, and it was way back at the time when you had to pay per minute because it was a long distance call for me to be on the internet. I was nineteen and at home—just hanging out at my parents' house. My mom came to me with this huge phone bill and she almost killed me. I was on the internet around eight hours a day while the stock market was open. There were a few phone bills that were a thousand dollars each, and needless to say, my Mom was pissed.

Bourquin: Yeah, I'll bet. When you were placing trades on a dial-up connection, you clicked the Buy button, and you let the thing spin for a few seconds. I remember those days, and it was like a minute and a half before you got a confirmation, right?

Gordon: I don't even remember. It must have been, but back then it didn't even occur to me that I wasn't getting the best price. I didn't have any knowledge of execution practices by the market makers and the games they would play. The spreads were huge and the slippage was terrible. You'd get crushed if you put in a market order because the price you'd get was nowhere near what you thought it was going to be. The software crashed all the time. You'd get disconnected from the dial-up connection. It was a mess. Back then, I thought that was just part of the game. I had to start somewhere. And I suppose that if you could make money in that trading environment, you could make money anywhere.

Bourquin: Yeah, absolutely. If you didn't go through that, you probably wouldn't be the trader you are today. So even bad experiences, I think, somehow add to your education as a trader. When you graduated from college, did you get a job as a trader right away?

Gordon: I went right to work looking for trading jobs. I found a company on Monster.com based in San Diego. I was just about to take my last finals during my senior year, and I called the number in the job listing. The guy who answered the phone wound up being my current business partner, Dave Floyd.

I talked to him on the phone, and I said, "I'm really interested in trading. I'm just out of college and I'll graduate here in a little bit." He told me they had open positions for traders, but of course, he needed to interview me. He was in San Diego and I was in upstate New York right before finals week. I wasn't sure how I was going to make it happen, but I knew this was an opportunity I shouldn't pass up. Who else was going to even consider hiring a trader right out of college whose only experience was a chat room, a few books on how to trade, and an E-Trade account? So I said, "Let me call you back." About a half-hour later, I called him back and I told him I would be there on Tuesday.

I flew out ahead of my tests and met him, interviewed, and immediately flew back home to take my finals. A few days later, he called me back and said I had the job if I moved to San Diego. I had a lot of family in San Diego at the time, and moving from the winters of upstate New York to the sunny beaches of San Diego was an easy decision. I had the opportunity to work as a trader and live in paradise. What more could I ask for? I lived in Pacific Beach, and it was a great move. I learned the ropes of trading from Dave in those first few months out of college.

Bourquin: Do you remember what he was looking for in a trader? Was he looking for certain qualities or a specific type of person? What do you think he saw in you?

Gordon: It's funny because most traders know that academic record does not always translate into success as a trader. Sometimes, people who have overly impressive academic records wind up being terrible traders because, basically, they're not used to being wrong. Trading is not like engineering or mathematics, where you have a formula and when you plug in the data, the answer is either right or wrong. As a trader, you need to be very okay with being wrong in the markets. Confidence and ego can ruin a trader who is determined they are "right" and the market will move in their direction. There is a saying all veteran traders know well: "The market can stay irrational longer than you can stay solvent." It is absolutely true. There is no right answer in trading, and you are constantly making decisions based on incomplete information. Some people have a very hard time with that.

So, my first boss and current business partner actually looked at my ski racing background and understood that I had come from a competitive background. He said to himself, "This guy's tough and did well in an independent sport." There's a lot of responsibility and self-discipline that goes along with ski racing, because it's you against the course—not really the other team. So, I think he saw the competitive spirit in me and almost everyone in this business knows it is an important quality when you make your living in the markets. He also knew that I came out to the interview right before my finals, which he said showed commitment to the job and to learning what it took to do well.

Bourquin: I love sports analogies as they relate to trading, Baseball is my favorite sport and I see correlations to trading all the time. In skiing, the thing that comes to the top of my mind is that you're always looking down the hill at the next turn and anticipating what it will take to get past that next flag without falling. Is there any connection there with skiing that you think helped you become successful trader?

Gordon: Yes, absolutely. It's actually one of the stock stories that I love to tell in my speeches at the Traders Expos and other conferences because it's so wildly applicable. If you turn on the Olympics during a ski race, you see the guys jamming down the hill at fifty miles an hour, but what you don't see is all the preparation that goes into the race ahead of time. There's actually a period of time called "course inspection." What they do is go to the top of the course and sideslip down the actual course they will be racing on later that day.

What you're doing is taking mental notes and developing a strategy to account for the different types of terrain on the course. You're looking at where the sun is hitting the snow, which is going to create inconsistent snow conditions. Or maybe there's a certain area that's shaded from the sun, so it's going to be very hard and icy. And maybe there's some rough terrain at a certain point on the course. You're taking into account all these known factors that will impact the course of your race, so you can build them into your game plan.

Preparation in ski racing is key because when you're doing forty or fifty miles an hour down the hill, you're not going to have time to think about these things before reacting. This needs to be built into your game plan before you even start the race. Inevitably, there will be unknown variables that pop up that you couldn't see ahead of time, so you need to be free while you're acting on your game plan to encounter those factors, and adapt and work through them on the fly.

Trading is really the same thing, especially the way I trade. I look at the market from all angles, and I'm constantly on the lookout for anything that could pop up during the course of my trade. If possible, I incorporate those factors into my trading plan before I actually place the trade. The fewer surprises, the better, and I know that, for me personally, I'm going to react much more objectively while I'm in a trade if I've already got a written game plan. Because inevitably, there will be things that pop up in the course of the race—or the trade—and you'll need to have your full attention to focus and make quick adjustments. So skiing and trading are unbelievably close in terms of preparation and execution during the course of your trade or a race.

Bourquin: I always hear very good professional traders say that they are confident making decisions without 100 percent of the information. They don't know everything there is to know, and yet they're still able to make a confident decision in the markets. Is that something you agree with?

Gordon: I think Paul Tudor Jones said it best when he said that some of the best trades are the hardest ones to put on. I think that means there needs to be a leap of faith. I'm not talking about blindly putting on a position without doing your research. But there's a point where you have gathered and assimilated as much information as you possibly can. You're never going to know everything. If you insist on knowing everything before you execute the trade, you're going to constantly have "paralysis by analysis." That's counterintuitive.

As human beings, we all believe that you can never have too much information. More information should equal better decisions, and that's true to a point, but you need to be able to make that decision to buy or sell knowing that you don't know what the outcome will be. So there needs to be a leap of faith. You can have the probability stacked in your favor, but there's inevitably a gut feel part that has to come into play.

There's an instinct that can be developed over time by watching the markets enough. You can get 80 percent of the way there by studying the markets and learning as much as you can about the behavior of a particular stock or option. Then 10 percent will be gut feel that you develop as your experience as a trader grows. The final 10 percent is that information that you just don't know. You have to be okay with that final 10 percent and still make good decisions without it.

Having all the information is not going to allow you to execute the best trade. At some point, you need to just feel when the market is going to make a move. I don't think you can quantify that. The best traders are not the ones that are the best researchers. If that were the case, scientists who are great at studying data would probably be clobbering us all. In the real world of trading, you gather the information you can and then you make a decision.

Bourquin: What markets were you trading when you first started?

Gordon: We were trading stocks at my first company, mostly NYSE-listed stocks—big companies. I'm a big advocate of getting to know the personality of a market, getting a feel for the market you trade so that you can begin to anticipate reactions to news and demand. One of the advantages of trading NYSE stocks was you were typically dealing with just one specialist. There's obviously one guy making the big "prints" and price moves on the New York Stock Exchange floor. You'd get to know his personality and the way he would handle his bid-ask spread and prints.

We knew the behavior of a couple of specialists so well that we'd always play games in the office and talk about what we thought the guy looked like, what we'd say to him if we were to go out for a drink with him after work. We could actually feel if one specialist was calmer than another during times of heavy trading. These days, with everything going electronic, you don't get that same feedback. But I still believe that with enough experience, you can begin to anticipate moves in whatever market you are trading just from watching how it moves day-in and day-out.

We'd also listen to audio from the S&P 500 futures pit. Even though we weren't trading futures, often times we could hear the noise in the pits increasing just a few moments before trading sped up on NYSE stocks. So, we would listen to Ben Lichtenstein, who does TradersAudio.com still to this day, and this was maybe ten years ago. He would call where the S&P futures were going and who was actively buying and selling. He would say, "There's paper in the pit," or "Paper buys," and announce where the prints were on the S&P futures. He'd announce when institutional sellers were starting to come into the market, and so forth. All the while, you could hear the low roar of the pit traders in the background, and it would get louder and faster when things were speeding up.

What would happen is when the S&P futures start to move, obviously the big listed stocks that make up the Dow Jones Industrial Average would follow very closely behind to catch up to the S&P futures. So, we would hear if there was big movement in the pit, and we would almost immediately see that translate over to movement in the stocks. The S&P floor noise and information would give us a slight edge as to where the big stocks would go. If we heard movement in the pit, and a buyer stepped in and pushed the price higher, we would jump in and get a buy order in on the New York Stock Exchange, and then watch how the specialists would handle the incoming order flow. We would then scalp in and out for ten cents or fifteen cents and do that twenty, thirty times a day.

Bourquin: Is the S&P futures pit still a viable leading indicator for short-term traders?

Gordon: Yes, to a certain extent, but not in the same way it was back then. I think the markets are a lot more complex and more efficient now. The spreads are much tighter on stocks because of penny pricing, whereas it used to be in fractions. The pit noise in the S&P futures can still be valuable to a trader in order to get a feel for the panic buying or selling, but it happens much faster now. Plus, now you've got algorithmic, high-frequency trading to contend with, which has changed things quite a bit. We were operating within seconds to take advantage of that delay, but that delay is gone, for the most part. The edge we had in those days—where we could get in and get out quickly because the futures market was moving ahead of it—is gone.

We could see the writing on the wall and decided it was time to move into the foreign exchange markets and trade currency. It's "adapt or die" in trading, and if you aren't able to change or tweak your trading methods as times change, you'll eventually stop making money. Nothing works forever.

Also, when I think of trading, it's a lifestyle business. To trade short-term all day—banging out thirty to fifty trades back and forth every day, trying to scalp a nickel or dime every time—after a while, you'll get burned out on that style. There's a lot of energy that's required to operate at that level, so from a trading lifestyle point of view, I knew eventually I would have to make a change. That frenetic pace every day can really start to wear you down.

Bourquin: Most day traders, when you talk about the early days of day trading, they started out on SOES [Small Order Execution System] and NASDAQ stocks. But you started out trading NYSE stocks. Why?

Gordon: The "SOES bandit" style of trading was popular a few years before I got into the markets. Dave Floyd did a lot of NASDAQ trading in the office in San Diego before I was hired. He was very active in the NASDAQ. I think Dave would tell you, his office had a couple of days where their volume alone represented more than 5 or 10 percent of the volume traded on the QQQs. So, in the late nineties, they were doing a ton of volume on that NASDAQ ETF. But then, I think after the internet bubble burst and all those tech stocks tanked, they started to go to New York Stock Exchange stocks because they realized they had a few-seconds edge by watching those S&P futures and getting to know the behavior of the specialists.

It goes back to the fact that with NASDAQ stocks, you're dealing with tons of market makers and ECNs who are providing liquidity. Whereas with the NYSE stocks, there's one guy running the book, which is the specialist, and there was an edge to be exploited there because, for a while anyway, it was less efficient.

Bourquin: Were you using any technical analysis when you were doing that, or was it just, "Listen to the pits and then go jump in front of it" on the NYSE?

Gordon: I was using charts, but it was very basic technical analysis. On my screens, I would have a one-minute and five-minute chart of the S&P futures, and a one-minute and five-minute chart of whatever stock I was trading at the time. On those charts, we would have Stochastics, Bollinger bands, and maybe a couple of moving averages.

The way we used moving averages was this: we knew the twenty-period moving average on both the fifteen-minute and sixty-minute charts was important to the market and that other traders were watching that price level. There always seemed to be a lot of volume around that area. But we were trading on the five-minute chart, so we wanted to monitor that level on our shorter-term charts. Doing a bit of math, we realized the 240-period moving average on a five-minute chart showed us the equivalent of a twenty-period moving average of a sixty-minute chart; those same levels but on our short-term charts.

Ultimately, we wanted to see the twenty-period moving average on multiple time frames. That's where there'd be a lot of volume. So, we looked at the moving average to know where volume would be or orders would accumulate, but then we looked at the stochastics to just confirm that the market was pulling back. When the stochastics began to turn up, we'd jump on board and scalp an upside trade.

Bourquin: Do you remember what your average share size was for a position back then?

Gordon: I started really small. When I first started trading, they started us with a limit of one hundred to two hundred shares. Once you could prove you could make money and be disciplined at that size, you would get bumped up to five hundred shares, and then one thousand shares, and then two years down the line I was calling our risk management bosses up in San Francisco, trying to get my limit upped to two thousand shares. Eventually I pushed it up to five thousand and then up to ten thousand shares. So, I would carry five thousand and ten thousand share positions for just a few minutes. In order to really make money scalping, you had to be trading that kind of size.

Bourquin: How did your salary look back then? Did you have some sort of base or draw plus a portion of your profits?

Gordon: There was no salary or draw. It was all based on what you made in profit. Back then, the deal was you'd earn 50 percent of what you made, and the firm kept the other 50 percent. And then, of course, you had to pay taxes. I was making a living, but only trading five hundred shares that first year. It was hard to make a living, especially living in San Diego. So, I lived very modestly for those first couple years. I think I ate about four to five meals a week at In-N-Out Burger, which I never grew tired of. Now that I live in New Jersey, I miss In-N-Out Burger! But I definitely paid my dues. Any new trader who thinks they are going to sit down at a computer and make big money right away as a trader is probably going to be disappointed. But it was worth living lean those first few years to learn how to trade.

Bourquin: You mentioned your transition to Forex at some point. What was it about your NYSE trading strategy that changed and made you decide to look elsewhere?

Gordon: It was perhaps 2003. I vividly remember the last big day we had trading on that style. It was right around the time they arrested Bernie Ebbers from WorldCom. I remember we came in the next day and the S&P futures were down maybe fifteen points—and this was when the S&P was around 850. As a percentage, that was a big move. The volatility was tremendous. I remember that the other traders in the office and I just killed it. We made the most money we ever made in one day, scalping back and forth. Dave and I actually finished with profits within a couple of hundred dollars of each other at the end of the day. That was just about the low in the market.

So, to answer your question, when the market started coming back from that, I think it was the 2003 low, the volatility just died. The style of scalping we were doing at that time really relied on a lot of volatility. Without the constant movement each day, making money as a scalper is extremely difficult. The market rallied from there, but the S&P went from trading twenty or thirty handles [index points] per day down to maybe eight. When we have no intraday volatility, that's when things really started to get lean for us in terms of trading opportunities, and Dave actually started trading the currency markets. So, he got me into it at that point and we just started trading the FX markets.

I really enjoyed trading with that office, but I wanted to expand my experiences a bit, so I went up to Los Angeles to work for Larry Connors at TradingMarkets.com and write about the currency markets. But Dave and I continued to stay in contact, and I continued to trade the Forex markets in my own account.

Bourquin: Let's talk about your next move to FOREX.com. Did you land there as a trader, or were you doing something else there first?

Gordon: I had been on the West Coast for a good three years, and I felt like heading home. You forget how bad those winters are after you're gone for a while, so I was ready to come back East. I was first hired to come in and write their Learn to Trade Forex courses. There wasn't a tremendous amount of information about Forex trading back then, so I set out to put together a strong intro course on how to trade currencies. So, originally, I was not hired as a trader.

I came on board and developed their first currency trading course. I was also doing some institutional sales, helping set up their big Introducing Broker [IB] relationships and communicating with money managers about bringing some of their money to FOREX.com. It was during that time that I really learned the business side of the spot Forex market and how the Forex brokers worked.

After a while, I started writing a daily report called "Strategy of the Day" for clients. Actually, at the time it was just for internal salespeople, so that they could get clear and straightforward analysis of the markets with charts to have something to talk about with their clients. Every day I would point out several things to watch on various currency pairs and offer some commentary along with the technical analysis. Basically, it was simply what I personally was watching in the markets in my own account. It served two purposes. First, by writing down my thoughts on the market, it really helped me to solidify my strategies in my own mind. Second, it helped to educate the sales team so that they could speak intelligently about the currency markets when pitching ideas.

I did that for probably six months or so, and then Mark Galant, the CEO at the time, started reading it. He thought it was well done and decided that he wanted to make it a research piece that would go out on the trading platform to every account holder. From there, "Strategy of the Day" for clients was born. I think that was in 2005. That strategy report really helped formulate my ideas, and I started to build quite a following from that research.

From there, I continued to trade my own personal account. I was not trading in our asset management program yet [trading firm money], but I was working very hard to show I could trade well consistently and get to that point.

I wrote an e-mail to my boss at the time, Glen Stevens. I had a unique idea as a way to get into that side of the business. I asked if I traded my personal account for three months and was profitable three months in a row, could I get a shot to trade on the hedge fund team? At that point, it was like a $100 million hedge fund. He gave that challenge the OK and agreed it was a good way to prove my trading ability. So, I worked hard to make profitable trades, was profitable three months in a row, and earned a seat on the fund. I think I was the youngest guy on the trading team of the hedge fund at the time.

Bourquin: Going from stocks, especially NYSE stocks, to spot Forex is a huge jump. What kind of things were you trying early on in that transition to get a feel for how to trade that market?

Gordon: That's a great question, because you can't scalp FX just because of something a specialist or market maker is doing. There's no central market-place for the spot Forex market, so I only know a few guys who can success-fully scalp, and then only for short periods of time. It has always been a much more technically-based market. When I was at TradingMarkets.com and during my time at FOREX.com, I was really studying a lot of different meth-odologies, because I knew short-term momentum trading would not work in the FX market. What I really needed to do was hone my technical skills in reading charts.

I started doing that "quest" for the Holy Grail, just like every trader does at some point in their trading career. We all begin looking for the magic setup or a magic methodology that will work in all markets and all time frames. Of course, it doesn't exist, but you still have to find a strategy and method that fits your personal style and risk tolerance. I searched high and low for a good couple of years before I found my current methodology.

I really had to work hard to make the switch from trading momentum to trad-ing on a more technical level based on charts. The point is you really need to get more technical to trade FX, because it's so much more of a chess game than a boxing match with an opponent [the specialist], which is what day trad-ing equities was.

Bourquin: I know that at some point you settled on Elliott Wave. When did that happen?

Gordon: That happened early in my time at FOREX.com. I had some knowledge of it, and we had access to a bunch of investment bank research. FOREX.com and the other Forex companies within the currency markets would hedge their business with the big investment banks, and we were big clients of companies like UBS, Barclay's, Goldman Sachs, and Lehman at the time, if you can believe it. Because of this relationship, we would get bank research, and there were a couple guys at each bank that I followed closely.

There was a guy at UBS named Jim Short who did Elliott Wave. There was also a guy at Goldman who did Elliott Wave analysis, and I would watch and read their stuff every day. I e-mailed them and bothered them all the time with questions about Elliott Wave. I read all the books. It was the early days in my time at FOREX.com, and I spent a lot of time reading that bank research. These guys were making calls and doing analysis that nobody else had. Their analysis was spot on, and I found myself asking them all kinds of questions about how they were doing their analysis. I began to seek out every piece of information available on Elliott Wave counts and read everything I could about the craft.

Bourquin: How did your compensation work once you traded your way onto the hedge fund team? Was it the same thing as before—all profit—or did you get some sort of base salary?

Gordon: Because I was serving in a dual capacity and was still on the research side, I was salaried for writing the research, and then I made a percentage of the profits from trading for the asset management team.

Bourquin: Okay. It was kind of a hybrid. You're a prop trader and a research writer, so you were doing it all.

Gordon: Yeah. It was a really cool job. FOREX.com was a great period of my life, and I got to work with a really good group of people and write a great research piece. I'm not saying the quality was great initially, but I had a lot of fun doing it. It also enabled me to clarify my strategies by putting them on paper for the world to see. There's no hiding or taking it back once it's been put out there. I gained a ton of confidence in my trading during that time.

Then I made a lot of good contacts with our clients around the world. My profile was on the rise there with the research report. I made it very clear that the trades and analysis I put in the "Strategy of the Day" report, I put on significant size within the hedge fund. It would drive our compliance department nuts! They hated me so much because I kept pushing the boundaries as much as I could by talking about real dollars that I traded. I drove them out of their minds, but in fairness to them, the National Futures Association—the NFA, had an office at the FOREX.com offices, and they were really cracking down on the Forex industry. FOREX.com was always very conservative and wanted to make sure they were in compliance at all times.

Bourquin: One of the things that drove them crazy was how you outlined actual trades from start to finish, right?

Gordon: Right. I always challenged myself to be as transparent as possible about what I was trading and doing in the markets. I wrote the compliance department and said I wanted to do something for the February Traders Expo in New York in 2008. I said I wanted to do a full accounting of my three best trades and my three worst trades from the previous month in the fund. I wanted to show readers of the "Strategy of the Day" report and my clients the exact P&L for the month. I did it, and I think I showed you the PowerPoint.

Bourquin: Yes, I remember seeing that. Not many people are willing to share what they made or lost.

Gordon: I forgot exactly what the breakdown was, but I made $25,000 or $27,000 over my three best and three worst trades, net, and I took clients through it step by step. I showed them exactly how I worked the trade setup. I showed them the chronology of the trade from start to finish. I took a gamble on being so public with the information, and it worked. My credibility as an analyst and trader continued to grow.

Bourquin: I read "Strategy of the Day" almost from the very beginning, and I think what made it different, why you got so popular with it quickly, is that a lot of people in chat rooms and in newsletters make a call on a trade and if it goes bad, you never hear about it again. They've moved on to the next call and they never go back and say, "I screwed up on this one." You would go back and say, "Well, obviously the dollar trade didn't work out so great. Here's why I think it didn't work out and here's what I'm looking at now." I think that kind of credibility and legitimacy is pretty rare, and I think people respect it.

Gordon: Definitely. There are a lot of people on the web in the trading industry trying to attract attention, and I always felt this was the best way to do it. In the trading industry, there are very few people who are willing to be 100 percent transparent. There are no secrets and no easy way to be successful as a trader. There is some horribly misleading marketing out there that makes traders—and especially new traders—feel like they can be right 90 percent of the time. That's not reality in the markets. If you're right 58 percent of the time and your average has shown you're losing 48 pips on those trades but you're making 82 pips, on average, on winners, that's a nice track record. That's enough to make a living in the markets.

I guess it was my mission to show people the reality of trading, because I've met a lot of really good traders in my career, and I'll tell you what: very few, if any, over the course of their lifetime is right more than 60 percent of the time. And that reality needs to be shared with people. I'm sick of the BS marketing out there. It's ridiculous. You can make money as a trader, of course, but it takes time, dedication, and hard work.

Bourquin: So Elliott Wave has allowed you to get to that winning percentage, but I've heard counting the waves isn't easy. You've got to count waves in a specific way, and it takes some practice. How long did it take you to get really confident with that strategy?

Gordon: I would say about four to five years. Anything that's a skill set that can yield a better-than 50 percent win rate, which is what a good trading methodology can yield, will take a lot of work. My old ski coach would always say, "If it were easy, everyone would be on the World Cup." It's a simple saying, but it always stuck with me. Elliott Wave is a methodology that allows you to quantify all the varied traditional technical patterns out there. There's a lot of breakouts, breakdowns, flags, wedges, double tops, double bottoms, and so forth. Elliott will actually tell you at what point of the trend or correction you'd expect to see these corrections come in or these patterns come in. You overlay Fibonacci on top of it and it'll give you expected starting points for trends and corrections, so that becomes your entries and exits.

But on a more macro level, what is Elliott Wave? All it's doing is helping you "tape read" and helping you understand what crowd psychology is driving the markets, and that's all it really is. It's herd mentality, crowd psychology that drives price change, not fundamentals. It's people's belief of what's going to happen in the future. Elliott Wave gives you a kind of a "cheat sheet" of what crowd psychological characteristics you would expect at each stage of the trend in a sequence.

It's so cool when you can step back and say, based on where I think we are on the wave count, I expect the crowd to be feeling a certain way. You pick up the newspaper and you turn on the TV, and you get a feel of what people are thinking and saying. You overlay that with the characteristics you look for at each stage of a trend or correction, and then you know where we are in the process and in the wave count. Then you go to work putting the trade on based on your validation or invalidation points. So, it's nothing more than a cheat sheet of crowd psychology. Once you gain confidence in counting the waves, the market becomes much more predictable. Does it always work? Of course not, but it gives you a better feel for where we are in the ebb and flow of the markets.

Bourquin: You mentioned that fundamentals don't figure much into your trading. When you place a trade based on your Elliott Wave counts, do you care, for instance, that on the day that we're doing this interview, the nonfarm payrolls [NFP] economic report has come out? Do you care about those events, or do you trade regardless of them?

Gordon: I trade through them all day long if the Elliott Wave count is strong enough. For example, today we had a long Australian dollar position that we put on this past Wednesday. We took half our position off for a profit before the announcement. We came into NFP today with a long Aussie dollar position, which would correlate to higher stock prices. Because the Elliott Wave count said we were in the middle of a good wave 3 breakout, I said, "We're carrying this position through NFP." I knew that, even if it were a poor report, the Aussie dollar would have gone higher anyway. The Australian dollar was nearing a high before the NFP economic report, but just because of where we were on the wave count, I was comfortable staying in half the position.

There are times that the wave count is so strong that it will override any other news. When we're in a bull market, markets will push aside bearish news and continue with the longer-term trend. Remember, Elliott Wave is a picture of the psychology of the markets. Even if an economic report is terrible for the markets, if we're in a bull market and the wave counts are strong, the market will head higher. Elliott Wave can tell you when we are in a bull market and when the market is willing to push aside poor data. So, yes, we look at fundamentals all day long. But we don't trade the fundamentals. We'll trade people's expected reactions to the fundamentals—and that's the key difference.

Bourquin: That's fascinating. So what that says to me is that you were so confident in the Elliott Wave that you're willing to disregard even a huge economic report. You're willing to trade through it because of what you see on the chart with the Elliott Wave?

Gordon: How many times have you seen a report that comes in on the weak side but then the market rallies? How many times have you seen a strong report but the market sells off and does the reverse of what you thought it would? It happens all the time. There's got to be greater forces at work than what the data was [showing] in that exact second. The way we substantiate it, or the way we fortify Elliott, is we do a lot of correlation analyses. We look for related markets. Obviously, commodities and equities are very highly correlated to the Australian dollar. So, what we'll do is we'll do wave counts on correlated markets and substantiate our analysis in the Australian dollar. So, if "risk is on" across commodities, international equities, and domestic equities, and we have good wave counts across the pattern, I don't care what data piece comes out. If markets are bullish and the crowd is seeking risk, those markets are going higher.

Bourquin: Let's jump back again in the timeline from when you left FOREX.com to open your own business. Talk about that decision and how that came about.

Gordon: It was always my dream to work for myself and own my own company. I've had the luxury to work with you, Tim, and the Traders Expo, and I've been around this business, this industry of trading, working with retail customers, for a long period. Through those relationships, I met a lot of traders who traded their own accounts but also had their own businesses. I wasn't sure that's what I wanted to do. I thought about going the investment banking route. I could have taken a job at one or two investment banks on the technical research side, but I chose to go with the retail side and work with clients directly and own my own research business. It's been terrific so far, and

I'm really happy with where I am. I love it. I really enjoy working with traders, watching them learn, and trading alongside them. It helps me improve my own trading.

During my career, I kept in contact with Dave Floyd, my first boss out of college. Dave had been running Aspen Trading for a while, and I started to talk with people at FOREX.com about going out on my own. They knew it had always been a goal of mine and that I was getting closer to making it happen. I talked to them for a long period of time about how I could transition in a way that would work for both of us. We worked out a way I could do this—I wouldn't call it an exit plan—but we worked on probably a six-month long plan for me to move out on my own. I worked very closely with them.

I maintain really good contact with them and work with them on several projects. I am incredibly grateful for the opportunities they gave me to build my skills as a trader and build a following online. It was a really nice departure and I had their full support. They treated me really well and it was a great experience. They gave me their blessing to go out on my own with Dave, and we relaunched Aspen Trading a year and a half ago. It's been the most amazing part of my life, in addition to getting married during that same period. It's been two years that I'll never forget. I'm doing exactly what I've always wanted to do: trade and share my analysis with clients.

Bourquin: And you're kind of doing something similar to what you were already doing at FOREX.com. You're doing research for clients on Aspen, trading your own account, and then you're also trading a fund as well, right?

Gordon: Yes, exactly. Just taking the same business model I've found success in previously. If we put out a research trade call, we will have supported it with hours of chart analysis, correlations, and reasoning. Our research clients are not at all surprised when we put on a trade, because we have typically been walking them through the background of the trade for several hours or even days prior. Dave and I also started a money management business called FGP [Floyd, Gordon & Partners], and we have some investors, so we'll execute our trading ideas there as well.

Our feeling has always been that if we're going to put out research and trading ideas to clients, there's no reason not to be confident enough in those ideas to place real trades on them. We have a tremendous amount of confidence in our research, so it just makes sense to actually trade them. We make money for our investors and add another level of credibility to our research side of the business.

I'm sure there are people out there who talk one way to clients and then trade another way in their accounts. I like to sleep at night and have a clear conscience. If I'm talking about it to our clients, I should be willing to put my own money behind those ideas.

Bourquin: I think that a lot of people are doing newsletters and putting out calls on Twitter or blogs, and they may be putting out a call and telling you what they're trading, but they don't give you the reasoning behind it. Maybe because they're afraid that if they tell their followers what their "secret sauce" is, a client or a subscriber won't stay. But you don't seem to have that issue. You explain exactly the reasoning behind it and why you're doing the trade.

Gordon: It reminds me of the movie *Blue Chips*, starring Nick Nolte. Did you ever see that movie? In it, Nick Nolte is the basketball coach and he's giving a pep talk to his team. He tells his team that, as far as he is concerned, he can walk over to the opposing coach and hand him their playbook and entire strategy for winning the game. It doesn't matter, because the plan and the strategy isn't the important part. The execution and implementation of the plan is all that matters. The skill of putting the plan into place is where the game is won. There is no Holy Grail in trading. There is no strategy that is unique or hasn't been tried. There is nothing new under the sun in terms of strategies, trust me. It's all about your skill, your discipline, and your execution.

I would love for every one of my research clients to know exactly what I know in terms of our style of trading, but it's not going to make them the best trader. They have to have discipline and execution skills, and that's something that only comes with tons of repetition and practice.

Bourquin: A lot of traders out there who are trading their own accounts dream of doing it full-time or trading for a hedge fund. Do you trade differently when you're trading with a fund than you would in your personal account?

Gordon: That's an interesting question. I've heard that some traders are more careful with funds they manage and take more risk in their personal accounts. But for me, my strategy is my strategy, and the risk doesn't change just because I'm trading the fund or my own money. Now, of course, I trade significantly larger size in the hedge fund. But the risk and methods are exactly the same as my own account. To me, if you believe in your trading ideas and have proven that they work, there's no reason to take on any more or any less risk in different accounts you trade. It's just a numbers game. If your strategy says you are risking 2 percent on a trade, all that changes is the dollars that 2 percent represents in the different sized accounts—personal or hedge fund.

We have a whole school of thought for what we call "T rankings" for our clients. We help them set up a risk profile for themselves and their trading accounts. We help them determine their goals in the market and then figure out a strategy that will yield a percent risk they will take on in their trades. It's just a numbers game. You execute the same way. It doesn't matter if you have a large amount of capital or a small amount of capital, it's all based on what your goals are in trading and what your percent risk is on each trade. Then you simply execute on that strategy.

Bourquin: What advice do you have for somebody who is starting out in trading and wants to cut their learning curve down from five years? Is there a way to do that? I don't want to say "shortcut," because I don't know that there are any real shortcuts, but are there things that you would do differently if you started out right now?

Gordon: No, I wouldn't change anything. Trading is a game of skill. The only way to improve any skill is with practice, discipline, and lots of repetition. It's something that is going to take you a while to get better at, and everyone who wants to make money consistently has to understand that. There are no "born" traders. Some people may pick it up faster than others, but no one just picks it up and is instantly wealthy. It's just like learning chess: it's going to take you a couple of years with a lot of dedication to compete with the best in the field, just like any skill game out there. Unfortunately, there are no shortcuts.

On the other hand, you can become good at this with good old hard work. It's a lot of fun, but it's a process. The only thing I would say to people is, don't come in here and, pardon the expression, half-ass it. If you want to be a good trader, dedicate yourself, study consistently, and get after it. This isn't something you can pay someone to do for you. The best chat room or stock-picking service in the world can't turn you into a good trader if you aren't willing to put in the hard work—at least for a couple of hours a day. If you want to trade for entertainment, fine, but if you want to get good at it and make a living or career in the markets, just like anything else, you have to work at it.

Bourquin: Talk about a typical day of trading for you. Forex is tough because it trades twenty-four hours a day for five and a half days. Lifestyle-wise, that's got to be tough.

Gordon: Yes, you can trade all day and night in foreign exchange trading, but our trading style means we don't have to do that. If you're a day trader, scalping in and out and trading London, Asia, and New York sessions, you might not get a lot of sleep. But these days, many things outside of currency trade around the clock. Maybe you're into stock index futures, trading the DAX and the S&P, and then the Nikkei during the Asian sessions. We certainly don't stay up late at night trading.

In our positions, we'll hold trades anywhere from half a session up to two to three sessions. For example, we've been in this Australian dollar trade since Wednesday. It's now Friday and we're going to carry a piece of it over the weekend. If we have a big trade on, maybe I'll get up at night to just check on it. I'll set an alarm for myself, so if the price gets to a certain point it will wake me up. But maybe one out of ten or fifteen trading nights, am I actually up looking at the markets. We have our stops and profit targets in place, so I don't obsess over the positions. We set our trades up so that they transcend intraday price action. We put our stops far enough away, and it's built into the risk profile so that a data report overnight is not going to really impact our trade.

While trading has become more global and information is released around the clock, this doesn't mean we need to be constantly monitoring positions in a way that adversely affects our lifestyle. As a new trader, you can certainly carry a full-time job and trade part-time. If you want to go full-time in trading, fine, but you need to start with a significant size of account. More than most people realize.

Bourquin: Good point. How much money does somebody need to start with to try to trade full time?

Gordon: You definitely need at least six figures. If you want to try to make a go at this, I'd say you need $200,000 to $250,000 in your trading account. That's separate from a savings account you can use to pay bills. I'd also recommend you trade part-time for several years first to get the experience you need and the confidence you must have.

Bourquin: Well, what if I had $75,000, but I had four times leverage? Does that count, or do I need cash in that?

Gordon: No, no, no. Absolutely not. You need that in cash. Leverage does not come into the equation when thinking about the money you'll need to quit your job and trade for a living. You need enough capital so that you can make smart trading decisions and not take an inordinate amount of risk. Too little capital equals too much stress because you constantly have to take on more risk than you should. If you're at seventy-five grand, you're taking a percent risk per trade of your overall account that is going to make you uncomfortable, and ultimately you'll have a loss that forces you back to your old job. People just don't make good decisions when they're very uncomfortable. You need to put yourself in the best situation possible to do that.

It's important to know that we don't encourage most of our clients to go out and trade full-time immediately, even if they do have the account size I mentioned. It's a highly stressful situation that few people can handle. Our trading style and our business is set up to cater to the people that like to work two to three hours a day on their trading, but they carry full-time jobs or they have other things going on in their life. Being a successful trader does not mean you need to go out on your own and do this full-time. If you have the means, the time, and the lifestyle that allows you to trade for a living, I would say, great—do it. But it's not for everybody.

Bourquin: How many hours a day do you think you spend on pure research?

Gordon: I wake up right around 6:00 to 6:15 a.m. eastern standard. I'll make the long trip from my bedroom over there through the kitchen and into my trading office, which is about a twelve-second commute—probably the same commute distance that you have.

Bourquin: Yep. It's one of the great things about owning your own business!

Gordon: No question. I'll work from about 6:30 a.m. after that first cup of coffee. Dave and I are in constant contact, and we will do research up until about noon. So, for about five and a half hours during the day, I'll monitor the markets closely—what our charts and any positions in play are, and then we'll move into the business administrative stuff and carry that into the New York close. Then we'll do another hour or two of research in the New York close. All in all, I'd say about seven to eight hours of research and about four to five of running the day-to-day business operations.

Bourquin: And so putting the actual trades on takes mere minutes. It's all the research that goes into it, I guess.

Gordon: Right. The hard work is done during those hours of research. Actually implementing the positions is the smallest part of my day. I also spend some time getting ready for my appearances on CNBC. That's one of the great things about having a business partner like Dave. CNBC can take a lot of time in order to get ready for a show, and I'll take off and Dave will run the business. It's good exposure for our small company, but I also really enjoy it.

Bourquin: How did the CNBC gig come about?

Gordon: Again, that was through FOREX.com. I got the ability to do some guest spots, providing currency commentary, because FOREX.com was a sponsor and ran TV commercials. The producers who run *Money in Motion* saw my spots and my opinions on the market and gave me the opportunity to try out for the *Money in Motion* show, which is the segment I'm on every Friday now. I probably went through three or four rounds of tryouts, and I think they probably brought thirty or forty people in, and I was one of the top three that made it for the show.

Bourquin: Once again, your transparent nature as a trader served you well! Are your strategies any different from what you talk about on CNBC, or are those the same kind of strategies you're trading every day in your own account and the fund?

Gordon: It's the same kind of strategy I am researching every day for my own account, the fund, and our clients. My research clients will know exactly what I'm talking about when I get on the air because I have been talking about it to them all day or all week. But it's difficult on a weekly show to really get the information out that I want traders to understand, because it's obviously just a weekly show, and markets change every day. But as far as the setups for the trade, the reason I'll want to be in a trade, they're the exact types of trading ideas that I do on the research reports. But the obvious difference is that I can't follow up and manage the trade with TV viewers as we can with the research clients.

Bourquin: You've got a lot on your plate as a trader, educator, and analyst. Where do you see yourself in a couple of years? Are there things in your trading strategy or personal style that you want to improve?

Gordon: There are always things that you can improve. That's the only certainty in the markets. But I'm really happy where our trading is right now and how the business is coming along. Right now, Dave and I are at this point where we're working with two quant guys who are analyzing all of our trading results. We want to understand how our strategy performs and how good we are at implementing it over a longer period of time. Currently, our win rate is very good. Around 63 percent of our trades are winners, and I'll tell you what, it's too high.

Bourquin: Too high? There's no such thing! What do you mean?

Gordon: I know it sounds crazy, but here's the reasoning behind that. Currently, our average losing dollar amount is too close to the dollar amount of our average winning trade. That means I have to be right less, but I have to be right for more average points per trade. Taking that another step further, I have to press winning trades more, be more patient with them, and allow them to work harder for us.

This is where Dave and I do well together as business partners and traders. Both of our collective thoughts go into one trade. We have to press our winning trades more with bigger size, risking being stopped out by hurting our average entry price. That's going to make our percent right—our "hit rate"— come down a bit, but that's going to separate the size of our average winner and average loser. So, I need to be right less on the trades that we do get right, and we need to be right for more dollars. Essentially, I want our winners to be much bigger than our losers, and in order to do so, our win percentage is going to come down some to make that happen.

Bourquin: That's interesting. Why not just move your stops closer? You may get stopped out more, but it'd be for less and then the winners will just run?

Gordon: It's a good point, and we've considered it. We don't do that because our strategy needs to have that wiggle room of a larger stop in order to give it time to work. I'm a good trader, but there are a lot of times where we'll get into a trade and it just doesn't immediately go in our favor. A lot of times, if we put a tighter stop loss, we will be knocking ourselves out of a trade too quickly that we believe, given enough time, will ultimately work out.

What we need to do is manage the trade well after the trade has shown evidence that it's working, and then quickly move the stop up behind us after it's working. We also need to add to the positions that are working well and still show room to continue in the direction we favor. So, we'll trail the stop behind and get more size on in the trade, and then allow the trade to work—and that's going to create more dollars made per winning trade.

If we kept our stop too tight, we'd risk not being able to see the trade follow through. But we need to be more aggressive with our winning trades, and that basically comes down to adding money to them once they are profitable.

We'd do all of that and still stay within our strict risk discipline. That can't change. We aren't willing to increase our risk on every trade and just hope it results in bigger gains. Traders have been slaughtered that way since the beginning of the markets.

Bourquin: That just shows how well you know yourself as a trader and why having a better than 50/50 win rate doesn't mean you'll make money as a trader. I think a lot of traders struggle and they can't understand why they can't get ahead, because maybe they are at a 60 percent win rate, but they are so impatient with their winners that they close them too early and they don't outweigh the losers in the right proportion.

Gordon: It's really simple to see, too. For my personal account, I write down all of my trades in an Excel spreadsheet, keep track of every trade, and I'll simply add up winners and losers occasionally to keep track of the win/loss ratio and net profits. One thing I didn't mention is that I rate each trade based on the conviction I have for that specific idea. It's my way of determining, before I put on the trade, the amount of confidence that I have in it working out favorably.

I have our four-tier convictions. We have a tier one [strongest] through four [not as strong], and I'll add up the averages for each trade—just doing the simple average win size, average loss size—for each conviction tier. Just very simple Excel stuff. After the trade is over, it shouldn't take any more than one minute to record that information on each trade. I then look back to see if my tier one convictions are making the most money. Sometimes they do, and it's always improving.

One of the best things you can do for yourself as a trader is go back and look at your trading results. It is amazing how many traders don't do it, but for me it makes all the difference. It started for me way back when I was writing those "Strategy of the Day" research reports at FOREX.com. If I were going through a period of poor trading, I would go back and look at times that I was trading well and then try to figure out what I was doing differently. I'd read what I wrote when I was trading well, I'd look at my tone, and I'd look at the market conditions during that time. I'd also look at what setups I was trading. Usually I would see something that I was doing during those good times that I had stopped doing, or the market had just changed and I failed to make the adjustment.

I'd recommend traders write research reports for their friends or family, simply because it's an excellent way to document your reasoning behind trades and keep yourself honest to yourself about why you are taking the trades you are taking. Having all those back editions of the "Strategy of the Day" report helped me tremendously and really set the tone for my trading for years. If nothing else, just keep a simple spreadsheet and put the trade parameters in—how much you originally risked, how much you made on the trade, and the rationale behind it. Keep it, store it, and then when you're going through a down period, look back in time to see what you were doing during a successful period. It's amazing what you'll glean from that.

Bourquin: You've mentioned that the "Strategy of the Day" report kept you honest because you're putting it out there to the world. There's no going back and saying, "Well, I didn't really think that way" or "Take that trade." It's out there, and the subscribers will hammer you if you try to back away from it.

Gordon: Oh, I had clients reading that thing so closely, Tim, that if I wrote in the report via a typo, saying we got out one price and it was actually ten pips away from that actual price, I'd have people writing in immediately and saying, "No, it was actually this price you got out." I mean, they had me honest to the pip. But it was good for me. There's no better way to stay disciplined and develop confidence in your convictions as a trader.

Bourquin: So if nothing else, certainly the strategies were great for your clients, but it sounds like that was a huge part of making yourself successful as well?

Gordon: It was a huge part of my evolution as a trader. I don't think there is a better way to learn. You know, the best thing you can do is get maybe five or seven of your trading buddies together and just come up with an e-mail circle and e-mail out to your friends what your strategies are and what you are looking at in terms of opportunities. If you put them to paper and try to get them in a logical format so that somebody else can understand them, it's amazing how much more honest you become. You're accountable to your trade and you're not going to just say, "I think XYZ is going to happen, so I'm going to put on a trade." If you can't explain in simple terms the reasoning behind your trades, then there is likely a problem and you'll lose money all day long. But if you have to back up your ideas with a reasonable argument, it's really going to make you think twice about taking a trade if you're unsure of the rationale. I was doing it with thousands of people all over the world, but you can do it with a small group of friends. You'll be a better trader for it.

It got to the point where I wouldn't put a trade on in the hedge fund that was any bigger than 50 percent of my allowed size, per my trading rules, unless it was in the "Strategy of the Day" report. I went through this enough or just found out the trades that I put in my research and made public were my best trades. The ones that didn't make it into the report were my worst, probably because I didn't justify to myself, to my readers, why I was getting into it in the first place. Funny how it worked that way.

Linda Raschke

Linda Bradford Raschke has been a full-time professional trader since 1981. She began as a market maker in equity options and was a member and floor trader on two exchanges. In the early 1990s, Raschke became a registered Commodity Trading Advisor (CTA) and started LBRGroup, Inc., a professional money management firm. In addition to running successful CTA programs, she has been principal trader for several hedge funds and has run commercial hedging programs. She was recognized in Jack Schwager's book, The New Market Wizards (John Wiley & Sons, 1992), and in Sue Herera's book, Women of the Street (John Wiley & Sons, 1997).

Raschke has been active with the Market Technicians Association for many years and has lectured in over 30 countries. She is well-known for her book with co-author Laurence Connors, Street Smarts: High Probability Short-Term Trading Strategies (M. Gordon Publishing Group, 1996).

Tim Bourquin: Linda, how long have you been trading for a living?

Linda Raschke: Thirty-one years. I started off on the exchange floor. I was fortunate that somebody else backed me, so I jumped into the pits right away and traded there for six years. I started off trading equity options but now 98 percent of my trades are in the futures market.

Bourquin: When did you decide to leave the trading floor?

Raschke: Well, I had actually had an accident and my shoulder and arm were in a sling, so I really couldn't stand down in the pits anymore. You need to be able to use your arms for buy and sell signs in the pit, so I moved upstairs. This was at the clearing firm First Options of Chicago. In those days, we didn't have the computers that we have now, so I was trading off of an old Quotron screen and calling my orders down to the floor.

Bourquin: Were there many women in the Chicago trading pits when you started?

Raschke: There weren't, but I was on two different floors: the Pacific Coast Stock Exchange and the Philadelphia Stock Exchange. I also had a lot of colleagues on the Chicago options floor—the CBOE—and there were always a few women down on those trading floors. In terms of traders, I remember there were about four females on the Pacific Coast Stock Exchange when I started down there. But there were still a lot of other females in clerical support-type jobs, so it was not so one-sided as you would think. Just not so many female traders.

Bourquin: Did you learn about trading in school, or who introduced you to the trading pits?

Raschke: No. I actually didn't even know that this environment existed on the exchange floors, although I had always been interested in the markets. I was an economics major in college and my dad always had chart books on his desk when I was growing up. Not that he was a trader by any means, but he followed the markets. Then, when I was living in San Francisco, I applied to a bunch of different brokerage firms to become a stockbroker because I thought that would be a great entrée into the markets. Of course, as you can imagine, a twenty-one-year-old female, "fresh out of school," got turned down by all of them, so thank goodness for that. I never became a stockbroker.

I did get a job outside of the financial industry, and the office was right across the street from the Pacific Coast Stock Exchange, so I could see in the morning the people streaming in and out of this old classical building, wearing their colorful trading coats and their ID badges. I befriended one of them, and that's ultimately how I got into the business.

Bourquin: Was trading in the pits a whole lot different from how you trade on a screen now?

Raschke: In some ways, it was. Obviously, you have a different dynamic in terms of watching the order flow physically in front of you, so that's something that's very different. You see the traders buying and selling, so you get a feel for the momentum of the markets. Once upon a time, there was an edge in the pits, especially doing options arbitrage, because you could use that sense of momentum as an edge. But that doesn't exist anymore. There's no edge to options at all because the market is so efficient now with electronic trading. But what really has remained the same for me was the approach of taking one day at a time and developing a routine for my trading.

In my case, my day starts 6:30 or 7:00 a.m. eastern, when I begin looking at the overall markets. I'm trying to always fit my views into a larger "macro" context, looking to see where we are in the one- to two-week cycle that the market always seems to repeat.

When I was trading equity options, it was a little bit more of a strategic game than one would be doing, for example, in a bond pit or an S&P pit, where you're "flipping the paper" and buying and selling for a quick profit on a move. With equity options, you definitely had to be very strategic in your positioning. So, it wasn't like we were making money buying an option and flipping it out a quarter point higher. It was constantly looking at the option Greeks and thinking, "The Gamma number is this and Delta is this. If I'm long calls and long puts, that's a positive Gamma trade, and now I need to trade the stock actively against that position in order to make money." So, you were forced to trade the stock back and forth against your position to pay for the cost of carrying the option position.

There are so many moving parts with profitable option trading. It is much more analogous to playing bridge or chess, where you have to think strategically a couple jumps ahead. Whereas I would equate a trader in the futures pit with more of a faster, blackjack type of game. Traders have to decide which type of trading they are best at and go trade that market.

Bourquin: Did you have somebody teach you how to trade in the pits?

Raschke: It's funny. There was a series of tapes that we could watch upstairs at the clearing firm that discussed the model for pricing options so that you could understand the theory behind it. You can't learn to trade from videotapes, of course, but it gave you the theory. Then it's like somebody throwing you into the open ocean and saying, "Sink or swim!" Nobody teaches you how to trade other than the mechanics of how you're going to bid or how you're going to offer. It's very much a "learn by doing" thing. So, I really have to say that, other than somebody explaining an initial pricing model, everything was pretty much learned by doing it.

It's pretty much the same thing today. A new trader obviously can be introduced to different concepts, like market profile or other theories that help them understand how pricing works in a free market, but the people I think that will make it in this business today have to find their own method and strategy to make money long-term. Successful traders need to find their own game and their own way, and I think it's pretty much through experience and trial-and-error trading where that happens. Everyone has to find their own edge in the market, and that can only come from just trading an account.

Bourquin: Do you think the people that start out trading behind the screen, who don't have that experience in the pits, are at a disadvantage because they don't really understand where pricing comes from in the same way you saw it happen?

Raschke: No, I don't think it makes a big difference. And honestly, of the people that were on trading floor, I would say that probably 85 percent of them have had an extremely difficult time making the transition to the screen, and the majority of them have not been able to make the transition to the screen at all. So, I don't think it matters much. Trading in the pits is just a different way of making money, and it is slowly dying.

I think that the learning curve for traders today is more about finding out what style works for them. Are they going to do spread trading or are they going to try and make money short-term, scalping for nickels and dimes, which I think is very difficult. Making a living scalping isn't my style, but some traders can do it and make a nice living. Most new traders may be able to pay the bills as a scalper, but I don't think they're ever going to get rich doing that. But there's always a certain sort of person that has an exceptional affinity toward doing that. Of course, how you trade is also going to be dependent on the capital that you've built up.

Most pit traders do one thing extremely well and do it over and over again to make money each month. Retail traders have to be more strategic and plan trades and use different methods based on the current market cycle. They need to take a macro view of the markets and understand how all the pieces fit together.

Bourquin: How has your trading changed over the last thirty-one years?

Raschke: I would just say that over the last twenty years, my trading has evolved to where I'm now able to trade a lot of markets and carry a lot of positions and manage several strategies at one time. When I began, I had to focus on one or two things and become an expert at those one or two things. It's a natural evolution. When you start out, you need to get good at one market—learn to do your execution well and specialize in doing one thing. Over time, you start to build up your capital and to put on multiple positions in several markets. Perhaps a stock trader will branch out and start trading currencies, gold, and crude a little more aggressively. It's been that same way for me. Most professional traders will make trades in many markets at the same time. To really succeed in the markets long-term, traders need to be able to accumulate that experience.

Bourquin: Do you trade from home or do you trade in an office?

Raschke: I have a home office. I prefer going to an office, though, so when I was living in Florida, I built a separate office twenty feet away from my house. Before that, I was in Jersey and actually built a separate office that was attached to the house. But when I'm in front of my screen or in my office, I might as well be one hundred miles away from my house because I'm so focused on my trading.

Bourquin: It sounds like separating home from work is important to you.

Raschke: I think a lot of it is just filtering out distractions. So, it could be distractions from kids or distractions from pets or from anything that pulls your mind away from the job at hand. I just think you need to remove yourself or put yourself into your game space, where you can concentrate and have total focus on the markets.

Bourquin: What kind of tools do you use in your home office for trading? What kind of codes and software, that sort of thing?

Raschke: I always have three separate computers. One is dedicated just to my execution platform. I think that's really important. I don't want to be running my execution software on the same computer that I'm running charting programs, or technical programs, or things that might hog up memory and risk having latency issues that slow down my orders. On the other two computers, I have two separate software programs that are basically redundant for backup. One looks exactly like the other, except both have separate data feeds and separate internet connections so that if there's a data latency issue on one, it's not going to interfere with what I'm doing.

Bourquin: Have you ever had both of your internet connections go down while you were in the middle of a trade?

Raschke: I've had everything happen. You name it—it's happened to me. Hurricanes, satellite dishes falling, having our internet and phone lines dug up by construction. That's why it's very important for each trader to address areas of weakness in technology and be resourceful and say, "Where are the Achilles' heels in my operations, and how can I build in some type of redundancy or backup?" I have positions of significant size these days, and if my data or execution went down, it could be very expensive.

Bourquin: How would you describe your overall philosophy in trading? Are you purely technical, or do you watch fundamentals as well?

Raschke: It's all technical chart-reading and tape reading. I've never been able to capitalize on the fundamentals.

Bourquin: What kinds of technical analysis do you do?

Raschke: Well, I hate to say it, Tim, but it's pretty darn basic. It comes down to support, resistance, and following the trend, and that's about it. There's either a support level or a resistance level to trade into. And you're either in a momentum, trending environment, or you're in a trading range environment. For my style of trading, the main technicals I follow are always the previous swing high and swing low. Price is everything, and areas where price has turned in the past are likely areas where it will turn again.

Other price areas I watch are the opening price, the previous day's high and low, and the swing highs and lows in between. All of my trading is based on that. I also do a little bit of volume assessment when the market opens because that's going to set the tone of trading for the day. It's kind of hard for the market to push the price to any extreme if you don't have decent volume in there to support the move. Otherwise, it's just going to be a light-volume, choppy day, without much direction.

I use a very simple system, which some traders find hard to believe, but it just works. There's no reason to overcomplicate this business.

Bourquin: You're right. The most experienced traders I talk to probably have the simplest of systems. When I start to hear retail traders talk about more complicated systems, that's typically a sign that they don't have a lot of experience in the markets. The more complicated their strategy, the less success they've had because they are looking for that magic strategy.

Raschke: Well, don't get me wrong. I've been doing modeling and research since 1992, and I can appreciate the complex mechanical systems.

Steve Moore at a place called the Moore Research Center used to do all my testing and modeling for me, and then I always had in-house staff that would sit there and grind stuff away to create a system around the ideas. But I just haven't yet been able to create or use any mechanical system that I felt comfortable or confident trading and that was going to be durable and robust.

But it's still part of the "asking questions" approach to trading, which I think is extremely valuable. If you can find patterns in the market based on what happens in certain situations, that's always good to know. For example, what happens the day after we've had three up days in a row in an uptrending market? Or, what happens if we take out the first hour's low in the second hour? Or, what if we take out the first hour's high in the afternoon? Does that lead to a higher close? If so, how often? So, it's always that type of question asking that drives successful trading. You can ask yourself these questions and build a base of ideas, and some people build automated systems based on the results. For me it's just another piece of information I keep in mind during the trading day.

Bourquin: You trade mostly futures. What types of futures contracts do you like to trade?

Raschke: I've always traded the E-mini S&P 500 futures. In fact, I have traded the S&P E-mini futures since the very first day that they were listed, and I've traded them almost every day since. So, I've always traded the index futures. I also trade the metals—I love gold and silver and copper. I also trade energy futures, crude, and natural gas. I've always traded the grains and currency futures, too. And, finally, I still trade the "soft commodities," like sugar, cocoa, and coffee, and I'm one of the idiots out there that still trades the meats!

Bourquin: Do you carry multiple positions overnight?

Raschke: Yes. I almost always have positions on in one currency or another, and I usually tend to carry five or six positions overnight. Some of those positions stay on anywhere from two days to two weeks.

Bourquin: It sounds like you're willing to trade whatever seems to be looking attractive at the time, or is moving, or you feel offers good opportunities.

Raschke: Yes. Trading is all about going where the volatility and liquidity are. Volatility and liquidity point me to the opportunities, and then, for me, it's just a matter of keeping the ideas that have worked and dumping the rest. I know that if I have eight positions on, perhaps five of them will be working, and I simply get rid of the ones that aren't working or just aren't hitting it right. It's like when you're dealt a hand of cards, you get rid of the crappy ones first and you keep the stuff that's working for you. Managing those "hands of cards" [trades] quickly and without hesitation is where success is had in the markets.

Bourquin: When you get into a trade, do you have an idea in terms of your profit targets and stop losses?

Raschke: I always have an idea of risk, and I always know where my trade is going to be "wrong." But I am just not a believer in looking at profit targets and deciding right away where I want to exit. I will watch the position, of course, to see how it reacts when it is near a previous high or a previous low. But once it has cleared those highs or lows, or it's trending, I just absolutely do not believe in putting a limit on my profits. Sure, I have rough guidelines, but why would I tell myself I'm only going to make "X amount and then I'm out" if the market is going to give me more? The market tells me when it is time to exit. That's not something I think a trader should tell the market.

Bourquin: Do you scale into and out of positions?

Raschke: No. I don't scale into trades as a strict rule, especially if they are losers. I do not average losing trades. I might "nibble" a position and buy a small amount in a certain type of market. If that position holds well, I might buy a little more. But I never scale into trades that are going against me. So, I'll nibble if what I am trading is in a range, and build up a position that way. I might have a spot where I'm very aggressive in adding to get to a full trade. More often than not, however, I'll try to put my entire position on at once.

Bourquin: How about exiting a position? Will you scale out or will you take it all out at once?

Raschke: That depends on the market I'm trading and why I made the trade in the first place. Usually, if it's just a short time-frame trade, what I would call a scalp, I don't scale out. For quick trades, I'm all in and I'm all out when I see a spot where I believe the trade is finished. But there are other cases when our models suggest scaling out would be a good strategy and we want to lock in some profit, but I'm not entirely convinced the move is over. In these instances, I'll put in a trailing stop and take some of the position off. Overall, though, I like to keep things simple and just go all in and all out at once.

Bourquin: Do you have a "favorite" type of trade you like to take whenever possible?

Raschke: Everything is so unique and fluid. No two trades are exactly alike. It bothers me that the industry talks about, for example, "bull flags" or "bear flags," like they are perfect chart patterns that are easily recognized each time. The markets just don't work like that. I like to think of patterns in terms of "bull traps" and "bear traps." A bull trap would be something like when markets flush out of a trading range and people get a little bullish on the false breakouts. Then, when they start to come back toward the range, they tend to create little vacuums as traders who were fooled by the false breakout start to rush to close their positions. Experienced traders can be very aggressive on those types of trades.

Even trades that look great don't always work out. I feel very, very lucky recently that I did exit some trades and didn't get nailed on a snapback or give back too much profit. A great trade for me is not so much that it worked perfectly because I got a perfect entry and perfect exit. I kind of look at my great trades as, "Did I dodge any bullets in getting out on a timely basis?" There have been a couple of times where I have fabulous profits in the bonds and I didn't take my trade off because my model was still saying there should be a continuation and it didn't happen, so I gave back profit.

What you have to keep in mind is that you really can't look at any individual trade as perfect. I think it's more important that you understand that whatever you do, do it consistently.

If you're going to trail stops, trail stops on every position and do it consistently the same way on every trade. If you're going to exit when it looks like the markets are getting choppy and take your trade off because you feel it has reached a climax, do that every time. But then don't cry when it goes up another ten days and leaves you in the dust. Success in trading is a progression—not trying to find the perfect trade every time.

I know I'm going to have good trades and not-so-good trades, and I never know which days will be winners and losers. What I do know is if I play my game consistently, then a certain percentage of the time I'll make profitable trades. I can't tell you how many trades I've gotten out of way, way too early and how many trades I've gotten out of a little bit too late. That's just the way trading works. Be consistent with your strategy, and over time you can make money.

All you can do is position yourself where there are opportunities and do it the same way every time.

Bourquin: Do you make most of your money trading on just a few trades each month?

Raschke: Sure. I probably make 80 percent of my money on 20 percent of my trades. Even for short-term scalpers I think that's the case. I was talking to a couple floor traders lately, and even when you're a pit trader on the floor of an exchange, maybe 80 percent of your year comes from just two or three good months. There are certain periods in the market when there is exceptional volume or volatility, and you just happen to be in sync with it and you've positioned yourself to profit from that opportunity. There will be other times when you just have no idea what's going on. It's those times where you have a good feel for the market and it is giving you those great opportunities that you make the bulk of your profits.

Bourquin: You've mentioned models for your trading a few times. Are you talking about computer models to help you find good trades?

Raschke: Yes, I always like to quantify everything just so that I know that my mind is not playing tricks on me because, trust me, as traders we all tend to see what we want to see in the markets. The computer models quantify things for me to make sure that I am reading things correctly. It's not some sort of automated program that buys and sells for me. It just helps me identify the things I should be monitoring.

It also helps put things in a historical context. For example, a model might show me that we've just traded three days low to high and it's still in a range. What are the odds that we're going to have another day of trading between the low and the high in a range? It might be time to watch for a breakout or breakdown outside of that range. Or, if I'm bullish on silver and it's had a huge up day, what are the odds that we're going to get a second, back-to-back big up day in silver again? It's probably going to be pretty remote. The models just keep me in check, and on a daily basis they help me read the markets.

Bourquin: You trade a lot of different markets. Do you find something to trade in at least one of them every day?

Raschke: I trade every single day. I'm not saying it's a great opportunity every single day, but again, I'm just positioning myself consistently to take advantage of opportunity.

Bourquin: Was there something you learned or did in your evolution as a trader that you really felt helped you accelerate your learning curve?

Raschke: With any business, you have to pay your dues. Even though anyone can open an account and start trading, there's a long learning curve. Even if you're going to become a doctor, or a radiologist, or an anesthesiologist, or something like that, it takes years of seeing different patterns and different environments with different pathologies to become experienced at recognizing problems. It's the same thing if you are set on becoming a professional golfer. You have to play in different weather, on different courses, and with different equipment until you find what works for you.

Trading is no different. If you want to be successful, then you need to engross yourself in the business and do your research. I've probably done over ten thousand hours of research, constantly studying charts, price action, and just thinking about different approaches to trading. There are no shortcuts.

Bourquin: How about monetary goals for your trading. Do you try to achieve a certain level of profit for your yearly trading?

Raschke: No. I don't believe in that at all. I think that's the most harmful thing a trader can do to their trading account. First of all, you can have all kinds of challenging market environments, and the trading opportunities might just not be there. Then, if you start falling short of your goal, you may start to place trades in a particular market environment that doesn't favor your game plan. Maybe your trading strategy is to play in certain volatility conditions. Maybe you're a seller of volatility and you like the market to stay in a contained range. Maybe you are a breakout trader and you like the market to turn. If those conditions don't exist and you trade anyway, you're setting yourself up for failure.

The best thing you can do is to keep positioning yourself in the right environment, and when the opportunity presents itself, you need to be able to recognize it and get teed up to hit it big. That's not something that you can do if you've only been in the market for two or three years. It takes a great deal of confidence and control to just say, "I'm waiting for that one opportunity where I can go in and really kill it."

Think of it like a tennis game. You keep the ball in play. You keep on hitting the ball back and forth and back and forth across the net, staying in the game. Then, if your opponent makes an error or is drawn off the court wide, that's when you go in and you hit the winner. You can't force your opponent to make that error. You can only position yourself to be ready when it happens and make that killer return.

I think setting monetary goals is totally inappropriate. I think a better thing to do would be to set goals for yourself to not make unforced errors. Keep yourself consistent and don't make spontaneous trades outside of your rules just because you think you should be in the market. Make consistency in your decisions the goal, not money. If you do that, the money will follow.

Bourquin: Are there areas of your trading that you are actively working to improve? Are there things that you want to do better in your trading, even after thirty-one years?

Raschke: Always. Every day. I'll never be satisfied. That's like asking a concert pianist, "Do you think you could play that piece a little better?" People who are good at what they do are never satisfied with the status quo.

One of the things I am working on is more complex trade management strategies that are automated. I want to be able to see certain ways to take advantage of little inefficiencies in the markets that I am missing now. That's what makes this game fun. There are boundless opportunities to come up with your own little nuances on your methods to make them just a little better.

The minute you think you've found the key to trading, I promise you the markets will change the lock.

Serge Berger

Serge Berger has been an active trader since 1998. During his career, he has been a financial analyst, dealt in fixed-income instruments at J.P. Morgan, and was a proprietary trader in equities, equity options, and futures. Exposure to a range of different asset classes has allowed Berger to identify which asset classes and strategies best fit his goal of achieving consistent profits.

Over the years, Berger has created a trading methodology that divides markets into different time frames and characters, allowing him to more clearly and without emotions determine which strategies to apply in given situations. His account and those of his clients continue to grow during all market environments because he focuses only on the highest probability setups and follows strict rules. At Berger's web site, TheSteadyTrader.com, he goes to great lengths each day to give subscribers only the best high-probability trading setups available and offers a friendly environment where questions are welcome any time.

Tim Bourquin: Serge, let's begin by talking about the type of trader you are—day trader or swing trader—and what markets you focus on.

Serge Berger: I use more of a swing trader's philosophy, but I trade on multiple time frames, which, of course, includes intraday time frames. So there is a day trading aspect to it as well.

Bourquin: So some trades are day trades, while some trades are swing trades. When you swing trade, is the duration of the trade a couple of days or a couple of weeks?

Berger: I divide my trades into buckets, and swing trades comprise bucket two. A swing trade is typically on for between two days and three weeks.

Bourquin: In what markets do you trade?

Berger: Again, it primarily depends on the time frame, but everything is based on US equity indices via futures and/or options.

Bourquin: Sounds like a little bit of everything there. Let's talk about your overall strategy as a trader. Are you a technical trader? Do you look at fundamentals? What are the things that you look at to find good trades?

Berger: It depends on the time frame, but I would say the narrower the time frame, the more technical it gets. Certainly for intraday and swing trades, it gets very technical, but there is a fundamental backdrop to it in terms of a macro view and based on economic data. All in all, however, near-term trading is certainly much more technical than trading on the longer-term time frames that we use.

Bourquin: As an example, what is your smallest time frame, and what technical tools do you use to trade it?

Berger: The smallest time frame would be intraday. Even something as quick as the opening gap in the S&P 500 E-mini futures. The technical tools we use there are candlesticks and basic, slow stochastic oscillators. What I tend to do there is go for a half-gap close followed by a potential full gap.

Bourquin: Can you explain what you mean by a "half gap" and "full gap"?

Berger: Sure. Let's say the S&P 500 closes at 1200 on Monday night and opens at 1190 on Tuesday morning. You have a ten-point difference there, so what I would do is buy the market at the opening once I get a signal based on candlesticks and some oscillators. Then, once the gap closes or the S&P goes back half way to the previous day's closing price, I will then take profits and keep the remaining position open until the gap closes fully.

Bourquin: So your theory is that if the market gaps up or gaps down from one day to the next, you'll take the opposite side of the move in hopes that it closes that gap?

Berger: Exactly. To some extent, it's a mean-reversion trade, if you will.

Bourquin: Right. Which slow stochastics do you use?

Berger: It's actually just the basic setup: 8, 20, 10, and 10. So, it's a slow moving average.

Bourquin: And what candlesticks are you looking for either on the close or on the open to indicate that, in confluence with those stochastics, the market may fill its gap?

Berger: The candlestick will always be something to look for at the open or within, say, the first thirty minutes of the day, and we're mostly looking for extreme candles. Most will have very long tails and small bodies, for example, or very big bodies that fully engulf a previous candlestick. We're looking for something that gives a very clear signal about reversion of the trend, and we can then go in and place a trade in the opposite direction.

Bourquin: You mentioned how you scale out upon a half-gap fill, but how do you decide how much position size to put on initially?

Berger: I consider the day and seasonal factors when determining position size, and the day is actually more important. For example, I will size a position much larger on a Tuesday, Wednesday, or Thursday than I would on a Monday or Friday simply because of the number of false signals I tend to get on Mondays and Fridays.

Regarding seasonality, I trade much less size around any US or European public holidays, and I trade less size in August, December, and January due to lower volume. The rest of the time, it's really the type of market environment that dictates size. For example, it is not the time to trade big size when there are central bank announcements. In fact, that's likely not the time to trade at all. In essence, I am looking to trade size only when there is tremendous volume and few planned economic announcements in view.

Bourquin: Your biggest trades are midweek. What would be a typical position size on a Tuesday, Wednesday, or Thursday, in terms of number of contracts?

Berger: Well, I do this for funds, so quite frankly, it depends on the size of the fund, but it could be as little as ten contracts and as high as two hundred contracts.

Bourquin: You've explained your method for locking in profits when the gap fills halfway, but how about the second half of the position? When would you take that off?

Berger: That's a very important point. Using our S&P example from before, when you get to that closing level from the previous day (1200), I would more than likely close the entire position. However, if it looks like there is a trend in place that could potentially move the market much further—maybe to 1220 in our example—I would keep about a quarter of the position open in hopes of capitalizing on that move.

One way I determine if such a trend could be in place is by looking at the Advance/Decline (A/D) line. If the A/D line has staged a major turnaround, that's a strong signal. Also, the strength of the candlestick reversal: a very long tail followed by a very strong candle to the upside, for example, is an extremely favorable signal that a stronger and more sustainable trend is at hand for that day.

Bourquin: What are the time frames you are using to measure those intraday trends?

Berger: I'm looking at a five-minute chart, a fifteen-minute chart, and a 400-tick chart.

Bourquin: Different traders tend to favor all kinds of different tick charts, from 612 to 340, and your preference is 400. Why do you prefer the 400-tick chart?

Berger: Honestly, that just came through trial and error over the years, and we've had to change it as the amount of trades per tick changed, but I think 400 gives you enough to be very fast without being too quick.

Bourquin: Let's jump over to the swing trading side of things and how you find those types of trades. If your intraday trades are based on gaps in the S&P 500, on what factors do you base your swing trades?

Berger: Swing trades depend on the underlying asset, first of all. So, for example, let's consider a basic underlying: a mid- to large-cap equity with a decent beta. In other words, an equity that has enough movement and for which swing trades are mostly based on breakouts and major reversals. So, when trading breakouts, we would just use basic laterals or any sort of trend lines or pennants coupled with momentum oscillators, and this is mostly done using daily candlestick charts.

We also use a lot of Fibonacci retracements, and we really try to focus on 50 percent and 61.8 percent, specifically 61.8 percent, because it has been a very good indicator for swing trades. In terms of profit targets, we tend to go as high as a 23.6 percent Fibonacci extension.

Bourquin: I don't think traders rely enough on extensions to help them when setting profit targets. We didn't talk about stop losses on the intraday trade. How do you set the stop loss on your intraday trades?

Berger: Well, going back to our gap trade example, I can only emphasize that as a very high-probability trade. I have friends whose funds are running entirely on just that strategy. I think you can make a lot of money trading that strategy, and extending beyond that to where you're not just trading the close of the gap because there are a lot of trades around it. For example, if you get a trending day like we mentioned before.

With the stop loss, typically I tend to put it literally just a couple of ticks below the major reversal point that we hopefully have gotten that day as a buy or sell trigger. Sometimes you get a fake out and the market will go back below that before going higher, but then again, on a five-minute chart, we will have another chance to re-enter that position.

Bourquin: Right, so if you do get stopped out because the market comes down and grabs your stop, you'll get back in again as long as everything is still telling you that it's probably going to fill the gap?

Berger: As long as we have a confirmation candle that is just as strong as the one we had initially, yes.

Bourquin: Going back to the swing trade on a breakout, what time frame chart are you watching for that setup?

Berger: On swing trades, it's mostly a daily chart. I find that a daily chart gives me a lot more certainty than an intraday chart, plus it gives a lot fewer signals. I want to wait until there has been a clear daily confirmation—like a candle coupled with a momentum oscillator or stochastics—and I wait for a daily signal most of the time.

Bourquin: And you said the momentum oscillator you use in that case is the slow stochastics?

Berger: Yes. I typically use slow stochastics.

My entire philosophy on swing trades is based on the concept of "the simpler, the better." I have traded for a long time and even worked at an institutional desk and so forth. I have met a lot of people who have very sophisticated models, and they work. I have just found that keeping it simple and sticking to profit and stop targets is just as profitable and sometimes easier to follow.

Bourquin: When you are looking for an underlying to break out on a daily chart, do you want to see an entire candle close above, say, a channel or a level where it's been consolidating before you will take the trade? So, for example, you might see the breakout signal one day, and then the next day you will take the trade?

Berger: I'll take the trade at the end of the day, within fifteen minutes to close. That's generally our window for a swing trade.

There are rare cases when, even if price hasn't really made that move but there is a very strong trend in—say, the oscillators and Fibonacci support lines—I will take the trade and just keep a tight stop.

Bourquin: How many positions are you comfortable having on at any one time?

Berger: I tend to have about ten to twenty positions on at once, and I try not to keep them in too many sectors. For one, I have a very clear sector focus, and it's mostly based on things I can understand: certain technologies, certain consumer cyclicals, and defensive titles. So, ten to twenty open positions is my usual range.

Bourquin: Do you have a basket of stocks that you chose from, or would you trade anything on the market?

Berger: No, I have a big watch list, and every once in a while something will pop up, depending on the environment. Given the European debt situation, there have been some European equities I've traded more recently because they presented good opportunities, but more or less, I have a watch list comprised of stocks that I have followed for many years.

Bourquin: Ten to twenty positions can be quite a bit to monitor. How are you actually scanning for these? Do you do your homework at night? And what software do you use to help you find these opportunities?

Berger: I use a Bloomberg terminal, which I still consider to be a great tool for cross-asset analysis, as well as for focusing on just one asset.

I have six big screens on my desk that allow me to monitor positions clearly. They're divided up by sector using different colors. I'm a very visual person, so I need a lot of desktop space and a lot of different colors to be able to follow everything.

Bourquin: There's a lot of information there to absorb. In gap trades, you're focusing on S&P 500 futures, but on the stock side, are you just flipping through the charts of the stocks in your basket, or are you somehow alerted automatically by Bloomberg when a condition meets your criteria?

Berger: I flip through the charts every Sunday and look at most of those stocks in greater detail. Every day I look at the S&P 500 sectors and their charts and I set alerts. I also set alerts on all the stocks on Sunday nights, and once I get an alert, I will wait until the end of the day to see if it does what I expected, and then I'll either pull the trigger or not.

Bourquin: Do you have a weekly goal that you set for yourself in terms of how much money you want to make?

Berger: I can't give a dollar amount, but what I can tell you is that the goal when trading the opening gap is basically to make between one and two S&P 500 E-mini futures points. If you do that, you make a very good living.

Bourquin: Right. And how did you go about learning to trade the opening gap?

Berger: I worked at J.P. Morgan as a fixed-income guy, and I always wanted to break loose from that and just trade, but I wanted to find something that would give me enough certainty of cash flow on a monthly or quarterly basis so I could leave, or at least get to a prop desk where I could survive. The gap trade is a very high-probability trade that allows me to do that, and that's really why I came around it.

Bourquin: Now, because the S&P may only gap a couple times a week and not every day, how often do you find that gap trade?

Berger: Well, even if there isn't a gap, I will also refer to a major intraday reversal as a gap trade. For example, even if the gap has already been filled, or if there literally hasn't been a gap, most of the time you will still get a reversal within the first hour or ninety minutes of the trading day that tends to go in the opposite direction of the previous day. So, opportunities come a lot more often, and even if there isn't a true gap, it's essentially the same thing as a gap trade, where I am literally just trying to take one to two points out of it as the market reverts back to the mean.

Bourquin: As opposed to looking for it to go all the way back to the previous high or previous low from the day before?

Berger: Yes, exactly. We're just trying to hit singles and doubles, and that's really all we're trying to do.

Bourquin: I was talking to somebody at a seminar about how some of the best traders are probably only good at one or two things, but they do it day-in and day-out in such a way that, after a while, it almost becomes boring, if you can call it that. Do you feel like the best way to trade is when you find something that works, you just do it over and over again, almost to the point where trading is boring?

Berger: I have a big sticky note on my desk that says, "*Don't focus on the money. Focus on the game,*" and that has helped me to literally forget about looking at my P&L on a day-to-day basis. Of course, for some accounts I have to look. But I try to separate the money aspect from my emotions because I have found that during my best months and best days, all I am doing is focusing on finding those intraday or swing-trade setups that I mentioned. And in the end, I won't even realize that I made that much money, and that there were no emotions involved at any point.

Bourquin: And that's one of what I call the "twenty habits of wealthy traders." While we're all here to make money, when you make your goal something else, you're able to make better decisions and the money comes more naturally as a result.

Berger: Especially if you trade futures. We've focused a lot of our discussion on the intraday trade on the E-mini futures, and there you have the biggest tendency to look at your P&L because you can literally see it tick up and down. There, especially, it is all about looking at the chart. If you see a signal that counts, take it, and then just take your stop and move on.

Bourquin: Let's talk a little more about the slow stochastics that you use. What do you want to see from the slow stochastics to act as a valid signal? Is it as simple as seeing those lines starting to move in conjunction with that candle?

Berger: On intraday trades, I mostly go for extremes. So, a lot of the time if we get an up gap, the stochastics will tend to get overbought quite quickly. Once those stochastics are extremely overbought on the five-minute chart—and preferably even on a fifteen-minute chart—in conjunction with a clear reversal candlestick, that will then act as a signal to go short.

It's different on a swing trade, and years of experience have taught me to go for divergences. If I have a stock that's making new lows but the stochastics are not, and I get other signals, including candlesticks and Fibonacci reports, I'll be much more prone to take that trade than if I have just an overbought situation in stochastics.

Bourquin: So, you're looking for some divergence there to say that price is not in line with what you're seeing on the candlestick chart, and it's not in line with what you're seeing in the stochastics, so therefore, it's a good trading opportunity?

Berger: Yes, exactly.

Bourquin: And on that reversal candle, at what point will you take the trades there? Is it the next candle, or is it at the close of that first candle, when you see that it's obviously going to close a certain way?

Berger: In the case of the intraday trade, I always wait for that candle to close. On the swing trade, I wait for the end of the day. I take the trade within about fifteen minutes of that day's close.

There is a very important distinction here, and I think that's why candlestick analysis is so important. If you're at the *bottom* of a trend and get a buy signal, that buy signal needs a confirmation candle.

If I get a buy signal on the daily chart with ten minutes to go for that day's session, I don't just buy. I wait for confirmation to come and give me another candle in the direction I want to go. And if I get that, then at the end of the day, I'll get in.

At the *top* of a trend, you don't necessarily need that. If there is a lot more room for a strong signal at the top, that might be enough to start going short.

Bourquin: You mentioned Tuesday, Wednesday, and Thursday as being most favorable for intraday trades. Let's say you get a good buy signal for a swing trade on a Friday afternoon. Does it concern you that it's a Friday, or will you still take that signal?

Berger: There is certainly a lot more reluctance to take a trade on a Friday afternoon. And I will say that's where a little more of the long-term analysis comes into play.

For example, fall 2011 was, in my opinion, a very difficult time to hold or buy things into a weekend because you never knew what news would come over the weekend. So, it depends a little bit on the macro and geopolitical backdrop.

Bourquin: So, news is still important to you, to some extent, especially on swing trades?

Berger: Yes. It's certainly important in the swing trades, and it becomes even more important in longer-term holdings that I tend to trade around with the other two shorter time frames.

Bourquin: That's interesting. I hear a lot of traders always have longer-term positions on, and while they'll routinely add and subtract from those positions, they're always holding some base amount and trading in and out all the time. Is that what you do on longer-term holdings?

Berger: Yes. I think the most alpha we can pick up as traders is by understanding the current environment. For example, I like to give the example of [fund manager] David Tepper from Appaloosa Management because it's a very prominent example and it's fabulous. He came out and said that government filings clearly indicated that they—the government—would buy Citigroup at "X" price, which was 20 percent, 30 percent, or I don't even know how many percentage points above the current price level! It was blindly obvious that he needed to buy the stock.

At the same time, it was also very clear that the liquidity injections were basically forcing investors to buy equities. Now, understand that was the most important thing in 2009. Valuations didn't matter. All of the bearish news didn't matter. The only thing that mattered was the liquidity injections, and in fact, that actually continues today.

It's very, very important to understand that sometimes fundamentals matter more. And other times, it's just news flow that matters.

Bourquin: When the government starts to get their hands in the markets, all bets are off in terms of technical analysis, because if the Fed wants to inject liquidity, that's going to override any technical signals you have. So, with that level of government intervention, you can ignore technical signals.

Berger: Yes, you don't want to fight that. And whether it's "Don't fight the Fed," or more recently, "Don't fight the ECB," it's not something you want to do.

However, technical analysis still works. You just have to understand the current situation. It has more or less been very punishing to be short over the past few years. If you understood that, then you understood that you basically had to turn into a trend follower—for lack of a better term—and buy the dips, which, of course, is a philosophy that can change quickly, but that's the current situation. Technical analysis will work, but it's not going to work for "trend reversal" analysis, if you will.

Bourquin: Do you keep track of your win/loss ratio, and can you share that with us?

Berger: I do. It depends on the type of trade, of course. The gap trade is probably the simplest example I can give, and the percentage of winners there is about 75 percent. That's pretty strong, but the bigger question is in regards to my size on any given trade. I can tell you that I am 75 percent profitable on those trades, which is true, but what really matters is how I size it.

Bourquin: Right. If you're sizing small on the winners and bigger on the losers.

Berger: Exactly. That's actually a big thing that some people don't understand. They are very happy to get a "tip" about a stock, but they don't know what size the other person is using—and to me, that's the most important thing.

Bourquin: Did you find the end of 2011 and 2012 to be a more difficult environment to trade because of all the news, or just as good a trading environment as any?

Berger: From a trader's perspective, it was very difficult, to be honest. Largely because of the lack of volatility. In early 2012, it was very difficult to see the magnitude of what was happening with the European Central Bank injecting money back in December for the first time. It was clear to me that there was going to be a rally, but it was very surprising to see it go so far.

I think it's been more difficult to trade, especially since late August through September. October 2011 was a beautiful time because of the volatility.

Bourquin: Yes, low volatility always makes it tougher. Because you're following the ECB and other central banks, are you trading currency futures at all?

Berger: No. I don't trade currency futures. And the main reason I stick with the asset classes I mentioned is because I think it gets too difficult to keep track of things. As I said earlier, I used to be a fixed-income guy and traded a lot of credit default swaps, corporate bonds, and even sovereign bonds, but it's just too much to keep track of.

Nowadays, with the advent of ETFs, if I want to get a general trade on, say, the euro or the Australian dollar, I can trade that using ETFs. Of course, I'm giving up some fees here and there, but I'm happy to just take it as a macro trade and not have to worry about the intricacies of dealing with foreign exchange and corporate bonds, because I'd then need different brokers and everything else.

Bourquin: Yeah, you're right. With so many ETFs these days, it makes it much simpler to initiate a position on any bias you may have.

As we finish up here, let's talk about any important lessons you learned that really helped you become more profitable and more confident in your trading. Is there something you can share that really helped you along the way?

Berger: Well, you always hear about the importance of simply taking your losses. There is nothing more humbling than that. It's an overused phrase, but it's very true. To me, it's all about discipline. The more I stick to my rules and don't focus on the P&L aspect, like we mentioned before, the easier I find it to make money.

The other thing—and this is just as important—is not to overtrade. Again, this is a commonly used adage, but it is true, and that's why it is such a common thread among traders. There is such propensity to overtrade—especially in near-term time frames, and especially when execution is as easy as hitting a button. Most of the time, that will do more harm than good.

Bourquin: I totally agree with that, and I've experienced it in my own trading. I took a stride forward when I realized that even if I wasn't actively in the market at that moment, or even if I hadn't made a trade that entire day, I was still trading. Trading does not mean simply that you're in the market. Trading can also mean that you're standing by while waiting for the right setup to emerge.

Berger: Exactly. The two best traders I know probably trade half as much as I do. Quite frankly, I don't trade that much myself.

Setups occur around the opening gap relatively frequently, but that's not typical. It's all about waiting for the right opportunity and then acting on it.

The problem is that, as human beings, our mind is always working, and it's difficult to turn it off. I've even gotten to the point where I've been doing yoga and some meditation just to make sure I can stay calm and focused. Alternatively, we can look to sports, or anything to keep calm and not jump the gun.

Bourquin: I agree that something outside of trading is critical, almost no matter what it is. It can be basket weaving, or sports, or some hobby to take your mind off the markets. That's very key.

Berger: Drinking tends not to be the best thing! But yeah, you need something to help detach your mind from the markets.

Bourquin: Yeah, drinking is probably not the answer! Let's talk about some recent trades. Maybe a good one and one that didn't turn out so well, and what you learned from it.

Berger: I can give you very good one on the S&P 500. If you look at the S&P 500 from a swing perspective, we had a low on February 16, 2012, and made a high just a few days later on February 21 in the overnight session. The market was very overbought at that point, and it then retraced 61.8 percent, almost to the tick. Of course, that's a very key Fibonacci support area and one we mentioned before.

We had lateral support. We had the momentum oscillators overbought, and, in fact, already showing signs of divergences. We had European credit start to tighten. Sure enough, we ended up reaching our 23.6 percent extension target at around 1375 just about a week later.

Bourquin: Wow, so that's a case where everything lined up and worked exactly the way it should.

Berger: Exactly. When things are so overbought, everyone understands it needs to pull back, but as a trader, you can't "be the ball." What I mean by that is the market can remain irrational for a long time, and much, much longer than we may think. To some extent, we all have the disease of short-termism, and from that perspective, it's very important to be able to disconnect your emotions.

Bourquin: And finally, the losing trade. What didn't go your way in that scenario?

Berger: Well, I like to leg into positions—swing positions especially—at the top or bottom of major swings. At the time, Apple was a big headline story, having busted right through the $500 level and now, at the time of our interview, tickling $550.

I went short using slightly out-of-the-money calls as we went up to that $500 level. Of course, now that we're at $550, that position is hurting. If you analyze it, however, there's a couple of very important things to be learned.

One of them is that I didn't short the stock. I instead shorted out-of-the-money calls, which gives me much more leeway. Those calls are several months in the future, so they give me more room to play with. I would then go in and short more stock once I see a major turnaround, but as we speak, that's a losing position. But important points to consider are that it was sized right and structured right, which gives me more room for error.

Bourquin: A lot of traders have really been hurt trying to find that top in Apple, and it just doesn't seem to be coming anytime soon. At what point would you be willing to buy the stock if it continues to not go your way, or at what point will you just get out?

Berger: That's a very good question. I strongly believe that stocks that go vertical—like Apple has been—inevitably come back some. Now, it doesn't have to be 30 percent, but a lot of them will come back between 5 percent and 10 percent, and that happens quite quickly.

If I see Apple go well above $570 in this specific case, I will start to take some losses on those short calls and then watch it a little bit more. But stocks that go vertical have a very, very high probability—in fact, it's almost 100 percent—of coming back. You can look at Google back in 2007 when it top ticked, or look at Netflix in 2011. Netflix rallied more than 60 percent vertical at the beginning of the year, and then cratered. That's an extreme case, but the point is that stocks that go vertical don't last. It's just a matter of when they're going to come back.

With Apple, it's not even the fundamental case. Now, I'm not a fundamental guy as much as I am a technical trader, but it's not a fundamental case that's going against Apple. Think about why Apple is going vertical. It's going vertical because of the momentum funds in there.

I have a lot of friends who are running momentum hedge funds, and they have good years and they have horrible years. Right now, Apple is being pushed up by momentum funds, and they will all leave on the same day. Again, that doesn't mean the stock has to crash into the abyss, but there is a very high likelihood of at least a 5 percent to 10 percent decline in Apple stock over a time frame of a couple of months or so.

Alex Foster

*Trading began as a hobby for **Alex Foster**, but after soaking up knowledge of count-less technical indicators and settling on three that best suited his style of trading, he has since made the leap to managing client money as head of Georgia-based AF Capital Management, LLC. His journey spans tumultuous market conditions, includ-ing the devastating crash of 2007, where his ability to remain safe and profitable not only confirmed the validity of his option-focused methods but ultimately paved the way for a move into the formal business of trading—a venture only some of the more experienced and battle-tested traders consider during their careers.*

While Foster may defy some conventional market wisdom, his track record and longevity shows that indicators don't have to be piled high and complex to be effec-tive, and that attention to risk and a propensity for keeping things simple can help anyone achieve unthinkable heights as a trader.

Tim Bourquin: Alex, let's start by talking about the type of trader you are—day trader or swing trader—and what markets you trade.

Alex Foster: I would say I'm more of a trend follower because I don't make day trades as often as I make multiweek or multimonth trades, and generally with options.

Bourquin: That's within the realm of swing trading, and weekly and monthly is how I trade as well. Let's talk about how you make decisions. Are you a technical or fundamental trader?

Foster: I use both, and I don't really think of them as being mutually exclusive, but I do tend to put more weight on the technical side because I see those changing more often than the fundamentals. I'd say the fundamentals influence me somewhat, maybe for broader trends, but when it comes down to making trades, it's almost always on a technical basis.

Bourquin: How do you like to conduct your technical analysis?

Foster: I use trend lines significantly and I am big into moving averages and Williams %R. I don't see a lot of people using that anymore, but it has worked for me for years and I have stuck with it.

Bourquin: I haven't heard a lot of people talking about Williams %R recently, either. So, how do you use that?

Foster: It's basically an overbought/oversold indicator, and people often aren't familiar with how the graph looks. The upper range is overbought, and that's generally seen as the 0 to −20 range, and the oversold is −80 to −100.

Now, I use both fourteen- and twenty-eight-day indicators to get a variety of time periods, and watching that tends to smooth it out. The fourteen-day gives me an early indication of what's going on, and the twenty-eight-day indicator generally gives me confirmation.

So, for any trend that goes into the overbought area—like in the S&P 500, for example—it might stay up there for weeks at a time. Simply getting into that overbought range is not a trade signal, but when it moves out—when it moves below overbought or above the oversold range—that's when there is a trade signal or a change in sentiment.

Bourquin: Interesting. So, a potential topping signal is when the Williams %R is showing overbought, and when it comes out of the overbought range is when you have confirmation that the market or asset in question is headed back down?

Foster: Correct, and that's the time to trade, whether it's a buy or a sell. I generally use it on a daily time frame, but I'll also look on a monthly basis.

Every couple weeks, I have a reminder pop up on my calendar to look at a three-year-long monthly chart, and I'll use the fourteen- and twenty-eight-month indicators to see how they are moving. That helps me not to get lost in the weeds of shorter-term charts, and I find that it pretty accurately predicts longer-term trends as well.

Bourquin: Do you find the reason you're better at trading on a weekly or monthly basis is because there is a lot of noise below those time frames and you're not able to get really good signals?

Foster: Yes, exactly. The longer time frames really cut out the noise and you can still see the shorter moves.

Bourquin: And how do you incorporate moving averages?

Foster: I look at everything—including a ten-, twenty-, fifty-, one hundred-, and two hundred-period moving average—but the most critical component of them is seeing a crossover. Anytime I see a shorter time frame move below a longer time frame, it's bearish. For example, if the ten-day moves below the twenty-day, or the twenty-day moves below the fifty-day, that's bearish. And the same thing is true in reverse. If a shorter time frame crosses above a larger one—like it might when coming out of a bear cycle—that's bullish.

Bourquin: So, for instance, if you had a ten-day moving average crossing below the twenty-day, and the Williams %R coming out of the overbought range and heading lower, those two things together would represent an ideal trade signal for you?

Foster: Yes, that would be an ideal trade, especially if it breaks the trend line. That's kind of a trifecta, when those three all come together.

Bourquin: And how often do those tend to line up?

Foster: Not very often, but if the basket of stocks you monitor is large enough, you can find one or two a month that do. It's those times when you really have to be willing to put on full size and scale, and even more if it's going well. When everything does align, it can produce some big, profitable trades.

Bourquin: So, are you trading options on the indexes or individual stocks?

Foster: I mainly trade options on indexes. I use some individual stocks occasionally, but especially since the middle of 2011, with everything moving in such a low-beta setup, I find that options on the indexes have been easier. Specifically, I use a variety of small-, mid-, and large-cap index ETFs, including SPY, DIA, MDY, and IWM.

Bourquin: When trading options on index ETFs, do you have certain straddle or strangle positions that you put on, or do you just buy calls and puts?

Foster: It depends on the setup, and this is why I add in both the long-term and the short-term trends and moving averages. If I look at the longer-term trend and see a multiweek or multimonth moving average crossover coupled with a shorter-term crossover—like the ten-day crossing the twenty-day, for example—I might buy a call to see how long I can take it.

The majority of my trades are naked puts, however, and depending on how bullish I am or how I read the setup, I might sell in the money. Otherwise, a lot of my trades are out of the money just to take the time value at a lower risk.

Like I said, though, it depends on the longer-term trends. If I see a long setup coming up on a multimonth chart, like the three-year-long monthly chart I talked about, I'll be more likely to sell in the money for shorter-term trades.

Usually, I'm still looking at first- or second-month-out trades, but I might go farther out if the long-term setup is there. Otherwise, I try to take smaller bites just to get about 1 percent a month and save the bigger trades for when I see a strong setup across the board.

Bourquin: When are you selling these naked puts? Will you typically wait for them to expire or close your position before that?

Foster: There are two different scenarios where I'd wait for them to expire. One, if they're still trading close to the price of the ETF and the trend is still in place, and two, if it's far enough out of the money and the trend is still going strong.

It also depends if it's in my taxable account or an IRA. Obviously, an IRA can't have margin, so I'm more likely to close out options there and move them higher. In my taxable account, I usually just let them roll and expire worthless.

Bourquin: How many trades are you comfortable having at any one time?

Foster: At any one time, I could have as many as twenty open positions. More recently, since the middle of 2011, my focus is more toward indexes, and it's easier to have more open positions that all come back to the same underlying ETF, in this case.

So, I'm not watching Monsanto and JPMorgan Chase and everything else under the sun, trying to figure out what I'm going to trade that day and what news lies underneath all of them. It's easier to trade multiple positions on one asset. So, you might have a naked put on SPY at 130, another at 135, and then call at 132, and you just monitor them all. It's still watching the same ETF or underlying equity, so it's easier to manage more full positions that way, even if they are all related.

Bourquin: That's a lot to keep track of in terms of what's profitable, what's not, and where your stops are. Let's talk about how you manage stops and profit targets, especially with so many positions open at any one time.

Foster: It all comes back to the trend, so it's completely variable and depends on where the market is, but I track everything in a basic Excel spreadsheet.

I like to keep things simple. As I said, I try to limit my indicators to two or three—the trend lines, moving averages, and Williams %R—and if there is any change in those, I can adjust all my positions quickly, which is why I like having everything there in Excel.

I always watch how much underlying value I have at risk so I can keep from going too far on margin in my taxable accounts. It's pretty easy to get ahead of yourself in those accounts, like I did when I began trading options. I'm sure a lot of traders have experienced that when first starting out.

Bourquin: How did you come across and settle on trend lines, moving averages, and Williams %R as the best indicator combination for your trading?

Foster: When I first began studying technical analysis, I read everything I could get my hands on—books, blogs, web sites, you name it. I began trying all the different indicators, and those are just the ones that really stuck for me.

Now, those three work for me, but they might not work for every trader. So, my advice is to work with a bunch of indicators to find out what works for you, but recognize there is a limit or middle ground to how many you can use before you start finding conflicting data. "Analysis paralysis" happens when one or two indicators say "buy," another one says "sell," and yet another one or two say "hold." That's when you end up not making trades at all and miss out in all directions.

I started cutting other indicators out when I saw that those three worked for me. Plus, they are simple, and everything comes back to keeping it simple.

Bourquin: We touched on this a little bit before, but let's go into more detail about which options you decide to buy or sell once the underlying has met your criteria based on those three indicators.

Foster: I'm first looking at what the overall long-term trend is by looking at a three-year-long monthly chart with multiple moving averages and Williams %R. If I see that, one—we are in a bullish trend, two—we're likely to move out of oversold conditions, and three—we've got the shorter-term moving averages above the longer-term, that would lead me to form an underlying thesis that over the coming months—with six months being the upper limit of that time horizon—the underlying asset is going to be higher than it is currently.

So, with that as the basis behind all the rest of my trades, I wait for the right opportunity where the shorter-term moving averages—ten-day, twenty-day, or fifty-day, if trading on a daily basis—are moving in the right direction.

Once I see that, I might go in the money on a naked put, and that will give me a chance to ride it up. And, even if it doesn't move up before expiration, I'll usually take the assignment so I can get a dividend while I wait for it.

Bourquin: That was going to be my next question! When will you take assignment, and when will you avoid it?

Foster: I do take assignments, but it depends where expiration is. If I don't take an assignment, it's because I'm going to roll the naked put lower.

For example, say I'm targeting a 135 naked put on SPY and it's in the money. A day or so prior to expiration, if SPY is working its way closer but I see that I'm most likely going to get the assignment, then I will probably let it be assigned in that case, unless I see the trend changing.

If the indicators have yet to move all the way to bearish but I see some wavering, like moving averages getting closer or a flattening out of a trend line, I might stay invested by selling it out of the money and buying it back by rolling it lower and then selling a 133 or 134 naked put. That way I'm still invested in SPY but at a lower risk or a lower probability of assignment.

Bourquin: Does the actual price point where you'll be assigned figure into your decision? In other words, does it have to be at a price where you don't mind owning the actual underlying asset?

Foster: It does sometimes, and that's when the fundamental side comes in. If it's moving down and we are at a P/E multiple for the S&P that's closer to eleven or twelve, I might be more likely to take an assignment at that point than when the P/E is around fifteen or sixteen because I'm more likely to go long and hold it when P/E is low.

Bourquin: How will you trade around important economic reports like nonfarm payrolls, or do you trade at all during those times?

Foster: I do trade through them. I used to let them influence my trades more often, but with the trend analysis and technical indicators I use, I sometimes—though certainly not every time—can get an idea of what's going to happen in advance.

Trends do not change based on fundamental input alone, and a lot of the time I think the trends tend to trade through it. Occasionally a trend will break, and I'm always ready to make a change in those cases. But if it's Thursday and big news or a data release is due out on Friday before the open, I'm usually not going to hold back from making a trade unless I believe the data is going to have a major influence.

Bourquin: Let me ask you a very market-specific question. Here in early 2012, it seems that every day, whether the S&P is up or down, it's always because of Greece. Do you follow that news, and do you care what they say about *why* the market is up or down at the time?

Foster: I feel the same way, and yes, I do care what the news is, but so often I think they are just filling airtime and trying to create a reason for worry or joy that doesn't really have logic behind it. Like you said, Greece has been the reason why the market goes up or goes down, but it's hard for any one factor to be both all the time.

Most folks who are looking at the underlying problems in Greece understand that even if there is a solution, like another gift from the European ministers to give aid or to take on debt, the likelihood of it being implemented and austerity measures going through is very low.

It's just a temporary fix—like a little Band-Aid on a big gash—and because it can and does move the markets, I watch it. But I don't think of it as long-term trading information.

Bourquin: Let's now talk about sizing and how you determine your position size when using options.

Foster: It depends on allocation, and for my account versus some of my client accounts, I might be more aggressive. I might use more small caps if I think small caps are looking strong, or I might use a heavier allocation towards small caps because I think I am going to get better performance there than I would with the Dow.

It also depends on my risk tolerance at the time. I'm usually pretty aggressive in my trades, but I do factor in current or upcoming events in my personal life and may become more hesitant to take risk under certain conditions.

Bourquin: What's an average option contract size for a trade in your personal account?

Foster: I typically only use two contracts at a time, and while I might use multiple contracts in a week, in any one day I only use two contracts at once.

I trade pretty small size and take small bites with most of my trades, and that comes back to managing risk. If after expiration I've done well and end up with a clean plate, and most of my options expired out of the money, I might start off building a new position with just a couple in-the-money trades. That way I have a lot of upside potential.

From there, if my position goes down, I'm not fully invested and can manage that position appropriately. Sometimes I'll buy it back, and depending on where I think the underlying is headed longer term, sometimes I might close it out. But I'll always start out small and can then keep adding to the position if it's going up.

An important point, however, is that I generally don't chase a position with my subsequent trades by using more in-the-money options. My third, fourth, and fifth trades, and any others from then on, will usually be out of the money.

Bourquin: Let's talk about trading client accounts versus trading your own account. When did you first start managing client money? And was that only after you had a successful run trading your own account?

Foster: I started managing client money almost three years ago, and yes. Trading was a hobby of mine since after I got out of college. It was always interesting to me, so I started studying up on it, and after taking business management, finance, and economics classes in college, it just drew me in.

I started making money investing and then built on it, and I was doing well and also talking to friends and other people about what to buy and different market models. I had a couple friends who were advisors, and they encouraged me to get into managing money, but at that time, I was focused on my own money and I didn't want to take the risk of trading other people's money.

The 2007 crash was the turning point for me. I heard so many horror stories about people not getting out, and while I'm not saying I got all the way out myself, I knew to reduce my exposure and wondered why other people weren't doing it, too.

People said to me, "Well, we are in it for the long term," but my view is that the long term is built upon shorter-term trades that can be managed on a long-term basis, though more on a tactical scale. So, although the strategic view is focusing on the long term, short-term trades can get you there better than just a buy-and-hold approach.

After that, I talked to people about making trades for them and giving advice, and then I talked to an advisor who explained to me that it was easy to get into business and still be independent. One of my biggest hang-ups was that I didn't want to work for a big brokerage house because I wanted more flexibility and to not have to push proprietary products or funds. So, it eventually just made sense to go out on my own.

Bourquin: How do you make money while managing other people's money? Is it a percentage of gains, a flat rate, or something else?

Foster: For me, it's just a straight percentage of assets, and it varies, depending on how active I am in the account.

If, for example, a client is interested in a more passive account that mainly employs a buy-and-hold approach and for which major market changes would only result in changes to a smaller percentage of the account—that would be a 1.25 percent fee.

Some accounts are totally active, where clients have more money with a big brokerage house, but they want to manage a portion of their account with me using what they call "play money." Now, that's quite an interesting term, and it would be nice to have that, but it's essentially the aggressive portion of their account. I would take up to 2 percent in those cases, and I might turn over the entire account every month or two.

This is very tax inefficient, but sometimes the inefficiencies work out because either the gains are worth it or the avoidance of losses makes up for it. Sometimes that's the case, too.

Bourquin: Going back to profit targets, do you have areas set ahead of time where you are going to close out your positions, or how do you decide when it's time to get out?

Foster: No, I don't figure that out ahead of time. I have heard of traders who have a 5 percent or 8 percent cutoff on losses and a 10 percent or 15 percent cutoff on gains, but I would rather let my winners run. When it comes to cutting losses, I count on the technical signals to help me get out at the right time.

It also depends on the account and its risk level, and I might set a broader barrier for an IRA account to maximize gains and not trade as much. But I will also use more out-of-the-money naked puts in those accounts.

If I think there is a 10 percent downside possibility for the S&P in a given year, I don't believe it's wise to sell at an 8 percent loss, because there might only be 2 percent left in the downfall. If, however, a technical indicator says to get out right away, then I would sell, although hopefully the sell signal would appear before sustaining an 8 percent loss to begin with.

Bourquin: It's interesting to hear more traders talk about getting away from setting arbitrary profit targets and instead relying more on what the market is telling them.

Foster: And here's a good example: if I had used an arbitrary limit at the beginning or middle of December 2011, when the S&P was making a near-term bottom, I would have missed out on 10 percent or 15 percent to the upside.

It's not really worth cutting a trade off based on numbers alone, and I don't ever want to limit upside potential. The way I look at it, I would rather miss 2 percent or 3 percent to the downside off the top than get out early and miss another 10 percent to the upside. I don't think I'm going to be able to pick the absolute top and bottom unless I'm extremely lucky anyway, but by using technical indicators, I can identify when a trend has changed or momentum has shifted.

Bourquin: Essentially you will catch the meat of the move and be comfortable with that.

Foster: Exactly, just catch the bulk of it and realize that if there is 2 percent, 3 percent, or occasionally even 4 percent off the very top or very bottom that you miss, that's small over the longer term compared to the 10 percent or 20 percent you could get in the middle.

If you're trading the short side in a bear market and can ride that for even 5 percent, then when you consider the S&P is historically going to gain 10 percent or 11 percent over twenty or thirty years, on average, you've not only erased 5 percent on the downside, but you've flipped it to become 5 percent on the upside. That's how to come out way ahead in the markets over the long term.

Derek Schimming

Through the different stages of his career, which spans 25 years, **Derek Schimming** *once managed over $275 million in client assets, studied under legendary trader Harvey Houtkin, and developed groundbreaking pure price-charting tools for the currency markets. His trading methods are applicable to all markets, and despite his vast experience and resources, Schimming quickly discounts the idea of an elusive "Holy Grail" of trading, instead favoring discipline and proper trade management as cornerstones of a successful trading strategy. His philosophy shows that breaking away from the confines of multiple lagging indicators, staying nimble in fast-moving markets, and above all booking hard-earned profits and limiting losses can pave the way for a highly successful and long-lasting trading career.*

Tim Bourquin: Derek, let's start by talking about the type of trader you are—day trader or swing trader, and the markets you trade.

Derek Schimming: Well, by design and by desire, I definitely would consider myself more of a swing or position trader. However, recent market conditions have not been conducive to holding longer-term positions, in my opinion, so as a result, I trade like a chameleon, changing myself and my behavior to fit what the market environment allows me to do.

I think a trader's style is defined by how they manage their trades. A great entry is just that, a great entry, but how I manage that trade and where I ultimately exit is what will really dictate my style.

I might come into a trade with one intention and end up with another one entirely based on what the markets dictate. Simply adjusting your stop and saying that you're a swing trader or saying that you're a day trader does not necessarily make you either one. That stop adjustment has nothing to do with your overall strategy. It only has to do with how much you're willing to lose if the trade doesn't go in your favor.

I don't really like to typecast myself into any one box, because although I do come from a fundamental background, given the more recent market conditions, I now find myself trading technically and with a fairly short-term time frame.

Bourquin: And are you specifically trading spot Forex or futures?

Schimming: I trade spot Forex because I believe that market has by far the most attractive opportunities for currency traders. But if there were charts for old tires and I could just see the prices moving, I could trade tires. Ultimately, I think anything is tradable.

Bourquin: I want to ask you about the type of technical analysis you do. What would be a go-to chart for you, in terms of time frame, and what indicators do you put on it?

Schimming: Every chart I look at is a pure price-analysis view. I don't look at time-based instruments, only at the price movement. I'm going to look at things based on a trading range and not necessarily just look at a one-hour chart and then make my entry on a fifteen-minute chart. My analysis technique has nothing to do with that, and that makes me different from the majority of other traders in the marketplace.

I do look at a broader pip range to see what's happening overall, and I call that "The Monet Effect," because you have to step back to really see it. Those familiar with Impressionist art know that if you come very close to a Monet, you see all the daubs of paint and how incredibly it was made, but you can't really see the picture itself until you step back, and it almost looks like a photograph. That's what's amazing. To me, trading is much the same. You've got to step back and take a look at what's happening overall, and then you can move in closer to see the finer details and be able to make your decision.

Even though the approach I take is fairly simple, it's difficult for me to put myself in any one box and say, "This is precisely what I look at," although I might favor twenty-five- and twenty-pip charts for broad searches, fifteen- and twelve-pip charts for looking at the last few days to get more of a swing view, if you will, and then a ten-, eight-, or even smaller pip-range study to actually take the entry into the market.

Bourquin: What is it about the price that tells you when it's time to start looking for a trade opportunity? Are you watching for price to approach previous highs or lows?

Schimming: I am first looking to identify what stage the market is in. That doesn't mean I'm always right about that, but I'm striving to identify where we are in the flow of the overall market or in the flow of a particular instrument. Only then can I make trading decisions.

Some typical patterns, like double tops and double bottoms, or breakouts and breakdowns, can be very consistent trading patterns for those who know how to analyze and trade them properly, but just looking at the simplistic nature of a higher high and following the subsequent higher low may create a new entry for me. So too might lower highs and lower lows, which are the basic components of a downtrend. I hate to make it sound so A-B-C basic, but that's really what it comes down to.

From there, it's just taking disciplined trades based on the patterns and trying to put the odds more in my favor, all the while recognizing that I can't be right every time. That's when patience and discipline really become key.

Bourquin: In speaking with traders who identify themselves as pure price-action players, many have said that it takes a while to learn to read the markets and get that "feel" you mentioned. How long did it take you to really become confident in your trading?

Schimming: This is where I respectfully disagree with the way most people feel about that. I think that's wrong. The only indicator out there that doesn't lag is price, and while so many embark on this never-ending search for the "Holy Grail" of trading tools, it just doesn't exist.

Too many traders get caught up in putting so much clutter on their charts that the only outcome is "paralysis by analysis." They're waiting for so many things to happen before they buy that I'm already selling to them when they finally decide to pull the trigger. The problem is that we want to see so many things line up in order to have confidence in a trade, and the reality is, at some point, each trader has to be decisive and put their money on the table if they think something is going higher or lower.

What I'm suggesting is that traders should require much less initial confirmation and then look for more things to confirm once they're already in the position. A trade doesn't need to look perfect when I get in, but I need for it to look better as I'm holding it, and if it doesn't, then I should get out. My philosophy is that by looking only at the price, I'm able to react much quicker.

I use only two indicators to qualify my trades, and while there are other things I look for as a trade develops, I mainly just deal with mistakes as they happen and allow winners to run while cutting the losers short.

Trading is always easy after the fact, but when we look back in retrospect, traders typically get out of winning trades too quickly just to book a profit, and they stay in bad trades for too long because they don't want to admit they were wrong and take the loss. It's unfortunate, but the natural mental cycle is usually telling us the wrong things.

Bourquin: You began to mention the two primary qualifiers you look for to confirm your trade entries. Let's talk some more about those.

Schimming: I created a tool called the Currency Strength Index—CCYX— and there is a lot of documentation on it on the internet, but what it does is disassemble the currency pairs. It's doing cross-currency analysis, but it's doing it from the large liquidity pools in the currency arena and allows me to see what's happening throughout the world, and not just according to one broker.

Using CCYX, I can see what's happening to the currencies on an individual basis and identify some basic trends. I always start here to discover which currencies are moving higher, which are moving lower, and which aren't moving at all.

Then, if I see, for example, that the yen and the US dollar are moving up while the British pound and Aussie are moving down, all of a sudden, my focus list is set, and I'll look at four currency pairs: GBP/USD and GBP/JPY, as well as AUD/USD and AUD/JPY.

Next, I'll take a Monet view of those four pairs and look at what's happened to them over the last few days and last few hours to gauge the cycle we are in. Obviously, there are several steps involved in that process, but when I'm ready to actually take a trade, I'll look at price pattern as well as two simple qualifiers: the TFXD oscillator, which is very similar to moving average convergence/ divergence [MACD], and also a directional movement system, like the average directional index [ADX]. I happen to put those two together just because they are the ones that I find most complementary to my style of trading and charting things, but that could differ from trader to trader.

By looking at price movement and patterns, I know which currencies are most—and least—in play and can shorten my watch list. Then, when I see a pattern develop—like a high that's looking to go higher following a pullback in the uptrend—I'll look at those qualifiers for confirmation to take that trade.

Once we're holding a position, trade management becomes most critical, and obviously, we want the earlier indicators, including CCYX, TFXD, and ADX to appear even stronger once a trade is on.

Bourquin: You mentioned that you came from a fundamental background. What role, if any, does that still play in your trading decisions?

Schimming: That's a good question, because we're dealing with currencies, not companies, like traders in the equities arena do. Obviously, in equities we would look at company data, like P/E ratio and earnings reports, news, and other factors to formulate a fundamental impression of a particular company.

In currencies, we don't have that information for particular countries, per se, but in reality, economic reports, like the Purchasing Managers Index [PMI], the

Producer Price Index [PPI], and nonfarm payrolls in the United States, probably represent the most substantial news events in any calendar month and provide that same kind of useful information.

I treat each country like a company and assess economic and fundamental data to see how it is making the nation's currency react. Now, I believe that sometimes things move fundamentally incorrectly, but the fact that a particular pair is moving is really all I care about as a trader.

I know a lot of people who don't like to trade nonfarm payroll reports, and I was one of them at one time in my career, but ironically, now that I have these tools available, nonfarm payrolls is my favorite day of each trading month. More often than not, I find trading around nonfarm payrolls to be like shooting fish in a barrel, not just because the dollar may tend to move against major currencies, but mainly because it means all markets are going to move. Things can happen quickly, and there's going to be plenty of volume and plenty of opportunities for those who know how to take advantage of them.

Again, when looking at pure price, I'm not waiting for a bunch of things to tell me what "should" or "could" be happening. I'm using price to tell what *is* happening. I make trade decisions and run with them, and I'll deal with the consequences when I'm wrong. The critical part is just to not get hurt too much in the event of a bad trade.

Bourquin: Can you recall a recent nonfarm payrolls announcement that serves as a good example of how you trade that data?

Schimming: Absolutely. I do the same thing every time, and as a matter of fact, the last few have worked out very, very well for us.

What I do is lay out a schematic that includes the expected figure, the median and the average, the previous report's figure, and how the previous print compared to its prior expectation. Next, based on what's expected for the new report, I analyze both potentially positive factors that could lead to more jobs being created, and potentially negative factors that could lead to fewer jobs being created. I'll then set some levels for those figures, typically using fairly round numbers.

You have to anticipate both sides and consider what data might surprise the market, as well as what might anger the market. That doesn't mean traders have to predict what's going to happen, but too many get caught up in that and then fail to take notice of what's really happening.

As traders, we don't have to know what's going to happen tomorrow, but we do have to anticipate what the possibilities are and be prepared to react when a move materializes.

On the morning of the report, I'm careful not to jump right in. I allow the news to come out and the typical knee-jerk reaction to take place. For example, if the news was good, the dollar should be reacting strongly, and currency pairs like EUR/USD and GBP/USD should be coming down. But those moves may or may not be happening right then.

We wait for things to settle down and for the trend to ultimately begin, and that may mean waiting five minutes or twenty-five minutes, but I can assure you that it's not five seconds. I don't have my finger on the trigger the moment that report comes out.

Bourquin: Do you have an entry point in mind before the report comes out, or do you wait to determine that until after you see the data and reaction?

Schimming: I'll look at ranges of key price areas where I would want to get in, but that's not necessarily going to be the end-all for me.

The human mind responds to round numbers, but regardless of the financial instrument, I never look at the market with one specific price in mind, because that can keep you out of trades that are happening as planned just because they didn't hit a certain number.

An even more common mistake might be when the market passes your specific entry point by a little bit and you wait for it to come back. It can be off and running from there, and you'll never have another chance to get in if you stay fixated on just one entry point.

It's fine to look at one specific price *range* for entries, but never break it down to a single price. You just can't make it that perfect, nor do you have to. I can get close and still be effective, and while the goal is to be very close, I'm not going to be spot-on at picking tops and bottoms. Nobody is.

Bourquin: Right. You just want to get the meat of the move after the trend has started.

Schimming: Yes, I'm not trying to squeeze out every pip from top to bottom. Just give me a chunk in the middle.

How often do we see traders get burned while reaching for "one last pip" or "one more dollar"? I can't tell you how many times I've seen reversals happen in those situations, and the worst part is that the trader saw their opportunity to exit and just didn't take it.

Again, the brain works in round numbers, but sometimes that's the Achilles' heel for traders. I want my stops to be beyond the specific levels of support and resistance, beyond a Fib or pivot level, and beyond a high or low so I have stronger protection. Then I want my limits to be inside those levels, and I want my ranges to be hit, because ultimately, even though I'm not constantly booking the top of a move—or even booking profits on every trade—I make consistent profits when trades go my way and limit losses when they don't. It's much easier to make money overall when maintaining that philosophy.

Bourquin: You mentioned placing your stops outside certain levels and your limits inside those levels, so let's expand on that a little bit, because I think that probably forms the basis for how you set your profit targets and stop losses, right?

Schimming: Absolutely. We can just use some round numbers and a hypothetical situation to help visualize this. Let's assume something is trading just above the round number 3,700, and just below that is a pivot level at 3,695.

We believe it will continue higher and know there is firm support near that 3,700 figure because of the round number and the nearby pivot for the instrument. If we enter fifteen pips above 3,700 and the known pivot level is five pips below at 3,695, as I'm taking it long, I need to set my stop so I'll be protected.

Some traders could have trouble here if they say, "Well, I use a twenty-pip stop." Personally, I like to use a fixed stop range as well, but mine is not a fixed number, be it fifteen, twenty, or fifty pips.

If I'm taking this trade at fifteen and I think the area of support is twenty pips back, in this case, I need to have my stop at ninety pips, because there's defense both at the round number and the pivot point below it.

Now, I don't want that hit, and if the instrument were to go below 3,700 and then below that pivot point, I would want out anyway. I think it can come down and scrape against them, though, so I place my stop according to the specific conditions. That's an example of trading "like a chameleon," as I mentioned earlier.

Regarding profit taking, let's say that 3,750 was the prior high, and as the instrument approaches, I want it to get above there. But my philosophy would be to take profits on half this trade at 3,740 and book a twenty-five-pip winner.

After booking those profits, I'll then bring my stop up somewhere between sixteen and twenty, so I'll put my stop at plus one to plus five. I'm going to see if the pair can still get over that previous high range and break out into new ground. But if it doesn't, I've already taken risk off the table. I've brought my stop inside my protection to let the trade move. I've set my initial price target based on a prior high or resistance point, or a Fib level or pivot.

There could also be factors that would cause me to exit the trade instead, but active management is likely how I would approach that.

The point I want to emphasize is this: I want my limits hit, so I've got them exposed where they can get hit. Also, I want my stops protected, and I'll adjust so they are somewhere in the fifteen- to twenty-five-pip range, based on where the protection is.

There is no easier thing to do than eliminate risk on a trade if it's moving in your favor. Myself and the traders in my group follow a written rule that says,

"Once profitable by fifteen pips or more in any trade, you should never allow that trade to go negative." If we're talking about trading as an art form, the art is really how you manage your trades.

Bourquin: That's why some traders are right a lot of the time but aren't making money and can't figure out why. It's probably because they're not managing trades properly.

Schimming: Obviously, we don't want to be wrong half the time, but honestly, if you can control your losers and keep them smaller than your winners, you can be wrong half the time or more and still be profitable.

Managing a winning trade is fairly simple, it's a lot of fun, and it's why we trade to begin with. However, it's how we handle the inevitable mistakes that's ultimately the key to long-term success.

You show me someone who can be disciplined and consistently manage mistakes, and I'll show you someone I can teach to make money trading. The problem is that the right decisions often go against our natural instincts, but the most effective traders will learn how to consistently win that psychological battle.

Peter Brandt

Since getting his start as a commodities floor trader in the 1970s, **Peter Brandt** *has happily made the transition to electronic trading, authored two highly acclaimed books—including* Diary of a Professional Commodity Trader *(Wiley, 2011)— and was regarded as one of the "30 most influential persons in the world of finance" by esteemed author, economist, and money manager Barry Ritholz. By placing his emphasis on classical chart patterns and longer-term time frames—and in the process de-emphasizing often misleading short-term or intraday price swings—Brandt has been able to take fewer trades without compromising his profit potential. His career spans multiple decades and ever-changing market conditions, but the pillars of his overall strategy—patience, discipline, and sound money management—are timeless and applicable for traders across all markets and time frames.*

Tim Bourquin: Peter, let's first talk about the type of trader you are—a short-term trader or a swing trader—and how you look at the markets.

Peter Brandt: I'm kind of a mongrel! It's tough to really pigeonhole the way I trade, but if you are looking at it from a time frame basis, I tend to be a swing trader *and* a position trader.

When I take new positions, I take them with the intention of being a swing trader on half and a position trader on half, but even though I live in both worlds, I don't have separate programs for swing trading and position trading. When I enter the market, I enter both swing and position trades at the same time; I simply exit them differently.

Bourquin: And since your background is in commodities, is that the market you trade most often?

Brandt: Yes, I was born and raised, so to speak, as a corn trader on the floor, so commodities are where I'm most comfortable. I like the futures market and I understand it well, but I will also dabble from time to time in stocks and ETFs.

I like being short the stock market, so I trade stocks on the short side, and I also trade Forex. Having started in the futures world, part of my history there was in currency futures, and I still trade them sometimes, but I also trade currencies in the spot Forex market.

Bourquin: I love talking to former floor traders about how they made the transition to electronic trading. For some, it was tough to go from the floor to the screen. How was the transition for you?

Brandt: Mine was surprisingly smooth, maybe because I always wanted to be an off-floor trader to begin with!

I was a niche trader on the floor, focusing on the September to December corn spread. I lived that spread. I knew rail, FOB, and barge rates, and I knew how much grain was being stored in Toledo and in Chicago. I was working the belts for Continental Grain Company at that time, and that was the door through which I entered the business, but even then I knew that my goal was to be an independent trader.

All the while, I watched all markets, and in the 1970s, I wound up getting involved in the sugar mills. That's what took me off the floor to trade, and I've never been back. I made the transition smoothly because off the floor was where I wanted to go all along.

Bourquin: It seems that one of the biggest differences between retail and professional floor traders is that the pros find one approach to the markets and just do it over, and over, and over again, while retail traders are always looking for new strategies. Do you still feel that the repetitive, "cookie cutter" approach is the best way to be successful in trading?

Brandt: Well, I would answer that in two ways. The first would be that every successful trader I know, from the most skilled traders on the floor in Chicago down to the finest electronic traders, all have a niche and understand it instinctively in their minds. Sometimes they aren't good at articulating precisely what it is, but they have found a way to understand the market as it applies to their own character and personality traits, and it's unique to them.

I know of no successful trader who has become that way just by mirroring the actions of another. Every successful trader I know has figured out a way to do it themselves. They borrow here and there, and they take select ideas from others, but they end up putting together their own collage, and that's how they operate.

So, first off, every successful trader I know, be it on or off the floor, has a niche. But, that niche can change, and that niche can be modified.

Markets have a way of taking some niches away, but good traders find a way to modify their niche and morph into something different. For example, those who traded successfully in the 1970s and 1980s but continued on with exactly the same strategy couldn't stay at the top of the game and inevitably encountered frustration.

Markets change, and traders have to identify that and be flexible whenever it happens. That has been especially true in recent years, with the increase in high-frequency and algorithmic trading, plus twenty-four-hour markets, electronic exchanges, and the quant world.

Even though the nature of the markets has changed, however, I would say for the most part that I'm still in the same niche now that I was in 1980. But there are subtleties within that niche—money management, most notably—that I have changed over time in response to changes in the markets.

Bourquin: Let's talk about that niche. How do you describe it when someone asks you, "Peter, how do you trade?"

Brandt: I'm a pure chart trader, but because there are a lot of people out there who trade charts, that means something different to everyone. I identify with what I call "classical charting principles," which are basically those laid out initially by Richard W. Schabacker in the early 1930s and then picked up in the Edwards and Magee book, *Technical Analysis of Stock Trends,* which was initially published in the 1940s.

That book has been referred to as the Bible of classical charting, and it is that for me. I have a worn and torn copy, and I refer to it daily. I'm a classical charter in every sense.

Bourquin: Can you describe what "classical charting" means? Is pattern recognition the essence of it?

Brandt: Yes. I'm a pattern trader, and that's become controversial these days, because some of the new quant traders are saying that classical charting doesn't work anymore. Now, I'm not sure exactly why they are saying that, because classical charting still works. It just works in slightly different ways and for slightly different reasons.

I look specifically at weekly charts. Being a day trader has never even crossed my mind, so I'm not interested in intraday charts, like hourly charts, five-minute charts, tick charts, or any of the others. My mind doesn't work that fast, so I like weekly and monthly charts for market analysis and for identifying broad technical themes, and I use daily charts only for market signaling.

Bourquin: Is "market signaling" how you find good entry points in the market?

Brandt: Yes, I'm looking to find the breakout. I don't like trading patterns within the patterns. I think that's a good way to lose money and get worn out by a market before it moves.

Specifically, I like patterns that are clear on a weekly chart and are at least twelve to fourteen weeks in duration, and I base that only on classical signals. I like rectangles and head-and-shoulders patterns with flat necklines. I don't really like symmetrical triangles, but they have diagonal boundary lines and a number of other patterns that I look at, so I will consider trading symmetrical triangles.

I hate trend lines and don't like the idea of trading them at all. To me, a break of a trend line doesn't mean anything.

As a futures trader, I'm generally looking to trade moves that I think can make somewhere in the area of $3,000 to $4,000 per contract and up. I'm not interested in a market that's going to move $300 or $500 per contract, because there isn't enough money in there to justify the risk.

Substantial moves, like one hundred points in the S&P or $50 to $100 in gold, are what I'm after. Although, in 2011, I had a gold trade that was a $300 mover. Those are the substantial moves that can only be launched out of weekly and monthly charts.

Bourquin: Do you think that the daily and intraday charts, like hourly and fifteen-minute charts, just have too much noise to really allow traders to identify and get a good chunk of a move?

Brandt: There is way too much noise, and a lot of those moves come from high-frequency traders. In some of the markets I trade, high-frequency trading [HFT] represents 50 percent to 60 percent of the volume on some days.

I think there is more volatility and far more intraday chart breakouts that end up *not* being sustained by the time the markets close. So, I really don't care what takes place during the market session. I only care about the daily closing price, because that's where people have to margin up.

When the markets close and create a settlement price at the end of the normal daytime hours, that's the price that goes to the clearing corporation. That's the settlement price, where people need to put up margin overnight. When you are dealing with only closing prices, you can wash out the high-frequency traders and the day traders, thereby removing a lot of the noise and enabling clearer price discovery.

Even beyond that, the single most important price each week is the Friday close, and that's why I'm interested in looking at not only open or high bar charts, but closing price charts as well.

I don't have a lot of time for candlestick charts, although they tend to be the hot ones that many traders look at today. I also do some point-and-figure charting, which is really old school, but I'm mostly interested in high/low bar charts and closing charts. Oftentimes, I will draw boundary lines through both closing prices and what I consider to be orthodox lows.

I'm looking for big patterns, and my goal is really simple: at the end of the year, when I look back over the forty or so markets I trade, I want to be able to pick out maybe twenty patterns that are the best examples of pure, classical charting principles—meaning that they were clear, they broke out cleanly, and they ran to their targets. I want to then be able to look at my purchase and sale [P&S] data and see that at least 50 percent of my trading was in these twenty patterns and that I caught at least 50 percent of each move.

Bourquin: Because you trade on a longer time frame, do you have to be even more patient and wait for the patterns to fully develop on the weekly chart before you get in?

Brandt: Yes, and I tend to struggle with that tension. I'm a discretionary trader, not a systematic trader, and as such, I'm always battling the human urge to be involved on my own time.

I think most discretionary traders will admit in their weaker moments that their emotions are a real hurdle to maximum profit. Our emotions tend to tell us to do the wrong thing at the wrong time and often can't be trusted. In my case, at least, I don't believe I can trust mine.

Because I look at long-term charts and trade long-term scenarios, I will often see things weeks or even months before the pattern is completed. There is a real urge to want to be involved, and for me, it's a constant battle to sit on my hands and remind myself that my paycheck comes from holding positions, not by actively trading them.

It sometimes takes weeks or months to develop the big price moves I'm interested in, and profiting from these moves requires having not only the patience to wait for a pattern to complete, but also the patience to wait for the market to run its course once a trade is on. Then, you still have to have the discipline to put on the proper size, as well as use sound money-management rules.

Bourquin: How many positions are you comfortable having on at any one time?

Brandt: I don't really pay attention to the number of positions I have on at any given time. I will have on as many trades as I have good signals.

I tend to trade underleveraged, however, and I can't believe the leverage that most novice traders use. It's remarkable that really good traders seldom risk more than one or two percent of their capital on any one trade, while novice traders routinely risk three, four, five, or even ten percent. That's one way to end your trading career very quickly.

I know a lot of very good traders who limit risk to a half or even a quarter of one percent on each trade they enter, and as a general rule, I'm in the 1 percent area.

As we speak at the end of May 2012, I've put on twenty-nine trades so far this year, and I currently have six trades open, which doesn't bother me. They could all go against me, and I would probably experience a 10 percent drawdown before I finally scrambled out of them.

I do pay attention to margin-to-capital ratio, or margin-to-equity ratio, trying to limit that to 15 percent. Seldom do I allow more than 15 percent of my trading assets to be committed to margin.

Bourquin: What would be a standard stop-loss area for your trades?

Brandt: Well, I focus on dollar risk and limiting trades to 1 percent of my capital. So, considering a $5 million account, when I enter a position I'm risking no more than $50,000 on that trade. Actually, I just went short the Russell using those rules today, although that trade has gone against me so far.

I want to enter at a logical place on the chart, where I can look back after the fact and identify the closing price that completed the pattern. I also want to put my protective stop at a natural barrier, where I would believe my analysis had been proven wrong, instead of arbitrarily using a money-management stop.

I also back myself into position sizing that way, by considering dollar risk and how much I have to risk based on the chart itself. With those two figures in mind, I can determine how many contracts to trade. While that can oftentimes vary, depending on how a market breaks out, as a general rule, when trading markets like S&P futures, gold, or soybeans, I trade one contract for every $100,000 to $150,000 in capital.

Bourquin: For that Russell trade you mentioned, what was the pattern that you saw on the chart, and how did you determine your entry point for that one?

Brandt: In the case of the Russell trade, we were dealing with a head-and-shoulders top that developed over about sixteen weeks. The market confirmed the pattern on May 16 by closing below the neckline, and although it nicked that line a few times in prior days, I ignored those because of the intraday nature of the trade.

I like to see those clear, decisive patterns, and I also like trades that have the right volume/open interest profile. I love going against conventional wisdom and not being part of a big crowd, and I prefer patterns with horizontal boundaries, as opposed to diagonal or slanting ones. That's why I don't particularly like trading wedges, symmetrical triangles, or trend lines.

Most of my trades happen in the last hour or two of active trading before the markets close briefly for settlement. At that time, I look at where the markets close, and I will either take action within the last thirty to sixty seconds of active trading or I will put in a limit order and trade it when the market reopens.

Bourquin: How do you determine profit targets for head-and-shoulders patterns? Are you looking to a previous area, where you believe the trade will be completed?

Brandt: The Edwards and Magee book I mentioned does a pretty good job of laying out how to establish targets, and I use that as a general guideline. The rule is that the height of a pattern that is projected in the direction of the breakout will give you a pretty good estimation of the magnitude of the move.

The target for this particular Russell trade is just under 710, but I don't like using exact numbers, so my limit order is in at 710 to 720—and that's the price range where I would "ring the cash register," as they say.

Bourquin: And when getting out, will you scale out of things, even if you think it could go a lot further?

Brandt: I do, as a matter of a fact, and I didn't get into that. I have had to battle with something that's a common concern among swing and position traders, and that is, once you get a nice profit in a trade, are you willing to ride that into a loser?

That's something all traders must think about, and I decided I wanted the best of both worlds: While I didn't want to give back large profits on trades, I also wanted to take advantage of continued profit potential. As a result, I strip out half of a position, sometimes within a week or two of taking the trade, and that gives me sustained power to ride out the other half of the position for the full extent of what the move may give me.

Bourquin: I want to circle back with you about something you said early on, and that was that you don't see value in trend line breaks. Can you talk more about that?

Brandt: I'm not a big fan of trend lines. I think you can give a monkey a chart book, a ruler, and a pen, and pretty soon even he's going to have a trend line that makes sense!

Technically, I think the violation of a trend line has no significance whatsoever, other than as an indication that there has been some change in market behavior. But that change can mean a lot of things. It could be a shift from a steady advance to a more gradual advance, or from an advance to a sideways congestion phase, or any number of other things.

I'm looking for fewer excuses to trade, not more, and if I added trend lines to my arsenal, the number of trading situations that would arise would increase exponentially. And because I'm now trying to limit my trading to five, six, or seven trades per month, I filter opportunities by using only patterns and pattern boundaries.

Now, I must qualify my previous statements by saying that if I'm looking at just a trend-line break by itself, I'm not interested. There are times, however, when a trend line becomes an extremely important technical factor because it combines with other developments on the chart. For example, a trend line that is violated in the process of completing a pattern or setting up a scenario that fits into a larger macro outlook would be a situation I'd be keenly interested in.

Bourquin: A lot of traders feel they have to be in the market at all times, trading frenetically and staring at their monitors for eight hours or more every day. In the end, it's about making money, and you've proven that by backing off your time frame to look at weekly charts and making only five or six trades each month, you can still make a good living while also reducing your stress level. That's a very valuable lesson for traders.

Brandt: I could go on and on about that, Tim, and back when I started trading, people paid up to $1 million to purchase a Chicago Board of Trade membership so they could go on the floor and, in essence, buy the bid and sell the offer. Basically, they could own the bid/offer spread, and while there are still bid/offer spreads in the markets today, those are owned by high-frequency and algorithmic traders, not private speculators—and that includes me.

When I buy, even if it's on a limit order, I'm buying at the offer, not the bid.

That bid/offer spread for active traders can amount to a lot of money over time, and because they now give away the bid/offer spread, I think the odds are stacked against day traders.

In those early days of pit trading, day traders who weren't on the floor were a really rare breed, because it was generally assumed that you could only day trade if you were an exchange member who had access to exchange rates and could buy the bid and sell the offer. Otherwise, the deck was stacked against you. Yet, somehow we now trade in a world where some people think they can just start day trading and make money like it's automatic.

I'll freely admit that if I sat and stared at my screens while looking at different charts and time periods and re-examining things, I would end up sabotaging myself. That would cost me money.

Maybe it's not true for everybody, but I know it's true for me that the fewer trading decisions I make, the better it's going to be in the long run. There may be individual cases where quick action might be profitable, but over a larger number of trades and a longer period of time, I know how I have to trade— and that's by holding positions, not trading them.

Bourquin: I completely agree with that, and I find it to be true in my trading as well. I could be following a trade on a weekly chart that is weeks or months in the making, but if I look at an hourly chart and perhaps see something there that goes against my idea, I could let that discount the quality of my setup on the weekly chart. So, along those lines, it makes sense to avoid short-term charts on these longer-term trades.

Brandt: I'm a believer in what's called "the fallen state of the human being," and I think that it is with rare exception that instinctual traders can be successful. There may be some who can be profitable in their trading—and perhaps extremely so—but I think those traders are the exception, not the rule.

I've had traders tell me that it drives them crazy when they are in a position—and it drives them crazy when they are not in one. That's the kind of double thinking that can lead to some pretty substantial losses.

For me, I think the key to trading is in risk management, not necessarily in signal generation. Keeping losses short and letting profits run is an all-too-common adage in active trading, but it can be very difficult to do.

Rob Wilson

*Many part-time traders naturally draw on skills that serve them well in their day jobs, but perhaps none are more fascinating than **Rob Wilson**, whose role as a commander for the British Royal Navy requires unwavering discipline and strict adherence to protocol. Wilson's military training has instilled in him the importance of quick, confident decision-making in the face of often limited or imperfect information. Whether he is at sea or in the markets, he knows that indecisiveness at the moment of action can have disastrous consequences.*

By trading only the EUR/USD currency pair, Wilson eliminates the need for extensive market research and analysis, and his ultra-short time frame and very tight risk parameters help him carve out small but steady profits while trading for only four hours early each morning before reporting for duty. His success and approach to the markets may serve as inspiration to any new or part-time traders who are looking to find their way and strike the proper balance between trading and the other important facets of their lives.

Tim Bourquin: Rob, you have a military background and an interesting story about how you got into trading. Let's start by talking about your military training.

Rob Wilson: I joined the Royal Navy as an officer cadet at the age of eighteen, and while I wouldn't call myself a high school dropout, I was the nearest thing to it. I managed to scrape by with the minimum qualifications and went to sea, and I never really came back. Here I am, twenty-four years later, still doing it, albeit I'm about to move to Australia and transfer to the Australian Navy.

My ambition was always to command warships, and I managed to achieve that when I was thirty-four and took command of my first one. I left my last command in 2009, when I was thirty-nine years old.

I attended Dartmouth Royal Naval College in the southwest of Britain and started my career watchkeeping on the bridge. I then learned to control fast jets using a radar and voice circuit, and I spent two years with the French Navy on the aircraft carriers Clemenceau and Foch. Afterwards, I returned to the United Kingdom and conducted my warfare training proper, then went back to sea, running the ops room on a warship, before I was finally ready to take command. I drove a minehunter initially, and was later promoted and took command of a destroyer.

Bourquin: Are you still in the Royal Navy?

Wilson: I am still serving, albeit on secondment to the US Navy while I'm instructing at their war college in Newport.

Bourquin: And how did the trading bug get to you?

Wilson: My father was trading indices and introduced me to it, but I wanted to pick a different instrument that I could really get to know and that was volatile enough for me to trade on a short-term basis. I really wanted to appeal to the side of my character that had been honed throughout my Navy training.

That was what led me to Forex, and from there, I got acquainted with Rob Booker, who actually came to trade with me on the destroyer at one time.

I wasn't happy trading on the one-hour or four-hour timescales because I couldn't generate the sort of discipline I wanted. I needed to trade on an even shorter-term timescale that was more in tune with what I was doing in the Navy.

Bourquin: Right. And because you were obviously working full-time, Forex was probably a good fit because you can trade it off hours. Is that part of what drew you to it initially?

Wilson: Actually, no. It was just the fact that I could see more than enough potential for profit in one pair, and that would take away the need for me to research and data mine. I could just focus on getting to know the personality of one currency pair, and that was really what made me choose Forex.

I didn't have a chance to start trading actively during the day until we moved to America, and then, all of a sudden, it opened up a window for me to trade between 3:00 a.m. eastern time [when the London Stock Exchange opens] and the time I went to work, and that's what I decided to do. I would get up at 2:30 in the morning, trade through until 7:30, and then go to work—and, actually, I still do that.

Bourquin: Wow. So let's back up. You said Rob Booker visited you to trade right from the destroyer?

Wilson: Yeah, it was great! In fact, we were just coming out of dock from a big refit, so Rob spent about three days with me in dock. Then we sailed the ship, and I took him down the River Thames and dropped him off at the head of the river to attend a few meetings in London from there.

We put him in a fast launch and went straight onto the beach, and much to the amazement of the bathers, Rob just peeled off his waterproofs, walked off the bridge, and never looked back. It was fantastic!

Bourquin: That's awesome! I know Rob and I can't wait to talk to him about that. That's probably a whole interview in and of itself that I should do with him!

So, after getting involved with currency trading, what were some of the things you tried initially to find good trades, and were you looking only at technical analysis?

Wilson: I started by stripping everything off my chart and trying to understand not necessarily what drove the market, but where I could identify opportunities to trade. I really started to make progress when it dawned on me that the currency market was a market just like any other. I saw on the chart where price points had turned and at least questioned the prevailing sentiment for whatever reason.

I then started testing very short-term reaction trades against those price points, and I found that I could make a very consistent profit from those, and that's really how I started trading.

Although I was using a chart, I was essentially placing market orders where I saw even the beginnings of a reversal pattern developing at those key price points. If price blew through those price points, then I would just trade them in the other direction.

That really chimed with my personality and the way I learned to work in the Navy, which was to be prepared to make a decision based on the best information I had at the time, but also to be prepared to reverse that decision if an event came about that proved my initial determination incorrect.

I loved the idea of being able to profit from being wrong, and you can do that just by adjusting your leverage. By using careful money or risk management, you can pop in a pilot trade at one of these points and look to take a few pips.

For me, I'll take fifteen pips, which will generate a 0.3 percent return, and I'm happy with that. If that trade doesn't come off, however, then my further aim is to learn from that and trade with what I now perceive to be the correct direction, only at a larger size.

Essentially, my aim is to get out of every session with a net profit, and that's all I'm trying to do. If I can earn anything north of 0.3 percent a day, I'm more than happy with that. The challenge is to be able to achieve that every day, though.

Bourquin: What are the time frames that you ultimately determined work the best in your trading?

Wilson: Well, I profile the session on a fifteen-minute chart and a five-minute chart, but I trade from the one-minute chart.

Bourquin: And in those four hours each morning that you trade before going to work, how many opportunities do you typically find on any given day?

Wilson: If I could get to where I want to be, it would be between six and ten. There's certainly that much energy in the market, and swings tend to be between fifteen and forty pips at any one time, but it really depends on what sort of market you profile going in.

Sometimes there won't be much energy or much volatility, and an opportunity that you spend four hours waiting for still won't come along. On other occasions, there will be many more.

The key is profiling the market: If we're in a trending market, I'll use dynamic support or resistance, and if I perceive that we're in a range bear market, I'm far more likely to trade from static or horizontal support and resistance.

Bourquin: How do "dynamic" support and resistance areas differ from "static" ones?

Wilson: Dynamic support and resistance would be determined using moving averages or Bollinger bands, for example—basically something that tracks price in a dynamic fashion.

It's critical to put yourself in a situation where you're learning something about sentiment if the trade fails. If you try to trade dynamic support or resistance in the middle of a range, your trade can fail and you will have actually learned nothing about sentiment.

Bourquin: A lot of traders who balance a career at the same time that they are trading can have difficulty deciding what to do if a trade setup emerges at the end of their session, right before they have to go to work. Do you close out all your trades before you step away, and how do you decide whether or not to take those trades that come in right at the end like that?

Wilson: Well, I stay in most of my trades for a maximum of half an hour. The market will have proven me right or wrong by then. So, as long as I've got half an hour available, I'll take the trade. But regardless of what happens, once it's time to walk away from the terminal, I'll close the book on any and all trades.

Bourquin: That's a kind of forced discipline to take the loss, if that's what it is at that time, or take a profit and eliminate the possibility for further gains.

Wilson: That's right, and I never want to end a session on a loss or even with a losing trade. So, if I've got one or two in the bag already, I won't take that last trade, no matter how good it looks.

Bourquin: Are there several currency pairs that you like to follow most?

Wilson: There's only one currency pair I follow—the Euro/Dollar [EUR/USD]—and there's a reason for that: It's the most liquid market, so it's giving me the clearest possible window on the psychology of the market, which is what I perceive I'm actually trading.

Whether the EUR/USD is trading at 1.3150 or 1.4150 really doesn't make any difference to me. All I'm doing is mapping key support and resistance points, trading against those, and then giving myself the opportunity to revise or even reverse the position to go in the other direction if they get taken out.

It sounds ludicrously simple, but I think the philosophy behind it is pretty strong, and it's certainly profitable.

Bourquin: And you're trading the spot market, right, not currency futures?

Wilson: Correct.

Bourquin: So, for a typical trade, how many units are you trading?

Wilson: At the moment, I'm normally trading about twenty bucks a point.

Bourquin: And since one pip is equal to one point, that's essentially two standard contracts.

For determining dynamic support and resistance, is there a certain type of Bollinger band or a certain moving average that you like to use?

Wilson: I use the Bollinger bands on the standard setting, so twenty-two, and I use the sixty-two-period exponential moving average [EMA], which seems to price pretty well in a trend.

Bourquin: I don't know that I've heard a lot of traders say they use the sixty-two EMA. How did you arrive at that one?

Wilson: I went right to it because Rob was using that on the one-hour timescale, and so I took it down to the one-minute to see how it looked.

Bourquin: How do you actually decide to put a trade on? Do you like to see it touch price before you'll enter an order, or do you trade as it comes to that area?

Wilson: I will time my entry so it's as close as possible to the close of the bar. As long as it doesn't fall through the line—as long as it just touches, or even if it's in the vicinity—I'll go for it. Only a close of the bar below the level I'm watching will invalidate the signal.

I also use the stochastic on 833 just to help time it a little bit, and believe it or not, although it's not a leading indicator, it can also give you a means of anticipating where divergence might exist.

Bourquin: And where and how do you go about setting stop losses?

Wilson: Some think it's a little crazy, but I only give my trades ten pips of room to work. I'm taking a scalpel to the market, really.

Bourquin: Wow, so it's got to work out right away. With such a tight stop, what's your win/loss percentage?

Wilson: On first trades, I achieve a win percentage of about 60 percent to 64 percent.

Bourquin: So, it's pretty reliable then. Will you trade either way, by putting on short positions at the top or going long at the bottom?

Wilson: Yes, I have no bias at all with regards to directionality. Given the favorable odds, and considering the fact that I only give the market ten pips and take profit at fifteen, it's enough to give me the edge I'm looking for.

Bourquin: Will you take profit at fifteen pips even if you feel like there's room left in the move? For example, if you're trading a bounce off of the bottom Bollinger band that looks like it might continue beyond fifteen pips, would you let that run further?

Wilson: Definitely, and a lot depends on the strength of the catalyst. I recently took a trade off the sixty-two EMA that started to move very quickly, so I extended my profit target out to thirty. That move eventually went to about thirty-four or forty before it retraced.

I have to bear in mind that I'm taking a signal for a one-minute chart, and having backtested so extensively, I've found the average movement of winning trades to be about thirty pips. Although you don't always get thirty, you almost always do get fifteen, and that's why I generally take profit there. However, if the market moves very quickly in my favor under those conditions, I may certainly extend out beyond fifteen pips.

I waited all morning for that particular trade to set up, and it was the only trade I took on the day. I was in it for thirty pips and happened to have gone in at double size because I was relatively confident in the setup. In that case, the trade was 1.2 percent of my equity, and I was very happy with that.

Bourquin: Some people—like yourself—are happy with their careers and don't intend to quit in order to pursue trading full-time, while others would love to do just that. Did you ever consider trading full-time, or do you like the lifestyle you have now, balancing both?

Wilson: I could see trading full-time someday. At the moment, for example, I'm mentoring a small group of people who hope to achieve what I have, and I like that human contact.

One of the determinants of my moving to Australia is that I can trade in the evening, and I'm open to the prospects of trading for a living. I'm getting to a stage in my professional life where I might get one more chance to go to sea if I'm lucky, but I want to be clear by the time I'm in my late forties, and that may well be the time I become a full-time trader. At the moment, though, I like the variety and the discipline that doing both enforces, and I like things just the way they are.

Bourquin: I like the separation and the sort of dual lifestyle for a lot of people, and I always caution those who tell me they want to quit their job to trade full-time. I think having a job and a steady income makes us less likely and less anxious to take undue risks. Would you agree with that?

Wilson: I would. For me, it's recreational, and I like that the risk is small and that it requires discipline and adaptability in order to grind it out every day.

My aim is to generate a very steady, upwardly sloping equity curve, and that really can take the pressure off, because if I can generate just 0.3 percent a day—if it were possible to do that every day, that is—that would equate to 100 percent equity growth over a full year.

For comparison, the big financial institutions regard 30 percent annual returns as their "gold standard," so to speak, and if I can beat that, I'm more than happy.

I'm mainly trying to align my trading operation in a way that enforces discipline for me and also looks relatively attractive and businesslike from the perspective of someone who may want me to manage their capital for them.

Bourquin: And are you managing other people's money right now as well?

Wilson: Yes, I am. I'm registered with the National Futures Association [NFA], and I'm a registered commodity trading advisor [CTA].

Bourquin: Do you take money out of those managed accounts to pay yourself, or, because you have a career, do you reinvest and let your profits run and continually build your account?

Wilson: All the management fees come out at the end of every month, and I just let those accumulate outside the account. It feels professional, like I'm paying myself, and I don't reinvest that money in the trading account. That's just a little additional income.

Bourquin: A lot of traders aspire to manage money and earn similar management fees to round out their existing income. Do you have any recommendations for traders who are thinking about that, and are there any especially valuable lessons you have learned along the way?

Wilson: The most important thing to bear in mind is that nobody who is going to trust you with their hard-earned capital is interested in you doubling it in a year. What they can't afford is for you to lose it.

As a result, my advice would be to focus on your equity curve. Get the volatility down as much as possible, and if that means trading a smaller size, then that's what you should do.

For example, one of my students, who was trading a $10,000 account, couldn't understand why his account was so volatile. There were 40 percent or 50 percent swings on a weekly basis, and though he was not comfortable with that, he sort of learned to accept it. The point I made to him was that it was all very well while he was dealing with an amount of money that he could understand and physically touch, but if someone with a million dollars asked him to manage that money, all of a sudden, he would be trading a sum of money that he never could have conceived before, and those volatile swings would then be completely unacceptable to him and his client.

No serious investor expects you to make them into a millionaire overnight. No one else could do it, so why should you? What they cannot cope with, however, are drawdowns. So, my advice to would-be money managers is to look carefully at volatility and sort it out so that their equity curve is going in the right direction and doing so at a steady, measured pace.

Bourquin: That's good advice even for those who aren't managing client money. Asking yourself, "Would I be comfortable taking the same risk with someone else's money?" can be a good measure of how much risk you are taking, and if you answer "No," then that's something you need to address right away.

Wilson: Absolutely, and the Forex education market doesn't help itself there, because it tries to convince people that they really can get rich quick. That's both absurd and highly disingenuous, because it masks the fact that Forex traders are going up against some very sharp minds in a zero-sum game.

Why should anyone sitting at home in front of their computer be able to take on the sharpest minds on Wall Street, with all the resources those traders have available to them, and hope to consistently come out on top? It's entirely unrealistic, but that's what people are being told, and that's why you see people take some obscene risks with their own capital.

If you genuinely hope to make this your business, then you should treat it like a business and prove to yourself, for example, that you can respect $1,000 in your trading account and limit the adverse effects of volatility. No one is interested in a spike up every so often if that spike is accompanied by a similarly steep downwards spike. That's unprofessional, and at some stage, you're going to wipe out that account. It might not happen this week or this month, but it's going to happen at some point, because you can't control the volatility.

If you can respect $1,000 and grow it into $2,000 over two years, however, then, all of a sudden, you're actually generating a steady equity curve. Now you're in a position to appeal to people who have sums of money to invest and can prove to them that you respect risk and are prepared to conduct business in a professional manner.

Bourquin: That's a great point. Yet when many people think of turning $1,000 into $2,000 over the course of two years, it can seem so agonizingly slow.

Wilson: Well, listen, turning $1,000 into $2,000 in two years is still 50 percent a year, and when you compound that, you are far outstripping the gold standard in the institutional market.

Bourquin: Right, no question. That brings up the idea of margin as well. So, do you use margin when you trade?

Wilson: I trade on a tiny bit of margin, and there's a counterparty on the other side of my trades, but I find it laughable that anyone would complain about a maximum leverage of "only" 50:1, because you can kill yourself very quickly at 50:1 leverage.

Bourquin: You can kill yourself at even 4:1 leverage. When the NFA took the maximum leverage in the United States down to 50:1, there was a lot of grumbling, but there was no grumbling from traders who really understand the dangers of using leverage.

Wilson: Totally. My maximum risk per trade will be about 1 percent, but that will be a third or even a fourth leg. My initial risk is 0.2 percent, and that might not change throughout the course of a session.

Bourquin: I want to make a point to ask you about news and data announcements, be it the US nonfarm payrolls [NFP] report, or interest rate decisions by the Federal Reserve or European Central Bank [ECB]. Do you follow news, and how does it impact your trading?

Wilson: I'm interested in when the announcements are coming out, because I know that's going to potentially fuel movement in the market. I don't care what the data ultimately is, and I certainly don't trade ahead of it. I'll only trade the reaction to it.

Bourquin: So, will you be in a trade when you know an economic announcement is coming out, or will you look to be flat?

Wilson: I tend to be flat during those times. Rob and I traded a recent NFP report together, though, and I threw a countertrend trade out there because it was a thin market and we were at a resistance level about twenty minutes after the news release. Once the spreads have gone back down, it's tradable at that point, but I certainly don't try to trade the news itself.

Bourquin: So, even if you've got a great setup on your sixty-two-period EMA, if you know a market-moving economic announcement is coming out in a few minutes, you'll likely avoid that trade until you see what happens afterwards?

Wilson: Yes, I'm ultra-defensive around major economic data releases because we all know that the news can—and often does—completely change prevailing sentiment in the markets.

Bourquin: Finally, Rob, what advice do you have for a trader that is struggling to make consistent money?

Wilson: My advice to a struggling trader would be to commit to learning to do one thing well. For me, this meant restricting my focus to one instrument and committing to trade it for a set period of time each and every trading day. Over time, you will begin to understand how to identify the highest-probability trade setups, how much room to give them, and what the expected post-entry movement is likely to be. This process will embed in you the traits of discipline, concentration, and decisiveness that are present in all successful market operators while reinforcing your positive expectancy and self-belief. All of a sudden, you are struggling no more. A positive equity curve has been established.

John Carter

*Having achieved worldwide acclaim for his market expertise, **John Carter**, author of Mastering the Trade (McGraw-Hill, 2012), is a mainstay on TV and at industry trade shows, and subscribers follow his insights and analysis each day at TradeTheMarkets. com and SimplerOptions.com. Carter is perhaps equally well known, however, for his candid accounts of the many thrilling successes—as well as a couple unforgettable missteps—he has experienced throughout his career. He primarily trades options using an uncomplicated technical approach and has managed to stay consistent and increasingly profitable, despite the internet bubble and vastly different market and economic conditions throughout the past 20 years. Carter's story is as inspiring as it is entertaining and features clear takeaways that can help new traders develop professional habits and motivate experienced traders to refocus on what really works—and eliminate what doesn't.*

Tim Bourquin: John, let's start at the beginning and talk about how you got involved with trading in the first place.

John Carter: Well, my stepfather, Lance, was a broker with Morgan Stanley, and at the time, I was in high school and spending the summer working at the mall and making about $4.25 an hour. I remember I had been working for three months and had saved around $1,000.

One Sunday, I come home, and my stepfather and his buddies are sitting around the table, looking at *Investor's Business Daily* and talking about how they were going to make some money that week buying call options on Intel. I had no idea what they were talking about.

We made a deal that they would spot me the $1,000, because I obviously had no time to open up an account the night before. If we made money, I would keep the profits, but if we lost, then I would owe that money.

They couldn't promise me that the trade was going to make money, and I hemmed and hawed before going ahead with it, but they bought calls on Intel that Monday for $1 and sold them on Thursday for $1.80, making me $800 in the process.

Afterward, I thought about how I had just worked forty hours a week for three months to make $1,000—and then did practically nothing and made $800. From then on, I was hooked and knew that trading was what I wanted to do.

Bourquin: Do you think that can sometimes be the worst thing that can happen for people, though? That's how people come to think that trading is easy and expect that they can just jump in and start making money trading.

Carter: Well, that's a good point, because there is that problem with beginner's luck. But for me, I think that set the tempo, because I actually didn't make or manage the trade. It was just my first experience in the market, and because it was so positive, I saw there was opportunity there. But they were very clear that I could just as easily lose money, too.

It was probably a month later that I had an account funded and was starting to do trades. But it's a whole other story of how long it takes to become consistent in trading.

I simply found that initial spark in knowing that it wasn't easy, or else everybody would be doing it. There were certainly times when you'd get overconfident and things would turn against you, but that first trade was really the trigger that made me think trading was something that I could do for the rest of my life.

Bourquin: Did you go to college after that?

Carter: Yeah, I did, and after college, I had no desire to be a broker, so I became a financial analyst and traded the whole time.

I traded all through college, too. The girl I was dating had about $15,000 in student loans, and they would advance her the money. I took some of that money and put it into a stock called Iomega and tripled her account. That same girl ended up marrying me one day!

Bourquin: That's funny. I don't know if that's allowed in the loan documentation, though!

Carter: It's not. You're absolutely not allowed to do that, but trading back then was way different than it is now. It was more about buying something and holding it for six or eight weeks at that time, and that was fun.

Bourquin: Did trading then become your job in the summers, or did you actually get another job?

Carter: I was trading all through college, and I was actually pretty active trading options. Then, when I went to work as a financial analyst, I swing traded and was watching the markets every day. I focused on the retail sector, watching companies like Kmart, Walmart, and Target, and actually got to go into the stores and help with inventory. That was how I really got my hands dirty.

Bourquin: Now, for what firm were you working as an analyst?

Carter: It was a small, boutique firm based out of Dallas, but it was later absorbed, and now I believe it's part of a Canadian firm. We had a group of about twenty guys, and the main focus was on retail. We actually did financial analysis on the companies themselves, but then also provided inventory and other services to retailers like Target and Walmart.

Bourquin: That's interesting. I didn't know that you had been an analyst. Did that knowledge of fundamental measures like inventory help you as a trader?

Carter: No, but it did help with seeing industry trends, and that was valuable. For example, changes to a company's inventory structure or other changes that would make for more efficient operations could be reflected in the company's stock price three months later.

I'm more of a technician at heart, but I like to pay a little attention to fundamentals after seeing how certain actions can actually impact earnings—or impact perception enough to where the stock price is affected because of it.

Bourquin: Were you allowed to trade those stocks at the same time that you were analyzing them?

Carter: There were no rules that said you couldn't, but I think I was the only one who was actively trading. There were people who were working with 401(k)s, but it was not a full trading desk as we know them today. A lot of the other analysts either didn't trade or were more focused on providing services to the retailers.

Bourquin: What was it about that job that made you quit and move on with your trading?

Carter: That was actually a good job and a good company, but I remember driving in one morning and thinking, "If five years from now I'm still making this damn commute to this same job, then I will have done something wrong."

I really wanted to push myself to take the risk and pursue my dreams of becoming a trader. Too many people wake up one day and suddenly realize that they're forty or forty-five and still at the same job. I was very conscious of that.

I don't know what the trigger was, exactly, that made me decide to quit, and I remember it was actually very difficult to leave that job, because I liked it and was part of the team. It was a situation where I could trade and still have a regular salary coming in, too, but I believed I'd reached a point where I had to make a choice—and I did.

When I put in my notice, they came back pushing hard. They weren't mad, but they wanted me to stay, and they were willing to offer a promotion and even relocation to another part of the country to keep me. After hearing that, I waffled for a couple weeks about the decision, but I ended up sticking to my guns, and I obviously don't regret it at all. It was a great move, but it was very difficult at the time to take that step.

Bourquin: Sure, walking away from guaranteed income and trading full-time, where nothing is guaranteed, is a very big step. Do you remember what year it was when you made the transition?

Carter: It was right around 1997.

Bourquin: That's before the whole internet bubble came to be. Let's talk about the first couple of days you spent trading on your own. What was it like?

Carter: It was a little nerve-racking. I remember I lost money on the first day, partly because I was overexcited. I had CNBC on right in front of me while I sat at my computer, and I thought I could just react to the news, but that just didn't work.

Actually, the first couple of weeks were pretty tough, so I took a step back and recommitted to doing what I was doing before that *was* working, which was centered on swing trading with options.

From there, the challenge was to learn how to do that while trading, because before, I would place a trade and then go to work, so I wouldn't stare at the chart every day. A big part of becoming a full-time trader is learning not to let the inevitable emotions screw up your trades.

Bourquin: Right. It's common for traders to start fiddling with stops or profit targets while trades are going on under those conditions. I've found that when I walk away from a trade after I have put it on, I actually make more money.

Now, you started out with options. Did you switch over from options to other things at that point, or do you still trade options?

Carter: I've been focused on options throughout my entire trading career, but I do trade some stocks and futures as well. Primarily, if I'm day trading, I focus on futures. But if I set up a trade that I plan to be in for longer—even if it's just two to three days—I'll use options.

Bourquin: Before you made the move to trading full-time, did you first want to build up a certain amount of money in your account?

Carter: Yes, and this is a painful story. I thought between $100,000 and $200,000 was the magic number for me, and at one point, I did get up to $150,000. That was after many ups and downs, and after making a lot of money and giving it back.

This particular time, I had $150,000, and I kept it for about six months or so. At the end of every week, I'd take out profits. If it was $2,000, I'd take it out, or if it was $10,000, I'd take it out. If I had a down week and lost money, then I had to trade back up to that $150,000 before I could start taking profits out again.

I was in a nice groove, and at the time, my fiancée and I were living in Minnesota, after I'd been promoted within the company. It was January, we were stuck in our apartment, it was about eighty degrees below zero outside, and my fiancée, who had never seen snow before, said to me, "Dude, if you don't get us a house with a heated garage, I'm out of here!"

So, I found a house with a heated garage and decided to put $30,000 down on it. The money was going to have to come out of my trading account, because back then, I put much of my trading profits toward collecting old coins. Even to this day, I'm still an avid collector, but I'd buy old silver dollars or gold coins, and they weren't really liquid. You had to hold on to them for years, and even then, the bid-ask spread was pretty wide. In retrospect, that wasn't really the best investment.

About a week before I was going to take that money out of my trading account, I was sitting there, thinking about it, and decided to take a couple of aggressive trades to build up my account to $180,000. That way, I could pull $30,000 out of the account and still keep the $150,000 balance.

I only had a week to work with, and the next day, I saw the stock market rallying up to a very key resistance point, so I bought some OEX options and put half my account into this trade. Well, it immediately started working out, and I was up about $8,000 within five minutes! I was thinking, "Great, this is going to work out fairly quickly."

Then the market spiked back up again, and the options dropped to $7.50. Since I had bought the first batch at $8, I thought, "Wow, that's a great price," so I bought another hundred and figured I'd be out of the trade. I had been trading long enough to know that if this trade went against me into the close, I'd get out and not even consider holding it overnight.

At the close, I was up about $10,000 or $11,000, and I thought, "Great, if we just get a nice little open, I'm out of here, and I've got my money." Well, the next morning, the Dow gapped up 150 points and traded sideways all day. It closed at its highest level ever, and for the next four days, the market rallied hard. I barely even remember those four days, but it was horrible.

I do remember that, suddenly, it was the day before we were supposed to close on the house, and I needed money, so I had to call the broker and just get out of that trade. My account went from $150,000 down to about $8,000. The options went down from around eight bucks to seventy cents. It was brutal. Nearly the entire account was gone.

At that point, there was no way I was going to tell my fiancée what I had just done, so I went to the bank, maxed out all of my credit cards, had just enough money for the down payment, and we ended up getting the house. But that was some serious stuff that really made me do some soul searching.

I was fortunate in that I had accumulated some coins and bought some real estate, so I could liquidate some assets and fund another trading account, but I really had to sit there and ask myself, "What the hell are you doing?" That was a gut-wrenching experience, because I lost money at a time when I really needed it.

Bourquin: Wow, so that was basically a $142,000 lesson in why you should never add to a losing trade or run your stops. Did you just become a day trader after that?

Carter: Surprisingly, no. I recognized that in that particular instance, I was trading only to make $30,000 for a house payment. I wasn't trading the setup like I should've been. So, the lesson for me wasn't to be scared of the market, and it wasn't that I shouldn't hold overnight. It was just to stay focused only on trading the setup.

You can't sit there and try to extract a specific amount of money from the market, and if you do, those are the kinds of mistakes that can happen.

If I would have taken that OEX trade and put on ten contracts, even if it went against me, I just would have been stopped out, and that would've been fine. Instead, I was trying to make $30,000, and that was my overriding concern. That's also what destroyed everything.

Even after that experience, my trading style didn't change at all. But I definitely came away knowing that you can't sit there and try to pull specific sums of money out of the market.

Bourquin: Would you tell people who come in targeting even $100 a day in the market that they're going about it the wrong way?

Carter: Yes. The reason it doesn't work is because you don't think of it as $100 a day. People start to extrapolate that over the course of a year. They say, "Okay, all I want to do is make $100 a day, or $500 a day," and then they think, "Wow, that's like $100,000 a year!" Suddenly, they're thinking about $100,000 a year, and when they're having a losing trade, that can really screw them up.

You can have expectations, because that's how you control risk. But you can't sit there and say, "I'm *going to* make $100 a day in the market," because there are going to be days that you don't. It can actually be limiting, too, because there could be a trade where just trailing a stop could make you $1,000 that day.

Actually, I think the best thing to do is go into a market knowing how much risk you're going to take and with no upside expectancy. To me, that's the best frame of mind to be in.

Bourquin: It sounds like, after that experience, you sold some assets to replenish your trading account and get started again.

Carter: I did. I actually took about four or five months off and came across Mark Douglas' book, *The Disciplined Trader* [New York Institute of Finance, 1990], and that helped me a lot. I talked to my broker, and I ended up going and sitting next to a twenty-year veteran trader at his desk for about a week and struck up a friendship with him. At that point, I realized that I could do this. I just had made a stupid mistake, and I really vowed not to do that again.

I sold two properties and some coins, because I didn't want to start with $10,000 and try to build up from there. I put a $75,000 stake back in, which was enough, and my goal at that point was just to trade for another year or so. I built it back up to right around that $150,000 level, and that was the time when I quit my job to trade full-time.

My wife was working, too, and she had a good job, so it was a good and calculated risk to me at that point. Of course, the worst-case scenario would be that it didn't work out, and I could always get a job again, though that's certainly not what I wanted to do.

Bourquin: This was probably right around the time when all those internet and tech stocks started to take off. Did you make money during that period?

Carter: That was interesting, because I honestly didn't know that there was an internet bubble at the time. I was just doing my trades. But I'd sit there and buy call options on Yahoo!, and it would spike up $30 a share, so of course the options would quintuple in price.

Just from history, I was very distrustful of that whole thing, and while I didn't rush in and start shorting, I wasn't super aggressive, either. I remember my skepticism actually caused me to miss some amazing moves, but at the same time, I was also able to live through the crash very nicely.

Bourquin: Right. One thing I didn't ask you about that is often an interesting topic is how your spouse reacted when you left your steady, six-figure income to trade full-time.

Carter: She was good, and although she was a little nervous about it, she also had the experience where I traded her student loan money and made her even more.

Her family always stressed getting a good job, though, and that's why I think she was nervous about it. In the back of her mind, she may have thought that I would just try it for a year and then go back and get another job.

Bourquin: Besides money, of course, what were you using to measure your success as a trader and make sure you were continually moving forward?

Carter: I set up two accounts, because trading is largely about keeping drawdowns to a minimum. I aimed to keep one account at a consistent level, like

$150,000, and my goal was simply to pull profits out of it every week. If I lost money, then my goal became to trade and build it back up to the point where I could take money out again.

I was just very conscious that I never wanted to put myself into a big hole again. But it was nice trading small in a big account, because there's a lot of flexibility—not because I could really push it and try to double the account, but because I had extra wiggle room if a position went quickly against me.

For example, if I bought ten option contracts and the position got hammered right away, that gave me the flexibility to buy ten more. I would do that sometimes and then look for a 38.2 percent Fibonacci retracement rally and get out of the trade with a much smaller loss—or maybe even get back to breakeven on that trade.

My measure of success, however, was being able to pull money out of that first account, and then my other account was strictly for swing trades. I didn't want to take money out of it and was just steadily trying to grow it by taking stock trades and some others. That was only a steady growth account aimed at keeping drawdowns to a minimum, and part of that meant taking breaks and not staring at charts all the time.

Bourquin: What did your friends and family say about your trading lifestyle? Did you get a lot of questions about what you were doing and if you could teach them to do it, too?

Carter: I did, and people would expect to sit down for three days and learn everything. But I knew what an excruciating road it is for new traders, so I actually tried to discourage them or at least say that it takes five years of ups and downs to learn to trade, and you can't just quit your job and start making money trading.

Bourquin: Let's talk about technical analysis, Fibonacci, and some of the other tools and how you began to use them every day in your trading.

Carter: One of the main tools I use today is called "the squeeze," and it's a measure between the Bollinger Bands and the Keltner Channels. I find that it gives me a lot of extremely helpful information about a stock, so I like that one quite a bit. Essentially, it measures the volatility—or the lack of volatility—in the market.

For most markets, and no matter what time frame you're looking at, sometimes they're quiet, and sometimes they're extremely volatile. The mistake I made in the beginning was looking for volatile markets and then jumping in on them. But I eventually realized that if I get into these markets when they are quiet and then sell to people like me when they get volatile, I can make a living doing this. That's essentially what I do, even to this day. I know that when a market pops up and is volatile, there's going to be a lot of people rushing into it, and I'm happy to hand off my position to them.

Bourquin: Did you learn technical analysis by reading books, or was it more about trial and error?

Carter: I read some books, but I think learning technical analysis is a lot like learning to play golf. If you've never picked up a golf club, you can go read the ten best books on how to hit a golf ball. But when you ultimately go try to hit one, you are still going to suck at it! You can't learn how to hit a golf ball by reading a book, and I think the same thing is true with technical analysis and trading.

One of my favorite books was Nicholas Darvas' *How I Made $2,000,000 in the Stock Market* [BN Publishing, 2007], because it really hit home and resonated with me, in terms of when to stick with a position and when not to stick with a position. A lot of the other books I came across just seemed to be different renditions of the same things, and while I could study them and get some ideas, there wasn't anything there that changed my life or anything.

I think learning about technical analysis and trading is just a matter of talking to other traders and trying things, and the irony is that you actually don't need a lot. I've heard it said before that you can pick one market, one time frame, and one indicator, and—using only that—you can figure out a way to make a living within three months. I really believe that to be true.

In trading, you don't want to be the master of all trades. You just want to pick a couple of niches and focus on them. That's really beneficial, because you get to know the setup, you get to know the time frame, and you become an expert in that area of the market. You don't need to know everything else that's out there.

Bourquin: In talking to somebody recently, they said to me that if most traders would just stick with what they already do—instead of trying to jump around between markets, indicators, charts, or time frames—eventually they'd be likely to make money.

The problems start when they try a few trades and don't make money, so they move on to something else, and then another, and another… Do you agree that if most people just tried to master one thing, they would eventually get it?

Carter: Absolutely, I do, and that's exactly what happens. It's like they're continually moving toward the next bright and shiny object without first having a base or understanding of their trading philosophy and what they are trying to do.

You can make a living with something as simple as a twenty-one-period moving average. You could actually look at that on five different markets, and that would be fine. If you're not making money with one thing, however, and then you go try to do the same thing in some other market, guess what? You're not going to make money there, either.

Bourquin: Has your trading changed much over the past eight or nine years, considering the dot-com crash and everything else, or are you still doing much of the same thing?

Carter: Gosh, that's a good question. It hasn't changed much, based only on the nature of the market, even though we don't have a huge bull run like we did in the 1990s. I find I don't hold positions as long, though. I now consider six weeks a long time to be in a trade, and from there, it is even shorter-term trading. Also, I'm more aggressive now about pulling money out of the market.

I've found over time that I actually care much less about what I'm trading. I don't think, "Well, I'm bullish on crude oil, so I'll buy this to capitalize." It's all about looking for opportunities to take money out of the market, and a lot of that simply has to do with what you see. For example, if I see a market coming down really hard, I know there's likely a lot of people getting flushed out of that market. I would look for an opportunity there, take it, and then get out. I can tell you that about 75 percent of the time I'm day trading, I am flat and am just waiting.

Bourquin: Let's talk about a garden-variety trade that you'd put on. What factors would lead you to take the trade?

Carter: I recently took a textbook trade on MasterCard, which I really, really like. I look for stocks, say, after earnings or other news. MasterCard popped and made highs after earnings and then started to pull back. At that point, I was looking for the stock to turn around, try to retest, and break through the recent highs.

I waited until the stock began to turn higher and then started scaling into that position. From there, I looked for a 127.2 percent Fibonacci extension of the move from the recent high to the retracement low after earnings. In this case, that was a potential $3 to $4 move, and that, to me, is a bread-and-butter trade.

What happened next was I bought in and held the position overnight, and the next day, it pushed up, broke the previous day's high, rallied up to that 127.2 percent extension, and that was where I got out. Now, it actually went up another ten points from there, but that was the setup and the move I wanted, so I'm happy to leave the extra money on the table.

This same strategy works to the upside and the downside, and what I like about it is that you're not sitting there, holding on for days while wondering where it's going to go. You've got a specific setup and a specific target, and you only need to decide how many contracts you want to use to trade it.

Bourquin: Will you take a trade on a stock purely for the technical setup, even if you have no idea what the company does, how their earnings look, and how other fundamental factors are shaping up?

Carter: That's a good question, but one that's tough for me to answer, because I don't trade a lot of stocks that I don't know. Really, the top stocks in my universe include Apple, Google, Priceline, and other very actively traded, fast-moving stocks with plenty of liquidity in the options.

I think, back in the day, it didn't matter what the stock was, but I don't run screens during the day just to find whatever stocks are making new highs that day or anything like that. I've got a universe of only about ten stocks, and I've gotten to know them very well. I watch them on an hourly chart, a fifteen-minute chart, and a five-minute chart, and there are plenty of opportunities just in that window.

Bourquin: Do you trade from home or in an office setting?

Carter: I have an office. I traded at home for a while, and then my wife had this weird affliction where she started having children! We have three small kids now, ages six, four, and two. I actually like working at home, and I miss it at times, but I found it difficult to trade with the chaos of children running around the house added to the mix.

Now I have three apartments that are just four miles from home, and there's one where I trade. The two others are where we operate our web sites, TradeTheMarkets.com and SimplerOptions.com. We employ a team of about ten people now, and they'll help out with the sites, they'll do customer service, and a couple even help me out with analyzing trades.

For the most part, though, I trade my accounts on my own and work on joint ventures with others, where we'll combine forces to trade an account, and that's a nice mix. It's valuable as a trader to not only have the independence of trading your own account, but at the same time be involved and work with other human beings. It can be fun, too.

Bourquin: Speaking of the business aspect of trading, have you ever thought about managing money?

Carter: It's funny you asked that, because I actually just started a commodity trading advisor [CTA] fund, called Razor Trading, as well as an options auto-trading service. Personally, I don't mind taking a lot of risk in my own account, and even though investors will initially always say to go ahead and do the same for them, they'll start freaking out as soon as they see the first drawdown. So, you really have to expect that and be prepared to deal with all the phone calls and e-mails that will come with it.

When I think about how many people out there have money making 0 percent at their bank, however, it doesn't have to be a huge fund. Even a small one that was making 20 percent a year would be a valuable service for those folks, as well as a nice additional income stream, from a business point of view.

Bourquin: Shifting back to your approach to trading again, do you do homework at night, and how much of your time is spent outside of market hours doing trading-related activities?

Carter: Surprisingly little. I used to look at charts for hours upon hours, but now I just spend about forty-five minutes at the end of the day doing it—and a lot of times I record that as part of a nightly newsletter.

I found that the reward is not proportional to the amount of time you spend staring at charts, which is strange, because conventional wisdom suggests that the more research you do, the more money you're going to make. But that's just not true in trading.

What is true is that those who come in open minded and with no expectations about the market have a better chance of making money. I think it's more important to have that going for you, so I always advocate things like exercise and other time away from the market so you can come back rested, relaxed, and ready to go, so to speak.

Bourquin: Earlier, you mentioned the five-year learning curve for new traders, but how long did it take you to feel confident enough in your strategy, your methods, and your ability as a trader that you could consistently make money doing this?

Carter: It probably took me a little more than five years. There are some things you can't really learn about in books and have to experience them instead. You've got to get "kicked in the teeth," as they say, and you've got to get into some situations that you didn't plan for. Through it all, the trick is not to get too cautious, because that's even worse than being too courageous. The fine line between caution and courage is a trader's ideal state of mind.

Bourquin: Do you still go through trading slumps?

Carter: Sure, and anytime I do, it means there's something serious going on, or it could be caused by outside factors in my life.

The single worst trade I took in 2011 was taken right before I got on a plane and went away for a couple of weeks. I had a great six months before that, but in that case, I got careless. When you don't pay attention to the garden, that's when it grows weeds, and the same can be true in trading.

Maybe sometimes those trades work out really well, but if ever I find myself getting a little too blasé about trades, I've got to reel back in and be disciplined. You always want to have a healthy discipline, a healthy fear, and a healthy respect for the market when trading.

Bourquin: Was that $142,000 loss you sustained early on the biggest one of your career?

Carter: My accounts have grown a lot since then, so I've actually had bigger dollar losses than that. But percentage-wise, I've never again been on the wrong side of a move as big and nasty as that one.

Bourquin: How about the best trade you've ever had? How much did you make on that one?

Carter: Well, the most I've ever made in one day was in an option trade on Goldman Sachs. That ended up being about a $250,000 up day.

It was a day that SEC news came out, and the stock dropped by about $20 per share. I saw it and just started loading up on options. At one point, I think I had five hundred option contracts on it. It was one of those trades that was right there, so I got focused and trailed a stop, and the result was a fantastic trade that happened very quickly.

Bourquin: When you start dealing with numbers that size, do you still get nervous while you're trading, or can you remain comfortable, even when dealing in such big volume?

Carter: I'm actually fairly comfortable, but I do get extremely focused. If it's a big trade, I'm not going to get up or leave the computer, but I won't be freaking out while I'm trading, either.

I always equate P&L management to exercise. The first time you do a bench press, you may be able to do one hundred pounds, and maybe a month later, you can go to one hundred and ten, and then one hundred and thirty, and so on. It's the same thing with trading. The first time I lost $1,000, I threw up, but the next time, it wasn't that bad. Then, the first time you lose $10,000, you might throw the keyboard against the wall, but the next time, it's not that bad. You actually build up your intestinal fortitude and what you can and can't handle as a trader.

The John Paulsons of the world are managing huge sums of money and dealing with fluctuations in the hundreds of millions of dollars, but they're just kind of used to it.

Today, if I'm taking a smaller trade, like ten contracts, or playing around with a couple thousand dollars, to me, that's as close to unemotional as I can get, because it really isn't going to have an impact on me. But for somebody else, who's just starting out, that could be their entire life. It's interesting to think of it that way, but it's just going to be different for everybody.

Bourquin: Should that be the goal for everybody: to try to get to the point where, regardless of the amount of money that is on the table, it doesn't trigger emotions, butterflies, or dreaded gut feelings?

Carter: That actually is the goal, and the reason everybody does well when trading a demo account is because they have no emotion in it. When trading real money, however, the emotions we feel are usually proportionate to the size of the trade.

I still consider that to this day. If I start feeling overly anxious about a trade and keep checking quotes, I'll sell a third of the position. Then, suddenly, I'm much calmer and more objective, which is where I need to be to trade well and avoid emotional mistakes.

Bourquin: Let's briefly turn our attention to the business side of things and TradeTheMarkets.com and SimplerOptions.com. How did you come to decide that there was an opportunity to start teaching people how to trade?

Carter: It was because we had reached a point where many people were struggling. Everybody looked like a genius during the tech bubble, but for many, it all changed after that. We still felt that it was a great trading environment, though, so we started posting ideas and showing people how to short something or buy puts. For some, it was the first time they had ever heard about that.

Bourquin: There's this idea in the trading industry that if you're really a good trader, there's no reason why you should have a service, because you could just make all your money trading. How do you feel about that?

Carter: That's true, and the usual question is, "Well, if you're so good at this, why are you teaching it?" I believe that's a valid question. There are people out there who are believable teachers but have never actually traded, and that's what I think makes it a legitimate question.

To me, the honest answer is because it's a great business. It's very scalable, it's repeatable, and if you can provide quality content and help people, they're going to stick around.

Bourquin: When it comes to those who teach and don't trade, sometimes the concern is that maybe the stuff they're teaching worked five years ago, but it doesn't work anymore, and that's why they're not trading.

Carter: I've seen that, too, and I think if you're going to teach, you absolutely have to stay current, and you have to be trading. The only way to be able to adapt and understand the markets is if you're actually trading yourself. This is why I teach all of my courses in the context of live markets and not with PowerPoint decks that look back on the markets in hindsight. I execute real trades in my own account during these courses, and my students can see my P&L. If I held a course where nothing I did worked and every trade I made lost money, I wouldn't have a reason to teach anymore.

Bourquin: Certainly aside from paying thousands of dollars for a course that promises to make great traders overnight, is there any way for new traders to legitimately shorten the learning curve and achieve results faster?

Carter: You're exactly right that the answer is *not* buying some $5,000 educational course. Nothing against those courses, but there is no shortcut, in terms of a course.

The shortcut is this: Treat *every* trade like a professional trader would. By that, I mean that you should size the position correctly, cut your losses fast, and let your winners run. That is the mindset of a professional, and new traders who follow it *without exception* can shorten the learning curve. Actually, they can do well from day one.

Unfortunately, the market is very good at reinforcing bad habits, and it often requires difficult lessons to learn what's right and what's wrong. Removing a stop may work the first time, so the new trader will keep doing that, but it's a bad habit that could come back and ruin them at some point.

Bourquin: Looking back over the course of your trading career so far, is there anything you would have done differently?

Carter: I think I would've favored the idea of scaling out more often, taking some money out of a trade, locking in a stop loss, and then just letting the rest go and checking on it once a day. Those are the times you can really catch some incredible moves without having to constantly stare at a chart.

You never know exactly what's going to happen in the markets, but I think I could have continued participating in some fantastic moves by leaving just one contract on—although that would've meant giving up the mental closure that comes with being completely out of a position.

Bourquin: John, in closing, is now as good a time as any to be a trader?

Carter: I think this is a trader's market, and it's a fantastic time to be trading. For retail traders, the dirty little secret is this: Especially in markets like futures and options, there aren't a lot of huge hedge funds trading those markets, because there's not enough liquidity for them there.

The big funds have to create synthetic positions that simulate millions of shares, but those are created off the books at Goldman Sachs or elsewhere and aren't transactions that we see as retail traders.

As a result, there is plenty of opportunity for smaller traders in markets like crude oil and gold, as well as in equity options, where big funds aren't active because of the lower liquidity.

I think there's probably more opportunity in trading today than at any other time. People always think the heyday for active trading was the late nineties and throughout the internet bubble, because anything you bought went up. But that was not trading. That was like having a surfboard, catching a seventy-foot wave, and just riding it all the way in.

Again, success goes back to having discipline. But even new traders can adopt that professional mindset, starting with their very next trade. Doing that can put them well on the proper path.

Anne-Marie Baiynd

*After being inspired by an introductory seminar on technical trading, **Anne-Marie Baiynd** made a daredevil's leap from corporate president to rookie technical trader in early 2005. Her expansive mathematics background and passion for analysis would later serve her well, but did not provide her immunity from the market's unkind initiation and substantial early losses. Undeterred, she worked tirelessly to simplify her process, methodically learning and testing technical indicators to produce a non-cluttered, clearly defined strategy that breeds confidence and positive results. She is regarded today as a leading expert in Fibonacci analysis and momentum trading, and while always aiming to continue her own quest for knowledge, Baiynd educates fellow traders at live seminars nationwide, as well as in her daily chat room. She is the author of* The Trading Book *(McGraw-Hill, 2011) and is regarded as one of the Top 25 Traders on Twitter.*

Tim Bourquin: Anne-Marie, let's start by talking about how you got into trading, because your career was in something else initially, wasn't it?

Anne-Marie Baiynd: That's exactly right. I had spent the last twelve years in a recruiting role and was the president of a small recruiting company. We called it a "boutique firm" because we only looked for certain types of very technical individuals.

I was tired of working one hundred–hour weeks and felt I had come to a crossroads in my career. Fortunately, I was in a space where I could choose what I wanted to do next.

It was late 2004 or early 2005, and although I didn't want to, my husband urged me to go to this *SUCCESS* Magazine seminar on technical trading. So, we went, and I loved listening to this gentleman describe the technique. Because of my degrees and my past, I really love analysis, and I like to think really hard. I found that presentation to be very, very entertaining. So, after I went home, I started investigating from there.

Bourquin: Was technical analysis brand new to you at that time, or had you ever studied financial charts before?

Baiynd: Technical analysis was brand new to me, and I could barely spell "stock market" when I began looking at it! I really had no interest in finance or the market, per se, but the technician in me was very eager to explore it.

Bourquin: Did you end up taking more courses they offered?

Baiynd: Only the introductory course. My husband wanted to take it, so we went, but they upsell in everything they do, and so it was pretty much only the surface layer of what the market is about. From there, if you really wanted to know more, then you had to go through their entire program.

I thought I learned better on my own anyway, so I just began investigating the markets. If it turned out I needed more education, I would take it from there.

Bourquin: Was your next step to start reading books about technical analysis?

Baiynd: Actually, I did something absolutely crazy: I just went for it and started trading—which was a very bad mistake!

Bourquin: Wow, let's talk about what you were doing and why it didn't work.

Baiynd: Well, in everything I've chosen to do before, I've simply focused and dedicated myself to becoming good at it and then worked hard to get it done. I thought this would be no different, but when I started trading, I had no idea what was going on! I had the introductory Investools book in front of me, and I was looking at it and the technicals.

My background as a mathematician means I can understand the basis of technical measures like stochastics, but as far as reading and interpreting them, I had no clue. Honestly, I was a tremendous gunslinger, and the only reason I stand here today is because I started with so much money that I was able to lose vast quantities.

Eventually, though, my husband convinced me that I had to stop trading and figure out what was going on first. Although I didn't want to sit out and not trade, that turned out to be the best advice I ever got.

So, I began paper trading, and I went from simple to mildly complex concepts, working through them piece by piece. I started by learning moving averages, and from there I fell into Fibonacci after seeing it on a Twitter feed. I knew what the Fibonacci sequence was already, and when I started looking at it, the wave retracements made so much sense to me. All of a sudden, I began to see the market in a whole new way!

From there, I spent about six months developing a system that would work for me. Now, the system had to be simple, and it had to be direct, because I was very prone to second-guessing myself, and with so much emotional capital already depleted from the massive losses I sustained early on, I really didn't trust myself in any form or fashion.

As a result, I vowed only to trade a particular setup, and doing that helped me to build up my confidence. That was how I started back in the market.

Even today, once I understand something, I try to expand upon it, and every day I look at the market, I learn something new. I'm always looking at it in a different way and trying not to box myself in, and that's why I never wanted to learn to trade from anyone else.

That doesn't mean that I ignored outside ideas, though. I went on to study multiple time frames after Brian Shannon inspired me to, and I looked at market internals because Peter Reznicek used them. Other than that, though, everything was of my own creation and is very natural to me.

Ultimately, that's how I had to do it in order to start trading with confidence and according to the rules.

Bourquin: And would you follow those guys on their blogs?

Baiynd: Well, Peter Reznicek did a show on thinkorswim, which was where I had my platform. He referenced the "king of market internals," and although I didn't know initially what he was talking about, when he pulled up a chart, I could see it.

After listening to him time the market using market internals, I thought I'd see if I could successfully integrate market internals into my existing strategy. I found out that one market internal in particular, the up volume minus down volume [UVOL-DVOL], was a very good indicator of where the trend was heading on the day.

As far as Brian Shannon goes, I used to watch his daily blog recap and noticed that he would look at things on multiple time frames, like five minutes and thirty minutes or hourly—or even on the daily and weekly time frames. That gives an entirely different view of what's happening from a broader perspective, and so I began to work with that as well.

In both cases, I borrowed outside ideas and notions and tried to combine them within my existing system. I am a firm believer that many traders fail because they simply jam a lot of technical indicators together, and that's not what a good trading system does. A good trading system has a few indicators that complement each other, so when those indicators conflict, there's a real reason why.

Bourquin: When traders first start out, they have so much information available, and there are so many people out there blogging, so many services, and so many classes, that they rarely know where to start. How did you know to start with moving averages and Fibonacci?

Baiynd: Truthfully, I was looking for something really simple that I could understand. I started with the simple moving average [SMA], which helped me realize that if my candlesticks were printing underneath the moving average, I should probably be short. Conversely, if the candlesticks were printing above the moving average, I should probably be long. Just that simple notion made me start there.

I went through all kinds of different technical indicators after that, however, and I commonly said I was trying to find the indicator that "lies to me the least." I finally settled on a couple of them outside of that moving average, but it was really by trial and error.

I went through every single one of them: MACD, RSI, Williams %R, you name it. Interestingly enough, I ended up working twenty-hour days doing that, instead of the twelve-hour days I was working while in the recruiting business!

I spent that many hours each day just studying and shuffling through indicators until I settled on something that meshed for me. I needed something to clearly guide me in my trading.

Bourquin: Talk about how you learned Fibonacci and how you now use it to find good trades.

Baiynd: Well, I learned Fibonacci as a mathematician, and so I understood that the sequence was just a set of ratios that are interrelated. Now, when I first started looking at Fibonacci as it relates to trading, I would just open up a chart and go from high to low. I had no understanding of wave action, but as I kept looking at the charts, I began to see them.

I then started to measure the waves and got to where I could anticipate the location of a potential rollover. Sometimes I would take the trade in anticipation of the rollover, but after getting blown out of those a few times, I learned to wait for confirmation before getting in.

Again, it was just by trial and error, and I did a little bit of live trading and many hundreds of hours of paper trading just to see if I could understand mechanically how the wave action works.

Bourquin: Is it Elliott wave that you're using in your analysis?

Baiynd: No, I'm just looking at the chart without doing any wave counting. I've tried to look at Elliott wave, but I found it to be very cumbersome. Everything is so contingent upon where you actually start the wave count, and if you start in the wrong place, it's just not going to work for you.

I just was trying to look at it simply and identify the repeatable patterns over and over again. For example, a pullback that reverses right back up and makes a double-top action before pulling back and again making a break to the upside signifies a wave extension. That tells me that the buyers rushed in, and the sellers were overcome. Now sellers are nowhere to be found, and that's my chance to go long.

The very reason I chose a background in statistics was because I'd been very, very good at pattern recognition all my life. That is the one skill that I brought into trading that I feel has really helped me to get over the top.

Bourquin: Since settling on Fibonacci as your primary method, are you continuously adapting how you do it, or does your strategy remain constant?

Baiynd: I'm always adapting. I aim to identify small market shifts and effectively respond to them. For instance, the 127.2 percent Fibonacci retracement level was once a very hard and fast number, but in recent months, I've noticed a shift in favor of the 138.2 percent level. I'm always looking for shifts like that and then adapting accordingly.

I must always remind myself that the market is fluid and alive. It's never going to do what we expect all the time. That's why I watch for changes in behavior, but most everything else—the wave count, the way I draw the waves, and my triggers—stays exactly the same.

The only things that may change would be my stop placement, depending on the level of volatility, or which moving average (fifty-, twenty-, or ten-period SMA) I use, depending on the level of momentum. Those discretionary elements I have to interchange on the fly, because every day is just a little bit different.

Bourquin: Just like Elliott wave requires that you learn where to start the wave count, with Fibonacci, you've got to pick the proper high and low in order to draw the lines correctly. How did you get good at that?

Baiynd: Well, here's the interesting thing: as long as you draw a high-low of any visible wave, Fibonacci is going to deliver a level that you can use to trade. And "clear wave action" means, for example, that the market came up into a high, reversed and came down into a low, and then reversed higher again. In cases like that, it doesn't matter which wave you use if you're trading the trend from one level to the other.

Now, that's a very bizarre concept to some, because people want things to be very rigid, but it really doesn't have to be that way. The market is fractal, so much so that it doesn't matter which wave we use, because there are going to be workable levels for trading there.

I determine which ones are workable by looking at the Fibonacci extensions and then looking to the left to try to match them with support and resistance. If I find support and resistance there, I know that particular Fibonacci level is a workable one. If there's nothing there, I throw it out and start again somewhere else.

It really can be as simple as looking to the left at support and resistance, though, and if it matches, then you can step through the trade just like that.

Bourquin: Do you trade all day, every day, and how many trades do you typically take in any one day?

Baiynd: If you would have asked me that eighteen months ago, I would have had the craziest number for you. I was trading about two hundred round-trip trades back then, but now it's typically ten round trips—or twenty, at the most.

Bourquin: What markets do you trade right now?

Baiynd: I trade oil, I trade futures, and then I trade the big three: Apple, Amazon, and Google. I look to see which is behaving the best for the day, and that's where I'll focus.

I'm at my trading desk by 5:00 a.m. eastern time, doing my analysis, and then I'll be prepared if one is going to break from whatever important level is nearby. If nothing looks good, or if they just stay flat, then I'll sit on my hands while I read or study something else.

Bourquin: When you first got into trading, it was partly because you were working crazy hours and didn't have much time for yourself. Has trading given you relief from that lifestyle pattern, or are you right back in it?

Baiynd: Well, I was definitely right back in it when I was learning and struggling —and even once I went back and was learning and getting it. Now my life is a little bit more in balance.

Early on, I used to look at fifty different instruments and just chase all kinds of things. Now I'm so structured that even though I still get up very early to study the market, I am usually finished trading by 11:30 a.m. or noon eastern time.

I might stick around and help my students or strategize for some kind of swing trade or longer-term investment after that, but I'll be done physically trading at that point.

Bourquin: A lot of readers could be at that stage where you once were, sitting in a chair at a beginner's seminar, and others may not have even reached that point yet. What advice do you have for those people to ease their transition into trading? And if you had to start over again, what would you do differently?

Baiynd: If I had to start over again, I would acknowledge and accept right away that my skill level was very light, if not practically nonexistent. Just because I was successful in one career didn't mean that I could just jump right in, start trading, and achieve great results.

People often think that there's a 50/50 chance that they'll win or lose, so they're overanxious just to play, and they think, "Well, how hard could it be?"

Trading, of course, is an extremely difficult occupation, and it's important to size up the playing field, realize where your skill level *actually* is, and then try to find a mentor or someone who knows what they're doing to help walk you through. I've actually done that for many, many people myself.

Another piece of advice would be that throughout your search for information, there is still so much more that you do not know. Work hard to get a clearly defined system in place, and then find someone to help you battle the inevitable challenges you'll face each day.

Bourquin: To be a trader, you have to be comfortable being alone, but the desire for interaction with other traders during the day has given rise to thousands of chat rooms out there. What advice would you share with people who use them?

Baiynd: Well, retail trading is a very isolationist game, and that was especially true before we had Twitter and chat rooms. When I started trading, there wasn't a ton of that around, but now there is.

It is my belief that you are doing yourself a great disservice if you choose a chat room that just spits out *where* the trades are. In order to be a good trader, you must also understand *why* you are doing something. You really don't need to understand precisely how a stochastic momentum indicator comes up with its level, but you do need to know how to read it and what it means when it's sitting in a certain space.

So, when looking for a chat room, look for someone who's willing to share precisely what they are doing. Frankly, that's very difficult, because chat room operators are often concerned about their revenue and worry that you'll find what you need and then move on. That's why a lot of chat rooms just reveal the trades and not the logic behind them. If you can get into a room that explains the logic, however, you will get a much better understanding of where your skill level actually is at that point, as well as learn more of the things you need to know to trade well consistently.

Bourquin: What do you tell people who aspire to quit their jobs to trade full-time, or maybe those who are retiring and looking to earn extra income trading?

Baiynd: For anyone trying to make it a career change, it's important to get as much education as possible before stepping into the space. Now, I believe that a new trader can learn to swing trade in a much more relaxed fashion than they can with day trading. The amount of pressure is totally different, but the mechanics and the psychological impact of making a bad trade are exactly the same.

Before making that first trade, however, make sure you have a good basis in your education and have come across a system that you want to implement. From there, just start slowly and move forward.

So many folks who try to make trading into a career come in so undercapi-talized that they want to double and triple those small accounts—but that requires tremendous exposure to risk. That's a dangerous formula, because their skill level is low and risk exposure is high, and the common result is that new traders often blow out their accounts and can no longer trade.

Before making this a career, it's important to realize that there are tons of lessons you have to learn before you can be successful, and there really are very few shortcuts when learning to trade the markets.

The best thing to do is practice. Open a paper trading account, size up the market to find good trades, then take and work through those trades. If you can't make money in a paper trading account, you won't be able to do it with a real account, either—no doubt about it.

Bourquin: And along those same lines, even if you are able to make money in a paper trading account, that's no guarantee that you'll make money in a real account, right?

Baiynd: Exactly. There is a different feel when trading with real money, as well as the added psychological stress, and that's the real kicker.

Bourquin: Some people say paper trading isn't worthwhile, because it doesn't indicate that you'll be successful when trading with real money. Yet, there's a lot of education to be gained there, and you really have to do it.

Baiynd: Yes, absolutely. It's important for understanding the rhythm of the market. But new traders must also understand that there's all kinds of slippage that occurs when trading real money that you don't see in a paper trading account.

Mechanically, however, if you are making the right trading decisions, you will really reap the rewards when you move to a real account, as opposed to not under-standing the mechanics and immediately jumping in and trading real money.

Jeff White

*After completing a standout amateur golf career and spending several years playing professionally, **Jeff White** made the transition to trading full-time in mid-2000. Having found some fascinating parallels between the two professions, White knows better than most that being successful is "a grind"—not the glamorous and leisurely lifestyle that many imagine. As a day trader and swing trader who is focused almost exclusively on equities, White looks for simple, repeatable patterns and uses only price and volume signals to isolate the most favorable trading opportunities. Still, he believes that good traders must continually build their knowledge and understanding of alternate strategies to stay nimble in fast-moving market conditions. White posts daily market analysis, commentary, and trade ideas on his blog, TheStockBandit.com.*

Tim Bourquin: Jeff, before you ever got into the business of trading, you were an NCAA collegiate golfer, and you later turned professional. Let's start out by talking about that.

Jeff White: I played college golf starting in 1993 until I graduated in 1997. I had some success in college and was an All-American. I was improving each year and wanted to give the tour a try, so I went out on one of the mini-tours.

I was a struggling professional. I went out there and gave it three years, and even though I got better, I wasn't doing so at the pace that I needed to. That's a grind. It's a lot of travel and living life out of a suitcase. It means long hours and limited pay, especially if you aren't on television every weekend. So, my drive for it diminished, because my results weren't aligning with my level of effort.

Along the way, however, I had been exposed to the market. My wife and I married in 1998, and we had a small amount of savings and no debt, which was a big advantage. We decided to invest our savings to build a nest egg, and because we were very young, we felt we could really get ahead of the curve, in terms of building wealth over time.

We met with a local broker and invested in some mutual funds in the summer of 1998, right before the hedge fund Long-Term Capital Management collapsed in August. That drove the entire market lower, and with our mutual funds exposed to that weakness, we lost some of our savings as a result.

That didn't sit well with me, so I decided to take matters into my own hands. I started going to Barnes & Noble practically every night and read every investing and trading book and magazine I could get my hands on. It wasn't long before I had taken money out of those mutual funds and was watching individual stocks on my own.

Like every new investor or trader, however, I made a lot of mistakes. But in 1999 and early 2000, throughout that bubble period, the market forgave those mistakes because of all the excess strength out there.

By the time mid-2000 rolled around, I was doing very well in my trading, and that was when I decided to transition from playing golf to trading for a living.

Bourquin: I found it very interesting that you characterize life as a touring professional as "a grind." There's an interesting analogy there between golf and trading, and I'm sure you've seen it, too. People often think that trading for a living is a glamorous lifestyle, just like they imagine traveling and playing golf every day is glamorous.

White: Absolutely, and I'm glad that you mentioned that, because there is a lot of grinding in both golf and trading. The only real difference is that there's air conditioning in trading!

I've found that there are tough stretches in both. There are times when you put in very long hours and don't get paid for it. The same can often be said in any endeavor when you are self-directed and self-employed, though.

Bourquin: Both golf and trading can make you a real hit at cocktail parties, too! When you were on tour, did people think you were living the dream life, and do they say the same things now, when you tell them that you're a trader?

White: Yeah. For whatever reason, people find that much more interesting, but I can tell you that my life is probably no more interesting than theirs.

Bourquin: Let's talk about your transition into trading full-time and how you went about getting started.

White: I walked into a day trading office in South Texas, where I lived, and there were several dozen traders in there. They were using very sophisticated software that I had never seen before and had access to leverage that I didn't, and that afforded them some unique advantages over traders like me.

It was a retail firm. Everyone was trading their own account, but with everyone in one big room together, there was a phenomenal exchange of ideas. People would be calling out their trades as they were getting in and out, or noting higher highs and higher lows in a certain market, or announcing when an economic number was about to be released. There were many sets of eyes just watching the market from different angles.

It was an excellent environment that helped me learn and grow as a trader. I had been a part-time trader for a couple of years before that, but when getting into trading full-time, I had a lot to learn. Even now, many years later, I still have much more to learn.

In a setting like that, you have a lot of traders and a number of different approaches. Some are momentum players, others are pullback buyers, and some love to play reversals. You also get people on different time frames. Some are day traders, some are swing traders, and some are position traders. By having that constant interaction and understanding of what strategies work well under certain conditions, it quickly multiplied my knowledge and experience level.

Perhaps more than anything else, though, I learned the most from the mistakes that people around me were making. That was a time when the market really changed from a roaring bull market into a bear market. With prices moving lower, it required people to adapt, because the market would no longer "bail out" bad trades on its own.

I remember one trader in particular who made money every day for about six weeks without having a down day. Basically, he was fading extreme news-based momentum, so when a stock would ramp higher following a news report, he would start to scale into a short position, looking for that "inevitable" initial pullback.

He had a lot of leverage at his disposal, but to make these trades work, he would have to time his entries well, scale in, and keep adding to losing positions whenever he didn't time them well. Inevitably, he would get that pullback, and that would bail him out of some deep holes. He might be down $20,000 and ultimately be able to close out a $500 winner.

Bourquin: Even though that's a really bad habit to get into…

White: It certainly is, but every profitable trade simply magnified his confidence. It was as if he was playing chicken with the market but somehow just kept on winning.

One day, that all came to an end, though. He blew out $186,000 in just a couple of hours in a biotech stock that went into free-fall mode after a news headline. He just kept buying and adding to the position until he ran out of buying power, and the brokers in the office had to close his position for him because he was out of money.

It was hard to see someone self-destruct like that, and it taught me a lot about the emphasis—or overemphasis—that so many traders place on being "accurate." Here was a guy who was more accurate than anyone I had ever seen, and even he blew out his account by being careless with risk and position sizing.

Many of the approaches I take to this day are rooted in some of my early experiences and the lessons I learned from watching other traders, especially in a case like that.

Bourquin: In trading, you get exposed to a lot of different methods, and while there are people like yourself, who take what they've learned and develop their own strategy, there are others who are constantly chasing the latest thing. How do you find the balance between chasing whatever you think is working at the moment and integrating outside information to create your own solid strategy going forward?

White: I think it's easy to try to learn too much all at once, especially when you are a newer trader. You understand that there are many different time frames and techniques you can choose from, so you try a little bit of everything and constantly switch from one to another. Ultimately, you only find yourself getting more confused, and you won't actually learn or make progress that way.

I learned to let the market dictate which plays to focus on, and then, naturally, you'll learn what you need to learn over time. That brings greater consistency and eliminates the need to learn multiple strategies all at once.

My advice would be to go to work on what the market is rewarding at the time, and keep paying attention when that's not working quite as well, too, because that's when you may need to adjust and learn something else.

Bourquin: Does that argue for having five or six different strategies at your disposal so you have an arsenal to choose from, regardless of the market environment at the time?

White: Absolutely, but you build up to that over time. Even a handful of strategies can be enough. You just don't want to be a one-trick pony.

The market isn't going to reward the same strategy forever, and when conditions change and your strategy doesn't, you only have two choices: lose money and become frustrated, or sit on the sidelines and wait indefinitely until the market comes back around to suit your lone strategy.

Having something else to roll into when conditions change can be an incredible benefit. Just three, four, or five favorite plays may not sound like much, but if they differ enough from one another, they can enable you to maneuver and navigate any market condition.

Bourquin: Sometimes traders have trouble taking the next trade after a string of trades they've made with one type of strategy goes against them. How do you know that market conditions have changed and it's time to switch, for example, from a momentum strategy to a range-trading strategy?

White: For me, it's a feel thing, and I don't have a set formula that tells me when conditions have changed. I must first be objective about each position, continually evaluating the price and volume action to see if those signals still warrant staying with that position.

Also, I have to be objective about the overall market environment and understand whether we're trending, momentum-based, caught in a range, or if there is complete indecision. Then, depending on the current conditions, I need to understand which strategies will work the best.

Having four or five losing trades in a row will happen. That's part of this business. When it does happen, though, it's important to act quickly to protect your confidence—and your account—by scaling back on your positions a bit. Then you should step back to identify the big picture and what's causing the losing trades. Don't take a losing streak alone as a sign that your strategy is no longer working.

Bourquin: To close the loop on your time spent working at that trading firm, when did you decide to leave that environment and start trading on your own?

White: That decision was almost made for me when the office in San Antonio closed. I started there in 2000, when there were about forty traders, but by the time I left in 2002, there were only a few of us left.

It was a process of elimination by the market. Obviously, the universe of tradable stocks really shrunk, and momentum died down, forcing traders to adapt. Many lost their money, and others just ran out of time. Since they weren't making money anymore, they needed to go back to other work.

After that office closed, I commuted to one of their offices in Austin, because I still wanted to be around other traders. I loved that camaraderie. I loved the interaction and the flow of ideas. That lasted for another couple of years, but that group also dwindled down.

Until that point, I had been uncomfortable trading from home because I wasn't confident in my equipment. By that time, though, the speed and reliability of the internet was much improved, and that allowed me to trade at home and still communicate with other traders throughout the day. So, in 2004, I stopped commuting and became a home-based trader.

Bourquin: Even though the technology and tools were the same as the ones you had before in the office setting, how was the transition, in terms of not having other traders around you anymore?

White: It was tough, not so much in terms of discipline or my ability to stay focused on trading, but I missed the interaction.

Trading is a very solitary occupation, and I missed having the opportunity to interact with people, even if it was just having lunch together. At the same time, however, that was definitely a time that made me learn and grow as a trader.

Bourquin: Let's talk strategy now. First of all, did your strategy change at all when you made the transition to home-based trading?

White: My trading did change around that time, but it wasn't based on my location. Instead, it was because the market itself had changed. As I mentioned, there was a much smaller universe of stocks to trade, and I found that the risk I was putting on to achieve the desired level of reward had really changed.

Initially, I could risk one to make three or four, and I had done very well with that. As the market got compressed and intraday prices weren't fluctuating as much, I found that I had to start zooming out on my time frame.

After that, I began doing a lot more swing trading, and I would hold positions overnight and look for multiday moves instead of just situational trades I could enter and exit within the span of about two hours. That was definitely a big shift for me.

Bourquin: So, would you say that you're now more of a swing trader who looks for bigger, long-term moves, as opposed to a day trader?

White: Yes, I'm more of a swing trader, but I still day trade, too. I like to operate on different time frames, because I feel there is always opportunity there.

I prefer the swing trades, because my tendency is to micromanage stocks. For example, when day trading, I'm naturally watching the tick-by-tick action, and it's tougher for me to stay in winning trades because I can't just bracket orders and leave the trade alone until it hits my parameters, like I would with a swing trade.

I'm very disciplined with cutting losses in both time frames, but the ability to better manage winning positions is why I favor swing trades over day trades.

Bourquin: Can you give a general idea of how you structure your trading day? How do you go about your "homework" when the market is closed, and what do you look for to signal good trading opportunities?

White: Being located in Texas, the market closes each day at 3:00 p.m. central time, so right after the close, I review the trades I took that day to see what I did well and brush up on any lessons I need to take from the day's action to improve my results going forward.

I then turn my attention toward research and dig through charts to help my planning for the following day. I start with the indices, and I primarily look at the NASDAQ and S&P 500, but I'll also look over the Russell 2000 and occasionally the Dow.

I want to know what the broad market is doing, where the important levels are, and what type of environment we are in. For example, is there a presence or an absence of momentum? I'll identify that and then determine what direction we are heading, because I know there is going to be a correlation between individual stocks and the overall market.

I look through a lot of charts and maintain some very basic criteria, in terms of price and volume. I like trading stocks that are at least double digits in price and have an average daily volume of a half-million shares or more. That filters out many low-priced and low-volume stocks, leaving those that are more liquid and likely to move.

I spend considerable time every day looking through several hundred charts and manually reviewing them. Software makes the process much easier, but I actually enjoy hunting for great setups and feel like doing the research this way gives me a better feel for the underlying strength, weakness, or indecision in the overall market at the time.

I set aside any charts that look interesting on my initial pass, and that usually leaves a short list of thirty or forty stocks I'll then go back over while trying to identify patterns, key levels, and any potential trade opportunities. At this stage, I'm thinking about where to enter a particular position and where I'd need to get out.

Bourquin: Do you use previous highs and lows, pivots, or some other method for determining entry and exit points?

White: I draw a lot of trend lines, but my charts are very clean and basic, in terms of indicators. I really like price and volume, so any indicators I use are derived just from those.

I draw trend lines along the highs and lows, trying to identify price levels that have been respected from one side or the other. For example, I'll pay attention to a prior support level that has become resistance, or vice versa.

One of my favorite plays involves recent momentum and then a little bit of a rest phase with some compression in price. It's a wedge-type look following a big momentum move, and that's really just a breather that helps me to identify a potential secondary move in the stock. I try to note any instances of those patterns and take a close look at the risk/reward profile each time.

Then, the final step for me is to determine whether the stock looks like it's ready to move right away. If it's starting to lean on a trend line, or if volume is starting to perk up and price is showing a bit more commitment, in terms of where it closed on the bar, those would be favorable signals for me.

For example, if I see a stock moving higher and approaching an overhead trend line amid increasing volume, and I also notice that price is finishing at or near the top of that bar. That suggests to me that the stock is getting ready to make a move.

A few ideas like that will make up my trade plan for the following day, and I always want to walk in with a plan so I never have to hurry up and find something to trade. I have my trade ideas and the important levels that go with them in mind already, and from there, it's just a matter of execution. I feel less emotion during the day when I come in prepared, and I feel much less guilt if ever I miss a market move—as long as I followed my trading plan.

Bourquin: That makes for built-in discipline and helps ensure you are only taking trades that match your risk profile and your trading strategy. Too many traders just try to chase whatever is moving that day, and that's often risky and tough to do.

White: It sure is. It also requires very quick decision making, and while you sometimes have to think quickly in the market, that's not a habit I want to cultivate, because it can lead to mistakes and a lack of discipline.

Bourquin: Do you trade differently on days where there are more setups, and how do you react on days where opportunities are thin?

White: On days where a lot of setups are prevalent, I know I have to be very focused and a little more aggressive, because there are more opportunities there. It's my belief and has been my experience throughout my career that as long as I manage my entries and exits well, being aggressive on these days will work in my favor.

When there are fewer setups, however, that's my signal to back off, trade less, and wait for the market to generate more favorable signals. I'm especially conscious not to force trades under these conditions, and I'll lower my expectations and be patient, instead of trying to find setups when they may not be there at the time.

Bourquin: Wealthy traders seem to understand that being successful isn't only about trading. It's about finding the right trades, and sometimes that means waiting for setups and not trading at all. Those traders won't simply dive in because they feel the need to be in the market at all times.

White: Absolutely. That actually brings up the cocktail party discussions again. A lot of people think being a trader means constant action and excitement, but I tell them that the fact of the matter is that there's a lot more watching and waiting involved than most think.

I honestly don't want to feel constant adrenaline when trading. There will be a few times each year that are that way, but most of the time, it's much more monotonous and just a matter of exercising patience.

Impatient traders are the ones who don't last very long, and it's not that they are impatient in terms of their time frame for a position. It's that they are unwilling or unable to sit and wait. That definitely takes practice, but those who pick their spots and wait for the market conditions that best suit their style are going to have much greater success.

Bourquin: You mentioned earlier that you are always learning and studying, and I love to ask professional traders to talk about the things they can still learn or improve upon. What are you still working on when it comes to your trading?

White: Well, for me, it's all about finding ways to stay in my good trades longer. I'm very good at cutting losses, but letting winners run is the part of the discipline equation that I have a hard time with. To get better at that, I try to scale out of winning positions so I can satisfy the urge to book some profits but also stay involved in the trade if the move should continue.

In terms of overall trading skills, I have always been an equities trader. I have dabbled a little bit in futures and options, but I never really added those to my core skill set as a trader. Lately I have been educating myself in options just to round out my abilities a little further.

I don't want to become stagnant and have only one market I can trade. Even though I've come this far trading only equities, I feel it's important to keep moving and growing. I'm not looking to make a major shift in my approach, and I'm not walking away from something I have always done, either. I'm just looking to integrate a little more of something new.

Bourquin: Finally, Jeff, how do you pay yourself? Do you take money out from your profits, write yourself a salary check, or maybe even trade through a corporation?

White: I've set up a combination entity through a traders' accounting firm that has some very good tax advantages, in terms of the deductions I'm able to take as a full-time trader, as opposed to being relegated to investor status.

From there, it's based on how much I want to pull out of my account at the end of the year. I factor in how much I need to live on and whether I have some money left over from the prior year in my personal account, because that might allow me to leave more in my trading account to grow the following year. It's just a constant give and take, but there is no set salary that I'm paying myself.

My wife and I are both very frugal people, so I never feel like I have to maintain a certain lifestyle through my trading, and that quite possibly has given me more peace of mind than anything else in all my years of doing this full-time. Obviously, I want to be highly successful, and some years are better than others, but I don't feel added pressure as it relates to money.

Patrick Hemminger

Spread trader **Patrick Hemminger** *began trading agricultural futures when the number of favorable trade opportunities in equities began diminishing as a result of more highly correlated global equity markets. Although it was borne out of necessity, Hemminger's switch to agricultural futures has proven a defining move in his career and shows that traders must be attentive and quick to respond to changing market conditions.*

The historically reliable and lucrative spreads in commodities like corn, wheat, soybeans, and even oil have allowed Hemminger to apply his unbiased technical strategy and achieve even greater success as a trader. By focusing on historical trends and non-complex technical indicators, Hemminger trades a variety of time frames, ranging from longer-term periods right down to intraday moves. His rather daring method of removing stops in the face of economic news and data may seem controversial to some, but as he explains, it helps him avoid being stopped out by the overly emotional market moves that are increasingly common in today's markets. Hemminger shares his positions, as well as regular market insights and trade ideas, on his blog, DirtyArbitrage.com.

Tim Bourquin: Patrick, let's talk about your trading strategies, and how you look at the market and find good opportunities each week. Let's start by defining your trading. What type of trader are you?

Patrick Hemminger: Sure. I'm a relationship trader. What I mean by that is I'm constantly looking at spreads and the value between two assets.

Most cases are very highly correlated. When it comes to an implied equity spread of E-mini S&P versus DAX—or in the case where a lot of my research and efforts are going right now—I'm looking at agricultural spreads.

Those could be spreads along a term structure, a calendar spread, or an inter-commodity spread, like corn versus wheat. But all of my exposure on the futures side is relationship based.

Bourquin: All right. So, when I think of spread trading, I think of corn and wheat usually trading together. But when they start to diverge, you see that happen, and you go long one and short the other to see if they will come back into convergence again. Did I round that out pretty well?

Hemminger: Yes, I think that's a good broad statement for spreads. You're looking to identify value, and opportunities can appear along many different time frames, including intraday, swing, or longer-term, seasonal periods.

Last year, corn and wheat were trading at par. That's an historical phenomenon that does not occur very often. There were many times last year when I was selling corn and buying wheat purely based upon the fact that the spread was an historical occurrence. I was more than willing to apply risk and looked for the spread to diverge back to the point where wheat was trading above corn, which is what has happened now.

Bourquin: And why did that happen? Do you focus much on the reasoning, or do you just say, "It is where it is, and I'm trading it"?

Hemminger: I tend to focus more on the technical perspective. Even looking back ten, twenty, thirty years, there is so much data—especially in agricultures—that is available. You can look back from a long-term perspective.

I try not to mix fundamental bias in with my technicals, as I'm aware of where the chatter is and what people are saying, but listening to the crowd has gotten me in trouble in the past. Now I tend to stick to my framework, framing out each trade, knowing where my risk and reward is, and sticking with the plan.

Bourquin: Now, previously I know you had been trading these divergences in equities—the Dow versus the DAX, as you mentioned before. What brought you to agricultures to try your trading approach there?

Hemminger: Well, that's a great question. Two of the basic tenets of being a successful longer-term trader are, number one, realizing that markets have changed and, number two, being flexible enough to evolve accordingly. Being a one-trick pony just is not a formula for long-term success, because, from a global macro perspective, the world is changing.

My specialty in equity spreads was US equity indexes versus European equity indexes. Because my main benchmark is the S&P, I would spread that versus FTSE, versus DAX, versus Euro Stoxx 50. But beginning in the middle of 2010, the opportunity in those spreads slowed down. There simply were not nearly as many daily opportunities to be involved in those spreads. When those spreads did diverge, they presented less opportunities and more risk in relation to prior historical performance.

Bourquin: Yes. I've heard that. Because trading has become more global, markets started to correlate a whole lot more than they had in the past, and there were fewer divergences. I think that's what you're saying, too.

Hemminger: Exactly, that's right on. It became very difficult to be long or short Europe, as those indexes and all of the financial futures there, including the Bund, BOBL debt futures, the euro, and the pound, were moving in relation to what the next news item was. People were paying attention to the news that was coming out of Greece, and it didn't make for good back-and-forth trade. It made for panic. In most cases, panic is a great thing, but in this case, everything moved in such a correlated manner that it just didn't provide the type of opportunity that I had become accustomed to.

The writing was on the wall at the beginning of 2011, and I knew that we really needed to start evolving our trading approach, the trends we followed, our trades, the asset classes we traded, and so on. Our evolution was really borne out of preservation.

Bourquin: Now that you have moved over to agricultures, what's your most common trade? Is it corn versus wheat?

Hemminger: The most common spreads that I'm participating in right now are mainly calendar spreads inside of a one-asset term structure. So, I'm looking for open interest and volume along multiple expirations in one single contract.

I'm looking for intra-term opportunities among calendar spreads of term structures and scanning the market for interrelationships—for instance, corn versus soybeans and hogs versus cattle. I do much less of inter- and much more intra-term structure positioning.

Bourquin: Can you give me an example of a garden-variety trade so that we can really break this down and understand your trading approach?

Hemminger: I'll start with the beans, which is a trade that I'm involved in right now. In this trade, I looked at the July 2013 versus the November 2013 spread, and the reason I zeroed in on that spread is because it exhibited price action that was very reliable and very highly correlated with past historical observations.

Let me back up. At the beginning of the year, I asked a dear friend of mine to develop a piece of software that analyzes historical data and identifies patterns in spreads that have proven to be highly reliable. The software brings those spreads to my attention and tells me the average win rate, as well as the average winning trade and the average losing trade.

Using my software, I realized that this particular bean spread was a 60 percent winner over the last five years from a time-cycle perspective. So, from mid-October to approximately mid-December, I can expect an average winning trade in this spread to make about forty-one cents and an average losing trade to lose five cents. That gives me an expected outcome of $1,200 to $1,300, which is exactly the kind of trade I'm looking for.

Bourquin: So, is the July contract historically overvalued while the November contract is historically undervalued? What are you actually looking at there?

Hemminger: Actually, the July 2013 contract right now is undervalued in relation to the November 2013 soybean contract. Historically, the middle of October is a reliable time of year to purchase that spread, and you should look to sell that spread somewhere before Christmas for an average profit of about $1,200 to $1,300 per contract.

Bourquin: So, you find areas where a futures contract in relationship to another expiring contract is over- or undervalued, and then you trade those two against each other until they come back into balance. Is that about right?

Hemminger: Yes, exactly. We are just looking to identify contracts that are offering an undervalued or overvalued proposition in relation to another contract. Then I try to zero in on the time. So, instead of just looking at risk-to-reward metrics, I've added a time function that gives me an added dimension to my trades. It allows me to really dial in, manage down my trades, and mitigate risk to a larger degree.

Bourquin: Your soybean trade sounds like it is a longer-term trade that you can hold for several months. Do these kinds of relationships or ratios happen intraday as much as they do over the course of months?

Hemminger: Yes. The bean spread is a fast mover. It's a volatile spread, and when you're looking at a forty-one-cent average winner, you have to be willing to take a certain amount of risk for that type of higher-reward trade.

A slower spread trade that I recently wrote about is the July 2013 versus the September 2013 spread in wheat. I'm short July and long September. In this trade, I'm looking at an average winner of ten cents and an average loser of three cents. This trade has a sterling track record in recent years as well.

In relation to the bean spread, this trade has much lower risk, but as a result, the rewards it offers are going to be capped as well. So, these two spreads definitely have different personalities. For instance, as the bean spread moves, you can see algorithms come in and bid the spread up, giving you an opportunity to scalp around your core position. In fact, a basic tenet of my trading strategy is to find core positions in agricultural spreads that I want to be in for one to two months and then trade around that bias in the direction of the historical pattern that I've identified.

Bourquin: How many trades or positions do you have on at any given time?

Hemminger: I would say that at any given time I have, on average, five to six different agricultural spreads on.

Bourquin: Do you set stop losses and profit targets when you enter these trades?

Hemminger: Yes. By utilizing the software program I mentioned earlier, I can get a real quick glimpse into how a certain spread has performed historically during a specific time slot each year. As I said earlier, this program provides an average loss and an average win, and I combine that information with technical indications of momentum, support and resistance, trend lines, and many of the other tools that I've acquired in the past ten years that I've been trading.

Bourquin: Talk about those indicators you are using. What indicators do you like to put on a chart in addition to seeing the ratios that your software program provides you?

Hemminger: I've never been a fan of oscillators. My whole life has been focused on keeping things simple and smart. I look at Bollinger bands not from a reversion perspective but from a momentum perspective. A group of guys that I traded with for three years taught me this way of reading Bollinger bands, and it's been a great addition to some of the other basic technicals that I watch, including trend lines, time cycles, and support and resistance.

I really try to keep things as simple as possible and avoid "quanting things out" in a complex way. It makes managing trades much easier.

Bourquin: Did you try a bunch of different things before you came across spread trading as something that finally worked for you consistently?

Hemminger: Yes, very much so. My first job was actually trading NASDAQ stocks in 2001. I had no idea what I was doing. Growing up, I couldn't tell you what a quote was. I had no idea, but trading really melded with my personality as a highly competitive athlete. It gave me a competitive outlet and a "hard way," as one of my friends says, to make an easy living.

When I first got into trading, I was very much engaged in quick scalp trades. I didn't do poorly, but I didn't do well. When I found pairs trading in equities, however, that was an eye-opening event for me. It gave me the opportunity to be a little more patient with my trades, because I was focused on relative value, not on whether KLA-Tencor [KLAC] stock was going to go up today or Novellus Systems stock was going to go down. Instead, I could trade the relative value in between the KLAC–Novellus pair. Those early days of equity statistical arbitrage pairs trading has really defined my career up to this point.

Bourquin: What made agricultural pairs trading more attractive to you than just straight equity pairs trading?

Hemminger: I enjoy the research process and looking through data, which are skills that I have continued to build upon as my career in the financial markets has developed and I have gained more confidence. I would say that process really started in 2006. As my confidence in relationship-driven trading started to build, I began to achieve consistent trading results.

I was trading along the crude curve, the Brent curve, and Brent oil. I was also trading heating oil versus ICE gasoil futures. All of these different relationships I was looking at were providing me with multiple trading opportunities. Some of the opportunities were based purely on statistical measure, some were based on technical measures, and some were based on pattern recognition measures. Regardless, each step along the way has equipped me in a different way, and all of those tools are what I'm now using to define my trading in the present and going forward.

Bourquin: If somebody wanted to get started in agricultural pairs trading, like you're doing, where is a good place for them to start? What should they be watching and monitoring?

Hemminger: The Chicago Mercantile Exchange [CME] obviously is great. That's the number one venue for trading agricultural spreads. For someone who is just getting interested or wants to scratch the surface of agriculturals, there is a lot of information and educational opportunities on the CME's web site.

Bourquin: I didn't ask you what your typical size is when you're doing these spread trades. What do you use to determine how much size you'll put on?

Hemminger: The number one factor that I use to determine position sizing is how much each tick is worth. You want to be very aware of what the margin is for the product in question. I go back to a simple average true range [ATR] and look back over the last twenty trading days to get an idea of the volatility of the spread. Then I bring that margin back to my account size in relation to volatility and scale into trades. I use a unit size that is related to volatility, margin, and the contract size.

Bourquin: Based on the ATR and other factors, you determine how much size you're going to take, and then scale in if it starts to work for you?

Hemminger: Yes, exactly—and these spreads offer a ton of liquidity. There is no lack of liquidity in most of these spreads, so traders should also pay attention to liquidity when attempting to trade agricultural spreads.

Bourquin: What if an economic announcement is released while you're in a longer-term trade? Do you leave the trade on? Do you monitor it closely? What do you do?

Hemminger: Obviously, you're going to monitor your trades during those releases. For instance, there is an economic release called WASDE—World Agricultural Supply and Demand Expectations—that's put out by the USDA.

I hold the WASDE. WASDE numbers come out every month, and most of my trades are going to go a little bit longer than three to four weeks. So, I constantly have positions on during those agricultural data releases.

Bourquin: Has the release ever stopped you out because the movement was so great?

Hemminger: I would never want to stop out on the emotional response, so I remove all my stops from the market. I wouldn't want an erratic market reaction or an algorithm going crazy and pushing the market one way artificially. So, during those times of higher volatility, I will actually remove my stops. I have never had an instance where that has gone against me, because when those numbers initially come out, they mainly elicit an artificial reaction in the markets.

Now, the release may obviously influence future market movements. But in some ways, thanks to the way that I position myself, I'm giving myself the option and the time to patiently look and see what's happening and how the market is truly digesting the news release. So, I tend not to allow those types of high-volatility events to take me out of a trade.

Bourquin: Now, it's got to be a little worrisome at some point to remove your stops. Perhaps some of the news is built in with agricultures, and so you won't be totally shocked if there is a drought or bushels come out less in harvest. But, still, I would imagine that the time you spend operating without stops has got to be a little tense.

Hemminger: Yes, it can be. It's similar to trading nonfarm payrolls. Every trader who is trading that release, regardless of whether they are taking a position or not, gets that little feeling of excited anxiety in their gut, and they react in accordance.

In my experience, I've found that reacting to what other traders are reacting to is usually not a good formula for stopping me out of position. In the past, I've made a decent amount of money by trading both economic releases and the spreads around them, and so I tend not to get too flustered or dwell too much upon the market's initial knee-jerk reaction. I let the market reevaluate where it wants to be before making any decisions to exit or enter a trade.

Don Miller

*Futures specialist **Don Miller** is a top-ranked fund manager, highly renowned mentor and trading educator, and member of the Chicago Mercantile Exchange (CME). Using a technical approach and multiple intraday time frames for his trades, Miller has learned to identify and buy pockets of value within the market and describes himself as a "liquidity provider."*

After starting out trading equities, Miller later gravitated to futures, where he found success through constant learning and adaptability. Despite achieving the consistency and confidence of a master trader, however, not even he was safe from the MF Global debacle. Having fallen victim to the scandal, he worked as an advocate, spoke candidly about his experience and the need for reform, and later recovered his missing funds— as well as his passion for trading. Thousands now follow his trade journal and blog at DonMillerBlog.com and his educational site at DonMillerEducation.com.

Tim Bourquin: Let's talk about the type of trader you are, in terms of your time frames—day trader or swing trader—and then about the markets you trade.

Don Miller: My time frame is primarily intraday. I trade the E-mini S&P futures, and I've been a member of the Chicago Mercantile Exchange [CME] since 2004. As such, I guess I would define my style of trading as liquidity providing, buying wholesale intraday, and selling retail.

My holding times are usually pretty tight. I am fairly good about reading the markets on a very short-term basis, and there are wholesale opportunities throughout the course of the day. I believe a bird in the hand is worth two in the bush, and that's typically how I have traded over the years.

Bourquin: Let me ask you about a couple of those terms that you mentioned. First, when you say that one type of trading that you engage in is liquidity providing, what do you mean?

Miller: Basically, one of the great things about the markets—and especially the E-mini market, which is one of the most liquid vehicles on the planet—is that, when somebody wants to buy or sell a futures contract, there needs to be someone on the other side of that transaction to allow it to take place. The more people that are able to provide liquidity, the more people that are able to be on the other side of that trade. And the more people on the other side of that trade, the more liquid the market, and you're going to see less volatility.

There is a stabilization benefit of providing liquidity to the market, and you also essentially serve as the party on the other side of a transaction any time somebody wants to buy or sell.

Obviously, we won't provide liquidity unless there is an opportunity for us as well, and we find our opportunities by taking advantage of and anticipating market cycles and markets that may get stretched one way or another, or markets that are moving toward a new path of least resistance. By and large, we're able to sell product at a better price than we purchased it. It doesn't happen all the time, but that's the intention. That's the goal.

Bourquin: How is providing liquidity to the market different from just making a directional play for profit?

Miller: At a very detailed level, I suppose the differentiation is that, if you are sitting on the bid or under the bid and you're allowing somebody to sell to you, then you are technically providing liquidity. On the other hand, if you decide that you want to get in the market, no matter what the price is, then you will go ahead and buy on the ask. In this latter case, someone else is providing liquidity to you.

It's a little bit of a gray area, in terms of when you're doing one versus the other, but overall, what happens is that the volume in the market increases, the participation in the market increases, and it makes for a more fluid market.

But is there speculation involved in liquidity providing? Can you engage in directional plays while you're providing liquidity? Absolutely. My most recent session was a good example. I didn't do much liquidity providing, except for at midday, when the market started coming in, and I was sitting on the bid and hoping that if people needed to sell, they could sell to me. Aside from that very limited window, I was making directional plays, speculating, and getting myself in the market.

Bourquin: Are shorter time frames involved in plays where you're providing liquidity and trying to buy at the bid?

Miller: Well, it really depends. The holding time depends on what cycle is in play. I believe that the market moves in a cycle on various time frames.

If the time frame happens to be a little five-minute consolidating time period and higher time frames really are questionable, in terms of whether you have wind at your back or not, the holding can appear to be fairly tight. On the other hand, if you are just busting out of consolidation or you're in a clear momentum trend on an hourly cycle, then the holding time can be a bit longer.

The holding period really doesn't depend on whether you are getting in proactively or you are getting in passively, in terms of providing liquidity. It really depends on the cycle in play at the time.

Bourquin: What about "buying wholesale"? That sounds great. We always want to get a discount or a good deal. But how does that work in the stock market? How do you buy on the bid and sell on the offer?

Miller: When I say "wholesale," that doesn't necessarily mean that you are always buying on a bid. If you are solely buying on a bid or selling on the ask, then what essentially is happening is you are always trading against the market's immediate direction. And if that's all you do, that's probably going to be a quick route to the poor farm.

Imagine if every single trade you got in, you were basically buying when others were selling, or you were selling when others were buying. That just wouldn't work. But through the mix of that, along with getting yourself in the market when you need to, that's where the opportunity is.

So, when we talk about wholesale, again, I don't mean that you're just sitting on the bid all the time, and that's the only way you're going to get in. What if the market's in a very clear uptrend or has busted out of a consolidation range, the path of least resistance has clearly shifted to the upside, and you want to get in the market? You would love to get that market as it is coming down after it breaks out—but it may not come down.

When I use the term "wholesale," I mean it more as a reference point. I think of wholesale as compared to where the market is going to be in the future—and that may mean five minutes, ten minutes, or maybe an hour from now. Wholesale means getting a product—whether it's E-minis or stocks, or Tiddlywinks or bananas down at the grocery store—at a price that is attractive, reasonable, and less expensive than it will be in the future.

Bourquin: So, are we talking about something you feel is undervalued in the short term? Is that what we're really talking about?

Miller: Well, I trade primarily by technical analysis. When I say "technical analysis," I mean using a set of indicators that in combination accurately define the flow of the market. And my trades are based on those indicators, which help frame the current flow and anticipated future direction of the market. Based on that information, it's usually fairly clear as to where the market is going.

I want to be really careful when using the term "value." When we talk value in this market, the value essentially is created by human emotion. You've got zillions of traders in the marketplace in multiple time frames and of varying levels of experience, and based on their actions, they're going to push the market into a position where moves are not sustainable.

Let's say you have a runaway market to the upside or downside that is just going bonkers. That market is not sustainable over the long term, and when you're able to identify those points in the market where moves are not sustainable, then, as framed by technical analysis, you're able to become a wholesale provider.

Bourquin: And technical analysis tells you if something is not sustainable and is ready to reverse direction or break out of some range that it has been in?

Miller: It helps frame the human emotion. When I was doing my live training last year, I was talking to somebody about how you would go about teaching someone to do this. He said, "Stop for a second. You just said something that I've never heard anybody else say. You're trying to teach market feel." And I said, "That's right." And he said, "That's crazy! You can't teach feel." And I said, "I beg to differ. The market and the opportunities that are provided are all based on feel."

Now, when I say "feel," I don't mean that you're waking up and just kind of feeling that something is going to go up. What I mean by "feel" is that you have a sense, based on experience and technical analysis, of what the market is going to do.

Once you've traded for a while, technical analysis becomes more of a confirmation. When you trade the same product over and over and over and over again, you're getting to know that product, just like you get to know your children. You get to know their tendencies, their personalities, and their rhythms. That's why I'm a strong believer in just trading one market.

As you get used to that child, if you will, you're going to know it very, very well. You're going to be able to anticipate its rhythms. When I say "feel," I mean technical analysis. It's like putting a scale or a ruler or some measuring device against a rhythm and a pattern that you're very familiar with, and you're getting confirmation of that with technical analysis.

Bourquin: How does being a member of the CME give you an advantage in your trading?

Miller: Reduced transaction costs. And for those that do engage in frequent transactions over the course of the day, which I certainly do, and as an incentive to help increase the liquidity in the markets, the exchanges allow people to either buy seats on the exchange or, in my case, lease a seat for a very modest monthly amount. In doing so, we are able to get reduced commissions.

So, it certainly helps our business and improves our cost structure. It also provides more volume, more liquidity, and more stability to the markets.

Bourquin: Do you still use a regular online broker to execute your trades?

Miller: Absolutely.

Bourquin: But because you're a member of the CME, they charge you less?

Miller: Yes, everybody gets their piece. The CME gets their fees, the broker that you're dealing with is going to get their piece, and there's a small piece that goes to the National Futures Association [NFA]. There are various bundles, and the broker is pretty much always going to get the same amount. I'm sure they probably get a reduced amount for high-volume traders, but by and large, those pieces are probably fairly constant.

The CME has a discounted rate schedule that is based on the type of membership you have with them and the volume that you trade. That will actually set your transaction price. The more you trade with them and the stronger your membership with them is, the more reduced your fees will be.

For example, if you were to purchase a seat, you'd get a more reduced fee as compared to even someone who leases a seat. I lease a seat, so I get a better transaction price than a retail investor, but my price is not as great as someone who has actually purchased a seat.

Bourquin: But whatever you pay for that lease is net-net. You're saving money each month, because you're doing enough volume to make up for the cost of the lease, right?

Miller: Absolutely. Actually, it's a very simple breakeven analysis that I'm walking traders through, in terms of determining what you're paying now and how many contracts you would need to trade over the course of the month so that the lease basically pays for itself.

The price of the lease has come down over the years. They really are at a price point where, if you're fairly active at all over the course of the day, it really makes sense to lease a seat. I think the rates right now are in the $400 to $500 range per month, and you can make that money back very, very quickly.

Bourquin: Talk about your evolution as a trader. Did you try a lot of different things when you first started trading before you finally arrived at your current method?

Miller: My trading evolved over time from stocks to exchange-traded funds [ETFs], when I was trading the NASDAQ, the QQQ, and the SPY. Then, in 2003, I migrated to futures, which, to me, is the most pristine realm of trading. You are actively buying and selling, you truly fend for yourself, there is no middle party, and you're directly engaging with somebody on the other side of the trade.

That's what my evolution was, but it really took a long, long time, and I suffered a lot of false starts.

The training program that I put together, which is called the Jellie program, is named for a jellyfish. In order to survive, jellyfish have to adapt. They have to be flexible, they have to eat wherever they're thrown into the ocean, and they can't provide self-momentum, so they've got to go with the flow. That's what it's all about in trading, whether it's determining which market is best to trade or diagnosing the current market environment and adapting accordingly.

I think those of us who have been fortunate enough to have crossed the line to success over the years have figured out that it's not about us, it's not about our egos, and it's not about what we think *ought* to happen. It's about identifying and understanding what really is happening and aligning ourselves with that.

Bourquin: Can you give us an overview of your technical analysis?

Miller: I believe in keeping it simple. I really do. It's interesting, because there have been a lot of studies out there that say technical analysis doesn't work. Those studies are actually probably right, but the fallacy in all those conclusions is that they look at indicators by themselves.

For example, a lot has been written about why moving averages, stochastics, moving average convergence/divergence [MACD], or support and resistance don't work. I would tend to agree with every one of those comments with the caveat that, by themselves, the indicators don't work. But I and many others who are successful view these indicators in combination.

If you understand that the market is trending and want to know on what time frame it is doing so, you can measure that by using technical indicators like moving averages, stochastics, and support and resistance points. Really, that's all you need. Throughout the hundreds of different indicators that are out there, you're just looking for a handful. You're looking for something to define momentum, trend, and the points in time where you really have to take action.

I could rattle off probably a dozen indicators that all measure momentum and a dozen indicators that all measure trend. People get caught up on the fanciest indicator for this and the fanciest indicator for that. But I keep it simple and use only a handful of indicators.

Bourquin: Do you have a favorite indicator for measuring momentum?

Miller: I use stochastics, but I'm sure MACD is fine. There are some custom indicators out there that also measure momentum, but I use moving averages, stochastics, support and resistance points, and that's it.

I also use an indicator called the Three-Line Break, which is a non-time-based line chart that is purely focused on price. As such, it helps define trends and reversal points. As long as the markets do not retrace below or go above a certain price point, the Three-Line Break is a wonderful indicator.

I also look at everything on multiple time frames. I've got a one-minute chart, a five-minute chart, a fifteen-minute chart, an hourly chart, and a daily chart. I don't just use technical indicators or technical analysis. I use these tools on various time frames to try to understand the time frame that the market is cycling in. The market may look flat, but it may just be consolidating a huge bull or bear fight in a higher time frame. It may be trending really, really strongly on a five-minute chart, but the hourly or daily trend may be substantially down. In other words, I make sure that while I'm chopping down trees in the forest, the forest is not burning down.

Bourquin: Let me switch gears a little bit and talk about one of the challenges that I know you dealt with in your trading career in the past year, and that was being a customer of MF Global. Can you talk about that time? How did you first find out there was a problem, and what was that like?

Miller: I found out there was a problem when, all of a sudden, I tried to place an order, and my order entry platform did not allow me to execute.

It was Halloween, and I knew something was up. I was flat at the time, and I called my broker and said, "What's going on?" Over the coming hours, everything started to filter out, and it turned out that my broker had turned off access to anyone with an MF Global account.

From what I was told, people who were trading on the floor were locked out of the building, and people who were trading electronically got turned off, and so that's what happened to me. That began a year-long fight within the industry and a very sad and difficult chapter not only in my trading career, but in the life of the industry.

It was just a very, very sad time, in terms of what happened, and then the true lack of appropriate action taken over the coming months was sad as well.

Bourquin: And this is a lasting issue. Were you trading at all during that time, or were you trying to regain access to your account and recover your money?

Miller: For a short period of time, all the funds were frozen. I forget how long that was, but I think it was about a month or so before the trustee actually made their first distribution. So, there was a time when I was on a bit of a forced vacation.

During that time, however, I worked harder than I ever had, even as a trader, because a number of us banded together right away to try to get the word out about how we thought this situation should be handled. For about a month or so, I was not able to trade, but then we eventually got about 80 percent of our money back. We got the bulk of our money back fairly quickly, but getting the rest of it back has really been a battle and a drawn-out process.

Bourquin: You've gotten 80 percent back so far?

Miller: Actually, I have since sold my claim. One of the things I learned in the process is that it seems like everything on the planet is traded. Even bankruptcy claims are traded. There are people who are willing to invest in bankruptcy claims because they believe that through the course of time and through settlement action, they will ultimately be able to sell those claims. They're buying wholesale and are going to sell those claims at a future date for a better price and make something off of that. There's a market for that, primarily in the bond market.

While we were advocating for how we thought the situation should be handled and continuing our business at the same time, we kept an eye on the prices at which these claims were being traded. Even though investors have all gotten 80 percent of their money back, based on what the trustee had told the courts and the information that had been gathered, we knew that we were ultimately going to be getting all of our money back—or close to it—and it was only a matter of time.

It's funny, because initially all these vulture funds came out and said, "We will buy your claim and we will pay you eighty-two cents on the dollar. Those who really didn't realize what was going on or didn't understand that most of the money would be found once the legal red tape had been sorted out probably sold at those prices, much to their regret. But those of us who did know what was going on watched the prices go up over time. Once they got to ninety-seven cents on the dollar, I made the decision to go ahead and sell my claims, because I could make back the small difference that was left in a very, very short period of time.

After almost a full year, I have put that effort behind me—as much mentally as anything else. But I will say that for a short period of time, my passion for this business disappeared. My frustrations grew as I tried to get people to understand how wonderful this business is and all the protections that were provided to people engaged in the futures industry. It was a big, big fight.

That chapter of my life is now 100 percent behind me. I can actively focus on what I need to do from a business perspective, and the passion is coming back.

Bourquin: Do you still worry about it, Don? We still don't know what happened at MF Global. They are still trying to figure it out. A few months later, Peregrine Financial Group [PFG] went out of business, and it seems as though the money is not there. Who knows what's going to happen with those investors? Are you concerned that it's going to happen again? I know people that moved from MF Global to PFG, and it did happen to them again. It was incredible.

Miller: I have substantially reduced my exposure on the futures side. I now have enough capital to provide the necessary backing for the transactions that

I engage in. The money in a futures account should be safer than the money in a bank account.

The analogy I give everybody is this: take a group of six people who are all holding hands in a circle, and put a safe right in the middle. Ask each of these six people if they would be willing to store their money in that safe. They look around and see that a bunch of protections are in place, so they say, "Of course we would." What happened in the cases of MF Global and PFG was the safe was broken into, ransacked, and burned beyond recognition without anyone ever realizing it.

That's how ridiculous this whole scenario was. There were so many protections and regulatory structures, rules, and laws in place to protect us—well beyond even having money in a bank that will pay you a small amount of insurance to cover losses up to a certain amount. What happened is everybody fell down. The regulators fell down, too. They didn't catch this in time, and when it finally did go down, everybody with a vested interest started pointing fingers at everybody else. The CFTC says, "Not me." MF Global says, "Not me." It's like a Family Circus cartoon.

What we've done over the past year is work very, very hard to hold people accountable, and that's one of the reasons that bond prices have floated up the way that they did. It is also one of the reasons that we got our money back sooner rather than later.

But I am concerned, yes. Will I ever have as much money as I had in the futures market? No. Will it stop me from engaging in business? Of course not. What do they say? "Fool me once, shame on you. Fool me twice, shame on me."

As I wrote in one of my blog posts recently, I don't intend on being Dick Van Dyke, the guy who trips over the ottoman every time. I plan on being the guy that walks around the ottoman next time.

Charles German

*While his career began more than twenty years ago on the floor of the Chicago Board of Trade, **Charles German** explains that his adoption of a trend-following strategy in 2005 was what ultimately led him to reach new heights in trading. He now uses an automated trading system that combs the markets for setups, places entry and stop orders, and executes with little or no human interaction required.*

While fully automated trading may be a dream for many traders, it was only through thousands of hours of meticulous backtesting and some costly, difficult lessons learned along the way that German made it a reality. By requiring that his strategy work in all markets and market conditions, he eliminates the need to chase trades or the flavor-of-the-day setup or strategy. German is an independent trader and trading coach at California-based CharlesGermanTrading.com.

Tim Bourquin: How do you classify yourself? Are you a swing trader or a day trader? How do you classify the type of trading you engage in?

Charles German: I would definitely be classified as a trend follower.

Bourquin: Being a trend follower can mean somewhat different things to different people. What does it mean to you?

German: Trend following to me means basically using a systematic approach to trade a basket of markets and attempt to catch any meaningful trends that develop in any of the markets I trade.

Bourquin: Are you mostly following daily charts?

German: Yes. I do more of a mid- to long-term following program. For day traders, my time frames would seem more like light years, but usually my trades last from five days to three or four months.

Bourquin: That's quite a range. We will get into what triggers your trade entries and exits, but why does trend following work so well for you?

German: I'm not really sure why trend following seems to work better for me than the other approaches. I think perhaps it's because it's a very strict, rule-based approach.

I have traded for a long time, and I always used the discretionary element and all these different indicators to try and pick tops and bottoms. But when I came across trend following as a stand-alone type of program, it really solidified what I have been trying to do all these years, which is to have a strict set of rules to follow that can be backtested over any market. That's really what brought trend following into the forefront of my trading.

Bourquin: When we are talking about trend following, are we just talking about following a market that is in a major uptrend or downtrend over several weeks? How is it that a trade initially appears on your radar?

German: I use hourly, daily, or weekly bars to determine a trend, and there are a couple of different approaches that you can use here. You can use a reversal approach, where you are always long or short, a breakout approach, a momentum approach, or a combination of approaches. For example, a reversal approach would be a dual moving average system. In dual moving averages, an indication that the trend is up or down will appear when the moving averages cross. If the fast moving average crosses above the slow moving average, you go long. If it crosses back below, you are short. You are always in.

With regards to breakout strategies, when a market breaks out of a range— and it could be a five-day range or a five-hundred-day range—you enter your position in the direction of that breakout, and you fine-tune your stop based on your testing.

Bourquin: Are you constantly backtesting markets to find where certain trends work best? Or have you backtested trades in the past so that you now know what approach works best in a given market and can apply it going forward?

German: Initially, trend following involves a lot of backtesting and thousands and thousands of tests, including millions of iterations on all kinds of different markets, with all kinds of different trend-following strategies and approaches to stops and profit targets. There is an initial period where you are backtesting for ten hours a day, but then you get into a rhythm where you determine what works, based on your backtesting.

I did a great deal of backtesting over a couple of years, which solidified the markets that I wanted to trade, the program that I wanted to follow, and what does and does not work for me. Now, every time we experience a drawdown or every time I want to question or test myself, I will do some backtesting. But at the end of the day, I always go back to my original set of tests, and that is what I have been trading off of for years.

Bourquin: Have you had to change your strategy at all? It sounds like you came across trend-following strategies that work for you, and they have continued to do well for years. Do you think that's the case with most backtested strategies?

German: Whether or not a backtested strategy does well over the long term depends on the way in which that particular strategy was backtested. A backtested strategy might look great on paper but not make any money in real life.

That said, I will not trade anything that hasn't been tested. Maybe I'm just wired this way now, because I have been backtesting strategies for so long, and it's kind of engrained in me, but when somebody says they are doing this or that in the market, I always ask them, "How do you know your strategy works? Have you tested it?" If they say, "No, I haven't tested it," I say, "How do you even know it works? How can you trade that? How can you have any conviction when you are experiencing tough times?"

Generally, somebody who hasn't backtested their strategy would get discouraged and quit trading when they are in a drawdown. The same thing goes for buying a system. You can't go spend $1,000 on a system and put any real amount of money or confidence into it. I always tell anybody who asks me about backtesting the same thing: you need to roll up your sleeves. You need to test everything in and out, up and down, and in all the different markets. You need to go through your system like crazy in order to have confidence when times are tough. Even then, there are no guarantees that it will work moving forward.

Bourquin: You test not just a strategy but also the specific markets in which it works best. Did two tests come together? Did one strategy work best in one market?

German: I tried a lot of different trend-following strategies, including stand-alone strategies and strategies that worked in combination with each other. I tried to test them over about thirty-five different futures markets, since I have always traded futures.

The theory is that if a strategy doesn't work across all of the markets, then you have done some curve fitting, or it's just not reliable. It's not robust. In all the backtesting that I did across thirty-plus futures markets, there were a small handful—maybe a half-dozen—that my strategy didn't work on in over thirty years. But it worked on every single one of the other markets.

I don't segregate the markets and say that my strategy worked really well in this market, so I'm only going to trade here. I think the key is having a portfolio of markets so that, when these ten are doing poorly, these five are doing great, and these four aren't doing anything.

Bourquin: What are the top three markets that you trade the most?

German: I don't have a top three. I trade twenty different markets in my portfolio right now. To say I have a top market that I trade would be like saying that I'm guessing where the trend is going to be this year, and you just don't do that. You have all these different markets, and you are hoping a few of those will trend. I really don't have a favorite market.

Bourquin: I like the idea of that, because you are not trying to force a trade if it's just not there. You have a base of other places to look, and you go where the trade is.

German: Exactly.

Bourquin: How many trades do you typically have on at any one time?

German: I could have zero up to probably ten to fifteen.

Bourquin: Let's talk a little bit about entries and exits. How do you set stops and find your entry points? Can you talk about a recent trade that you have done in the past week or month? What is a good, garden-variety, Charles German trade that you can talk about?

German: I recently had a really good month, and that's because I had entered long positions in the grains at an ideal time. They were breaking out of this consolidation that they had been in through six months or so.

We are in the middle of the worst drought in fifty years, and the prices of corn, soybeans, and wheat all went through the roof. You can look at that chart right now and clearly see that there is a major trend that somebody is making money on.

Bourquin: When you are talking about a breakout of something that's been in a range for a while, do you want a single daily bar to close above it, or do you want an entire bar above it? What, exactly, is the trigger for you?

German: There are different ways to enter a trade. Some people require a close above a breakout, some require a close above a trend line, and others require a close above a moving average.

Bourquin: Does your entry strategy require a lot of confidence?

German: Yes. Sticking to the entire system requires tremendous confidence. But, again, you go back to your backtesting, and I have tested a close above, a close below, and a breach by x number of ranges or x distance. I have tested all the different entry points, I have found the entry point that works best for my psychology, and I have a lot of confidence in it.

Bourquin: Do you use testing to determine your stops, or do you use a different method for that?

German: Yes, absolutely. There are three things that trend followers need to test: their entry, their stop loss, and their exit. Those are the basic tools of a trend follower, and you need to test all three of them at once.

Bourquin: How far away do you set stops?

German: You want your stops to be dynamic. You want them to adjust on their own to market conditions. I generally use a function of the average true range [ATR]. I will set stops just far enough away from my entry that my trade has enough room to work. My testing tells me exactly where that is.

Bourquin: That makes sense. You don't want to set your stop so far away that you could get hurt pretty badly.

German: The whole premise of stops is that you are cutting your losses short. I don't place my stops too far away from my entry price. If a trade starts to move and then immediately reverses, I just get out. Then I will wait for it to start its move again. Once a trade is in and it hasn't hit your stop, you just let it go.

Bourquin: I think one of the toughest things for newer traders to do is to take the stop loss and then be ready to take that exact same trade a day later, or ten minutes later, if the same signal approaches. Was that an issue for you originally, or did you just say, "This is what the test says, so this is what I'm doing"?

German: No, I knew all about that. They call that a whipsaw. But, you know, that's part and parcel of trend following. You get whipsawed all the time. Even when you get whipsawed ten times, though, if you have one good trend, it makes up for all of those small losses, because you are taking big wins and small losses.

Bourquin: How about your exit point? Is your profit target a function of a previous high above the range that a trade is breaking out of?

German: I guess the simplest explanation is that I use a trailing stop. As a trade moves higher, the stop trails behind it, and there are dozens of different trailing stops you can use. That's what I use to get out of a profitable trade.

Bourquin: Can I ask what software you use in your trend following and your backtesting?

German: I use a bunch of different software. I don't want to go through all the different software that I use, but I can say that there are several inexpensive options for doing basic backtesting. It gets tricky, however, when you start to think about the cleanliness of your data and how to fuse different contract months and roll-over periods for longer-term backtesting. That said, when I started, TradeStation was the easiest to learn. That's really all you need to get started.

Bourquin: Once you're into a green trade and the trend continues to rise, do you allow for scaling in more or building up size in an existing trade?

German: I don't, because it's never tested out for me. Richard Dennis and the famous Turtle Traders used to add positions every half ATR. It worked for them, but as far as my testing tells me, it doesn't work anymore, so I don't add to any positions. I have a core position that I put on, and that's it.

Bourquin: How about scaling out? What do you do there?

German: I've been messing around a little bit with some scaling-out algorithms, and they seem to be testing fairly well. But, by and large, I just operate on a one-in, one-out basis.

Bourquin: It sounds like your trading is very data driven. Was your previous career in a data-driven industry?

German: There was no previous career. I moved to Chicago during a summer off of college and started working on the floor of the Chicago Board of Trade when I was nineteen. From there, I immediately jumped into technical analysis and started trading all the different futures markets over the phone using daily bars and technical analysis. I've been trading for about twenty years with varying degrees of success until 2005, when I really took hold of trend following.

Bourquin: Did you have a mentor in this space, or did you read books? How did you get started in trend following?

German: I didn't have any mentors. I was on the floor, and floor traders are, by and large, scalpers. They basically trade tick for tick, trying to gain an edge. Nobody that I had access to really did any computer trading or any long-term trading. I learned about trend following from independent study—essentially by reading every book I could find on trading over twenty years. Perhaps I got lucky that I focused on trend following and it has been working.

Bourquin: Let's talk a little bit about risk management, in terms of the size of your trades. Is there a typical size that you put on as part of your testing?

German: No. When you trade a bunch of different markets, you can't say that you are going to trade one size across all of them, because a tick in bonds would be $31.25, while a tick in corn would be $12.50. Markets have different tick and range sizes, so from day to day, a range might be $5,000 in one market and $500 in another. Logically, it's best to normalize all of the market ticks and ranges using a fixed-fractional type of money management sizing algorithm or method.

Bourquin: So you use just a fraction of a portion of the funds that are in your overall account?

German: Yes, exactly. You take a fraction of your equity and determine how far away your stop will be in dollar terms and how many contracts you can put on while maintaining your overall risk level. So, if you have a $1,000 risk level and the stop is $100 away, you can put on ten contracts.

Bourquin: Is that calculated for you in your trading platform, or is that something you do in your head?

German: Everything is calculated by the system. The system is actually so systematized that you can literally turn it on, walk away, and just let it run, and it will do its thing. It doesn't take any decision making at all.

Bourquin: That sounds pretty attractive to me. I have to walk away from my trades, because I am just no good when I am sitting in front of the computer, watching them. Is that the same for you?

German: No, because there is no decision making for me to do. I could sit there and watch the numbers move around, but if I am committed to my system and know that I'm not going to mess with it, there is nothing for me to do. It could be going up or down, and it doesn't matter, unless the system says buy or sell.

Bourquin: Talk with me a little bit about when you first got started in trading. I know that the floor is a little bit different than screen-based trading. In 2005, when you started trading full-time behind the screen, did you lose a lot of money? Did you make a lot of money right away? What was that experience like?

German: It was an expensive lesson in backtesting. I was 110 percent all for trend following. Markets were moving big, I committed a decent amount of money to my trading account, and I had a system and a set of rules in place, but the rules had not been tested. It was a very logical set of trend following rules, but when I started trading, things did not go very well, and I lost a good chunk of capital following those rules. I was so sold on the theory of trend following that I did not even backtest my system. That is when I decided that nothing gets traded unless I have performed rigorous testing and decided it is viable.

That was one of many expensive lessons. You can look at a chart and pick out different trades that would work, but for every one hundred ideas I have, I am lucky if one of them works. That's why I go back to my original saying: you have to test, test, test. If you don't test, then how do you know your system works? How are you going to be able to risk any real money in it?

Bourquin: In that experience, when you were losing money, I think that's when people develop into either systems-driven and strict rules-driven traders or discretionary traders. There are some people out there who say, "I'm a discretionary trader, and it has always worked for me," but the data guys say, "I don't know how anybody is discretionary, because at the end of the day, discretionary traders eventually lose." What are your thoughts here? Is using data really the only way to achieve long-term success in this business?

German: I don't know. You look at the long-term, managed futures guys who have been using trend-following strategies for years, and a lot of them make substantial, double-digit returns every single year when compounded over twenty-five or thirty years.

On the other hand, I haven't seen any evidence that a mutual fund manager can make 15 percent or 20 percent compound annual real returns over twenty-five years. If you know of any, then maybe you could tell me. But it's just hard to deny the long-term performance of some of these managed futures guys.

Bourquin: At some point along the way, you started managing money, correct?

German: I did. I started managing some money, got a handful of investors, got my web site going, completed my documents, and started taking in some investor money. But, honestly, with all of the new regulations and scrutiny that money managers are facing these days, I am not sure that I want to continue going down that road. It's hard to manage money for people. I think I would rather trade on my own terms and share some of my research with others who are interested in trading.

Bourquin: With the regulations that are coming down after MF Global, the Peregrine Financial Group [PFG] debacle, and everything else, I am sure that money management is going to become pretty onerous. If you don't have somebody dealing with compliance issues on a full-time basis, I can see how working as a money manager could become pretty difficult.

German: Yes, and I am not in that mode. I don't want to have a big staff, and I don't want to deal with red tape. That's one of the reasons I chose trend following in the first place. Once you have your system in place and you believe in it, you set it up and let it run. It gives you time to do other things.

Bourquin: Let me ask you a little bit more about the strict rules-based aspect of your trading. Are these rules that you have programmed into your computer system? Is the computer looking for certain opportunities, and will it trigger a signal for you when one appears?

German: Yes. Like I said before, I can turn the system on, walk away, and not look at it again for weeks, and it will automatically calculate where my entries will be and where my exits will be. It automatically calculates everything.

Bourquin: You don't put the trade in and then walk away? The system can buy and sell, open and close, and do all that for you?

German: Yes, depending on what software I'm using. With the software program that I'm developing right now, I can leave it on, and since the program is on a dedicated server, it just runs itself. I don't even need to be there. The way I currently use this program is I download the market data at the end of the day, press "run" on the system, then press "generate orders," and the program generates the orders, which are all stop orders. I can put in my ten or fifteen stop orders for the night, and then I check it again the next night.

Bourquin: Wow! And you can see which orders have hit and which orders haven't, right?

German: Yes, exactly.

Bourquin: Getting to that point would seem to be the goal of a lot of traders. I know it took a lot of hard work to get there. What recommendations or advice do you have for somebody who is where you were in late 2004, coming into 2005? Are there any lessons you learned that really helped you get to where you are today?

German: I firmly believe in trend following. Markets have been trending for thousands of years, and there have been major trends all over the globe for all of time.

The first thing you need to do is find what really grabs you. If you don't believe in your trading theories—if you don't believe in your system—then you are dead in the water. You are never going to be able to commit enough to make money. You need to know what you believe in.

I give my friends and family Michael Covel's book, *Trend Following* [Financial Times Prentice Hall, 2004]. I say, "Read this book." Then, if they read it and they believe in it, I'll step them along and say, "OK, now read this book."

If you believe in trend following, then learn the lexicon, get some software, and get a programmer on board. You can hire a TradeStation programmer and start testing some of this stuff, or you can learn the programming language yourself. You just have to dive into it and do it.

Bourquin: I know Michael Covel, and he seems to be the guy in trend following. He blogs quite a bit about it and talks about it, so I know he is a good resource for that.

German: Absolutely.

Bourquin: A lot of traders out there say, "Just show me what works right now." But I like the idea that you have to believe that your trading strategy is going to work for a long time—especially if you're programming software and setting up a system to trade on its own. That's a key point, because you have to believe that your system works.

German: It's not what works right now. It's what has worked over long periods of time.

There is no way that I'll trade a strategy that doesn't work over a portfolio of markets or that hasn't worked for a very long time. Those are my two basic requirements.

Bourquin: At the end of the day, no matter what market you're in, trading is about price action. It doesn't matter if you're trading corn or wheat or oil. It's all about price action.

German: Yes, for me, it's about price action. I look at price action only. I don't look at volume. I don't look at indicators. I don't look at supply and demand. I look at zero fundamentals. How can you sift through all the fundamentals and still have time to trade them on a day-to-day basis? The price is what tells you what the fundamentals are.

Dr. Andrew Menaker

*In addition to his own successful futures trading career, psychologist **Dr. Andrew Menaker** has worked as a psychological consultant in all corners of the trading and financial industries, as well as at the government level with the US Department of Defense and Navy. Professional and retail traders alike have enhanced their performance as a result of his coaching.*

Menaker believes the markets are ultimately people-driven. He also firmly asserts that a solid understanding of the social and behavioral factors that move prices can often separate the traders who achieve long-term success from those who fail. Psychology, he says, can even help traders overcome the adverse effects of high-frequency trading. Menaker offers consulting services, as well as various products and resources, on his web site, AndrewMenaker.com.

Tim Bourquin: Andrew, I'd like to start with a very broad question. Is high-frequency trading making it tougher for retail traders to make money these days?

Dr. Andrew Menaker: Without a doubt, it's changed the landscape of the markets. There is more automation and more machine-generated volume coming into all markets.

But I think the impact of high-frequency trading depends on which market you're looking at: stocks, indexes, futures. There are different issues in different markets. I will tell you what I see from my own perspective, because I trade my own account, work with a lot of traders, and come into contact with a lot of traders across a wide spectrum—from people who are trading at banks and hedge funds to people who are trading their own account. I hear a lot of people who are looking for the easiest or most convenient excuse as to why their performance is poor. The most common excuses that people are latching onto nowadays are high-frequency trading, automation, algorithms, and things like that. But, like I said, those are a reality, and undoubtedly they have changed the way that price action operates.

I also want to point out that trading has never been easy. There's that famous line that trading is the hardest easy money you'll ever make, and it's true. There have always been challenges, and I think the current excuses that people are using now are the algos and high-frequency trading.

There are going to be different amounts of high-frequency trading in different markets. In June, for instance, about 13.5 percent of all volume on the New York Stock Exchange [NYSE] was dark pool volume. But I know that in the E-mini S&P futures [ES], which is what I tend to trade a lot, we're seeing, on average days, 50 percent to 70 percent—and sometimes even more—of machine-generated volume.

Bourquin: What about the argument that we're just making the markets more liquid? You can now get in faster because we are there and making markets in the securities.

Menaker: I am definitely aware of that argument, and to a certain extent, that's a valid argument, right? I'd have to say, though, that high-frequency trading does change the landscape, and there is also the argument that high-frequency traders are getting in front of everybody for a sliver of a penny.

I can tell you what's really interesting, because I've been out to a few institutional hedge fund conferences. Even the guys and the gals who are trading large size for funds, hedge funds, and banks are having a lot of issues with high-frequency traders. So, it's kind of an interesting situation. I don't know where we are going to land or what's going to happen, but I would say that people need to understand that, because the markets have changed and we have more automated volume, we have to be even more on top of managing ourselves and have a good approach to trading.

If you were to look at one thousand random traders and, in that group of one thousand, you had a large number of automated systems traders along with a good number of discretionary traders, what you would see is that there is a larger percentage of profitable traders who are using automated systems. However, there's a big caveat here. The *bigger* winners are in the discretionary camp. In other words, it's harder to become a successful discretionary trader, but once somebody does, they tend to outperform the automated system traders.

Bourquin: That begs the question: what are the people who have figured it out doing differently than everyone else?

Menaker: That's a great question. I think what's happened is that they figured out that markets are more social than people realize. I think that it's easy to forget that markets are still social, given all the different arguments that we see on CNBC and read in the *Wall Street Journal* about automated trading.

Let's use a poker analogy. I have a good friend who is a trader and who used to be a professional poker player, and I asked him one day, "If everybody at the table at a high-stakes game has the same level of ability, and everybody has all the same probabilities of cards memorized, why do some pros consistently make more money than other pros?"

What he said was on the surface, poker looks like a game of numbers and probabilities, and it is to a certain extent. But where the real edge lies is in reading the table, being able to bluff, and reading other people's bluffs. I think markets are the exact same way.

As traders, we watch our screen, and it's so easy to forget that the blinking lights and the moving lines and the colors that we see on our screens are just representations of something else. That something else is the buyers and the sellers who are battling it out, so, to your question, I think the people who have figured this out really understand that it's people who move markets.

Another way to put it is this: if you buy stock XYZ today, there's only one reason in the world why stock XYZ is going to be higher an hour from now, a day from now, a week from now, or a year from now. There's only one reason: people are willing to pay higher prices than you paid and will continue to pay higher prices, for whatever reason. They might say the reason is because they like the company, or they feel good about the economy. But it doesn't matter what the reason is. The action is what counts. The action that's required is other people have to pay higher prices. As soon as other people—fund managers, hedge funds, whoever these people are—decide to not pay higher prices, stock XYZ will no longer go up.

In order to predict markets, the people who really figured out the game are predicting people, and I can tell you that some of the more successful hedge funds understand this. They're looking at the market not so much through fundamental analysis and technical analysis. They are trying to *sense* it. They want to predict what people are going to do.

I'll tell you, there's a real interesting piece of research that came out a couple of years ago from the California Institute of Technology. The research was conducted by some financial engineers—these guys are quants, right, they are mathematicians—and they had two groups of traders. They had a group of traders who were experienced and another group who were total novices, and when they had them trade against each other, of course, the experienced group outperformed the novices. But then they did something interesting. They provided some training to the novice group of traders. They trained them on how to interpret or assess other people's thinking and their intentions. In other words, they taught them how to read other people, and then they had those novice traders apply that training in the competition, trading against the more experienced traders.

After the novices had been trained, what the researchers found was that these novices were able to match and often beat the more experienced traders. You might think that's kind of a fluke. Well, they've actually done the same study about twelve times, and they've gotten the same results every time.

Bourquin: I think that's one of the big arguments that people have against high-frequency trading. They say, "Look, I can read supply and demand, and I can read Level II buy and sell orders, and I see phantom orders come in and out that are trying to fool me into believing that supply or demand is there when it's not." But I think they actually have a hard time reading those things.

Menaker: Exactly. First of all, yes, algos are used in execution a lot, and not just by high-frequency traders. Even non-high-frequency traders are using algos, and that kind of throws off the queue and makes things look different.

Here's an interesting tidbit: on a trend day or a strong directional day, when the markets are really moving in one direction pretty much the whole day, the high-frequency traders and algos are generally getting crushed. Those are not good days for them. They tend to do really well on the range-bound days, rotational days, and days where we're trading in between some pretty known levels that everyone is watching. Those are good days for them. But they don't make money every day. They also lose money, and the days when they don't do well are trend days.

Bourquin: I imagine those are the days when a discretionary trader should be doing well. Maybe the lesson here is to stay away from range-bound days?

Menaker: It depends on your style. For my style of trading, my job in the morning involves constantly trying to figure out if the day is shaping up to be a directional trend day or a range day. If I think it's one of the two, I'll keep my eyes open to see if we will be switching back to the other at some point that day, because I have two different ways of trading. If we're looking at a trend day or the possibility of a trend day, I am going to want to go for a ride with the momentum. But if it's looking like a rotational range day, then I'm going to want to fade the levels that I'm looking at.

Bourquin: Do you decide what type of day it is based on the charts you're using to look at the ES?

Menaker: Yes, and I use a lot of market profiling and volume profiling, so I'm looking for responsive and initiative activity. I'm a psychologist, so when I see levels on a chart that some people might call supply and demand, what I see is emotionally charged areas on the chart.

In other words, everyone else is saying, "Hey, here's a trend line," and while I might look at that as well, I'm going to see it differently. To me, it's not just a line on a chart. To me, it represents an area of a lot of emotion, and when price gets back to that area, I'm going to want to look really closely at internals. How many stocks are ticking at their high of the day? How many stocks are ticking at their low of the day? How many stocks are above or below their volume-weighted average price [VWAP]? I'll look at stuff like that as we come into an important area, and how price and internals behave at that area will tell me what to do. I listen to the market and want to get as close to the market as possible in my trading.

Bourquin: Let's talk about that, because, as a psychologist, you think that the way to alleviate some of the problems that high-frequency traders are bringing to the market is through trading psychology. Talk about why that is and how to use trading psychology to get around this.

Menaker: Sure. I'll give you a really specific example of trading ES. Let's say that a big player in the ES market knows that there's support at twenty-eight, because they look at their charts and they can see the same levels that everyone else can. Now, they can afford to sell five thousand contracts at twenty-eight and then offer another two thousand at twenty-seven. While you and a hundred other small traders are busy covering your long positions at twenty-six and twenty-five, that big player is covering his short positions—and he is even buying those twenty-fives back from you.

The big player will sell enough to get price to go past your pain point—and everyone has a pain point. Everyone has a pain threshold, so you need to know what your pain point is, because once you reach that point, that's when you start to get irrational. Know what your pain point is. The big player knows that if they can just push it one or two ticks past your pain point, of course, they can set off your stops. This happens a lot. This is how they operate, and they use algos to do this kind of execution.

We have to remember that the lines on a chart just represent what people are doing out there. No matter how many algos are active, it's people who are responsible for writing the algos and turning them off and on throughout the day—and they're always switching algos in all day long. The same algos do not constantly run throughout the day.

Bourquin: Does this argue to just use areas of support and resistance on the chart, and don't worry about time and sales, because it's just going to be a fake out anyway?

Menaker: Time and sales is not a fake out. In fact, time and sales is really important to me. I watch time and sales like a hawk on the ES, and, unfortunately, time and sales scrolls by pretty darn quickly, so you have to use filters.

If there were a ton of volume hitting the bid, you'd think that they are market sell orders. But, let's say price only ticks down one tick. Let's say ten thousand contracts have hit the bid in the last five minutes, but price is only ticking down by one. That tells me that it's quite possible there is a large, passive resting order on the other side of the trade. And if this is all coinciding with an important area on my chart and I see internals doing something interesting, I might decide to get active at that point and put on a trade.

To me, order flow is really important. Time and sales is never a fake out. Time and sales tells the tale. It's difficult to organize, understand, and interpret it, because it's constantly moving. It flows past really quickly.

Bourquin: At least time and sales is the actual sales. It's not orders up there for a split second and then gone again, like a Level II might be.

Menaker: Right. I don't really trade stocks anymore, partly because I think that there is really no advantage to looking at Level II anyway. I mostly trade index futures.

I think, when we're in the environment that we're in now, with a lot of high-frequency traders and algos, it's really difficult to trade really small, short time frames for a few ticks here and there. I think, for people who are trying to scalp the market nowadays from home on their computer, it's almost impossible, because you're going to get scalped by the computers. Instead, what I have found is that we have to lengthen out our time frames and look for bigger moves. For instance, I'm not going to come out and trade in the ES unless my target is at least four or five points away—hopefully more.

I'm not trading for just a point or two because, if I do, I'm directly competing with the algos, because that's their playing field. Algos can really push the market around a few ticks here and there, but they're not going to push the ES up ten or fifteen points. Algos can't do that, although they are involved in a move like that.

What happens is that some algos will trigger another move, which triggers another move, which triggers another move, and then people see it. They jump on, and all of a sudden, the market moves twelve points, and what set it off was some algos earlier. But algos themselves didn't say, "Hey, let's move the market up twelve points." People need to understand that all algos do is execute orders. They don't make the decision to move the market up or down.

Bourquin: Let me ask you about those four or five points you mentioned earlier. I'm always curious as to how people set up their risk-to-reward ratios. How do you decide whether or not a trade has the potential to have four or five points in it?

Menaker: Well, I use a lot of volume profiling, so I'm looking for an area. If I see an area where there has been a lot of volume or a small amount of volume above or below a certain price, that could represent a target area for me. If it's too close to where my entry is, however, that just doesn't represent a favorable ratio for me.

I will say that I'm probably a little different than a lot of traders out there. If I'm sensing that we're in a really strong directional day and it seems like we're still pretty early in a move—or at least it seems like that's the potential—I will sometimes just jump in the market. I'm not going to worry about my risk-reward ratio, because my biggest days occur when I catch the trend early on in the day and ride it for a good part of that day. I want to have as many big days as possible, and if I'm only looking at each trade through a risk-reward ratio, it's going to keep me from jumping in on those days.

Bourquin: If you catch the trend and it's working, will you keep adding to your position?

Menaker: Definitely. But it's not for everybody, because most people buy breakouts that don't work and sell breakdowns that don't work. Jumping in with momentum is tricky. Unfortunately, and here's where I put on my psychologist hat for a second, it just dovetails too perfectly with a lot of the vulnerabilities that we have as human beings. Let's say that we've missed out on all the morning's trades or have been stopped out. When price begins to make a big move, we feel like we're going to miss out again, so we had better jump in. We don't want to be burned again and lose out, so you can see, unfortunately, that momentum trading makes you vulnerable.

Most people don't succeed at it because they're going to be jumping on too many moves. But from what I've seen in my own trading and in that of a lot of traders who I've known over the years is that momentum trading is where a lot of the more successful traders are from. It's either that, or trying to catch a falling knife, or trying to pick reversals.

Now, having said that, if we're in a day that's clearly a rotational range day and the NYSE TICK is not putting out any extreme prints, high or low, that's the kind of day where I will trade a lot differently. I'm obviously not just going to buy something that's going up and sell something that's going down. I will fade levels. I will actually look for a range and fade it.

Bourquin: It sounds like you're looking for moves where volume seems a little meek or tepid, but yet you still have price moving up. Have I characterized that correctly?

Menaker: Yes, that's one way. There are different criteria. I have to remember that the ES are a reflection of the underlying market, which is the S&P 500. I go to the S&P 500, and I want to look at its strengths and weaknesses. What are its big components? What are its top five or ten—or even twenty or thirty—components? I will be looking at those to see how they are behaving, what their volume is like, and what their price action is like, because that's going to lead the market.

I look at that, the NYSE TICK, and certain risk-on and risk-off sectors. If financials, XLF, and transports are all above the prior day's high and the ES is in the middle of its range, it might look on the surface that the ES is not going to do much. But, look, the underlying equity market is showing some strength! I'm going to look for additional signs that maybe this could be a sneaky breakout brewing for midday.

The best way to describe my style of trading would be that I try and get as close to the order flow and the social context as possible so that I can pick my trading spots.

Bourquin: Does social context include watching the news to see what they are talking about? Most people say, "No, I'm not going to watch CNBC, because it's a bunch of nonsense anyway." But if we're talking about social moves, the news might be one of the best places to find social context.

Menaker: That's a really good question, and I've personally gone back and forth on that myself over the years—paying attention to the news or not paying attention to the news—and I think people can succeed going both ways. What I will tell you, though, is that there are hedge funds that are scraping social media, like Twitter and even Facebook, and they are scraping CNBC and Bloomberg for keywords and sentiment. Then they will apply that to an automated trading system.

That's happening more and more. I was in Japan in June for a hedge fund conference, and I met a Tokyo University professor there who's a financial engineer. He showed me how he and some other guys were starting up a hedge fund using this model that I just explained, and they thought they were the first to do this. And I said, "Actually, no, there are six or seven funds in the United States that I know of that have already been doing that in the last three or four years, and there are probably more than those six or seven. I just know of only six or seven myself."

Bourquin: There's a web site where you can actually do that. I know who the founder is, James Ross. He started HedgeChatter.com, which does exactly that, too. That kind of information is starting to be made available to the individual.

Menaker: It is. Going after market sentiment is really important, and I think it's going to become more and more important.

Let's look at where we are today. As we're talking in late 2012, we are near 1,400 in the S&P 500 and ES. Back in March 2009, we bottomed out close to six hundred. Is the economy twice as good now as it was back in 2009 because the S&P is twice as high? No, it's not, and what's the difference?

Bourquin: Any time that I try to justify or correlate the economy with the stock market, it's never a good thing, because it never makes sense if you try to do it that way. That's why you see so many articles in the *Wall Street Journal* saying, "Can this rally be trusted?" That doesn't make any sense to me. A rally is a rally—either the market is going up, or it is going down. Just because it's happening within a crappy economy doesn't mean that it's not happening. I think that trying to make the two of those jibe together is very difficult.

Menaker: Exactly, and I agree with you 100 percent. I will just add to what you were saying. The idea that, "Oh, we need volume. We have seen decreasing volume in the last three or four years, and that's why this whole rally is suspect." Well, here's the thing: we don't need to have high volume to support higher prices. We've had higher prices for three or four years. All that we need for higher prices—or even lower prices, since this works on both sides of the spectrum—is to remember that the market is an auction. This is how I approach markets, and this goes back to the social context of trading.

What is an auction? Well, an auction is a marketplace where buyers and sellers come together to strike a deal. What's going to happen is that price is going to auction up—sometimes we even call it a price discovery—and it keeps going up as more people are willing to bid up whatever it is that they're willing to buy, right? But it will stop going up as soon as those bidders get tired and enough sellers get interested and start selling. Now, that happens regardless of the amount of volume or the amount of activity.

That, combined with the introduction of automated trading, has changed the nature of volume and the way that volume is measured and calculated. There are some strange mathematical things going on in the markets. But because the last three or four years have shown a decrease in volume at the same time that the markets have moved up, a lot people are suspicious. I hope that those people are not all holding onto short positions.

Of course, we've been going up in a monster rally, but nothing goes up forever. Something is going to give at some point. But for people to say, "This is not real," well, that's just not realistic.

Bourquin: Earlier you mentioned VWAP, and I know a lot of readers will be curious as to how you use it. Can you talk about how you use VWAP in deciding whether or not you're going to trade something?

Menaker: There are a lot of different ways to use it. For one, look at the slope of VWAP. Let's say it's the second hour of the trading day, and VWAP has been pretty much flat so far. That's a sign that we are in a range-bound market. If VWAP is sloping up and I see that the NYSE TICK slope is pointing upwards, that suggests that there is buying bias and that buyers are perhaps more in control than sellers.

Those are some of the things I start to look for. There are a gazillion ways you can use VWAP. Some people use it as a pullback place. When a strong price trend pulls back to VWAP—or maybe one standard deviation away from it—they'll use that as a place to jump on the trend.

It's not a be-all and end-all, though. I don't ever execute a trade just because of VWAP. It just goes into the mix. It's all about context for me. Where was the market yesterday? Where is it right now? Where are we in relation to other points on the chart? What are people thinking and feeling? Did the shorts not get any love this morning because we're now above yesterday's lows? Are they getting nervous? At what point are they going to puke? What do the internals look like?

I don't actually even use any fixed setups with my trading. The majority of my entries are created on the fly based on what I'm thinking and feeling about the market.

Bourquin: You talked about your profit targets in an area where there has been a lot of volume and price. What about your stop? Where do you decide, "I'm wrong, it's time to get out"?

Menaker: In trading, it's all about the exits, right? It's not really the entries that determine how much money you make—or lose, for that matter. It's about our exits. I want to make sure that I'm entering as close to an exit area as possible when something tells me that I'm going to be wrong.

Now, for me, if I'm thinking that we're in a strong directional day, I'm going to give my trades a lot more room. But if I'm trading on a rotational range day, I'm going to be tighter with my stops. My basic, fundamental objective is to try and determine which strategy I should be using, and I'll approach stops differently, depending on whether I'm using a trending directional strategy or a range strategy.

Bourquin: I was talking with John Bollinger the other day, and he has done a lot of work outside of Bollinger bands in the past few years. One of the things he has been doing is bringing back equivolume, where he takes time off the charts entirely and is just looking at price and volume. The wider the bar, the bigger the volume, and the thinner the bar, the smaller the volume is at that price.

It seems like people are starting to just use volume and price. Some traders will say, "Duh, I've been doing that forever." But a lot of people are so used to that one-minute, five-minute, or fifteen-minute chart. To get away from that and look at the market a little bit differently is unusual for them. It's uncomfortable for a while, until they get used to it.

Menaker: Right, and I'm glad to hear he's been doing that, because I think that more traders need to be doing that. I have been doing that for a long time.

Bourquin: I always like to finish off an interview by trying to figure out the one takeaway from each conversation that I've had. It would seem to me that your takeaway lesson would be, "Forget about time—or make it less important. Start looking at how much volume occurred at a given price level." Did I sum that up pretty well?

Menaker: I wouldn't completely ignore time, because it gives you an idea of acceptance and rejection. When price moves away from an area very quickly, that's rejection. If it does so in the midst of a lot of volume, that says something different than if price had stuck around that area in the midst of a lot of volume. Time is a factor, but in order of priority, I would say that volume and price are more important.

Brian Lund

*California-based **Brian Lund** is a trading industry executive and part-time equities trader whose ability to liken the art of trading to some facets of everyday life has earned him a wide following across the web and social media sites. While his approach to the markets is somewhat controversial, Lund has found success as a trader by ignoring economic news and fundamentals and instead scanning a universe of hundreds of stocks in search of simple, repeatable patterns to trade.*

New and more experienced traders alike will appreciate Lund's candor and the rationale behind his decision to operate in only one market. They also can benefit from his unbridled honesty on subjects like high-frequency trading, P&Ls, and those popular yet often overused trading/poker analogies. Followers may read Lund's unique insights and commentary about trading, life, and the intersection of the two on his blog, BCLund.com.

Tim Bourquin: The first question I always like to ask traders is: what kind of trader are you? Are you a day trader or a swing trader, and what markets do you trade?

Brian Lund: I would say that I'm a hybrid trader. I like to look at patterns that are setting up for swings but then take intraday trades off of those charts. Basically, I am an equities trader. I do a little bit of options trading, and I have dabbled in futures here and there, but I'd say that 95 percent of the time I'm focused on equities.

Bourquin: Do you have a basket of stocks each day that you're watching, or will you trade anything?

Lund: I've got about three hundred and fifty stocks that I'm always looking at, and that list ebbs and flows. I pare it down or add to it, depending on what sectors are hot, but I generally am looking at about three hundred and fifty stocks on the weekends and pulling at least ten to twelve ideas for the week that I want to focus on. What happens with me is, if I get too many stocks on my list, I lose focus and can't follow them all. I would say the most stocks that I'm looking at during any given week is twenty, but it's better if it's somewhere between ten and twelve.

Bourquin: Chart-wise, are you just flipping through the charts in search of specific patterns?

Lund: Yeah. I use TC2000—I've used it forever—and I'll put the charts in there, hit the spacebar, and give them each maybe a two- to three-second look. Over the years, I've drawn support levels and resistance levels on the charts, so they're already on there from previous times that I was looking at the stock. But I'm looking for things that jump out at me, like flags, double-bottoms, ascending triangles, and really any of your basic, technical analysis-focused patterns.

Bourquin: Once one of these patterns jumps out at you, how do you act on it?

Lund: I'm looking for a swing setup, and then I'm going to zoom in on an intraday chart—usually a five-minute chart. Let's say I see a stock that's got a nice flag pattern. I'll know on the daily chart where I think that breakout is going to happen, but during the course of the week, I'll be looking at it on a five-minute and maybe a thirty-minute chart. What will often happen is, if you have a breakout point on a swing chart, you just look at the chart and say, "Oh, I'm going to buy it." But the breakout might actually be really extended on the intraday chart before it gets to that daily breakout. Often when that happens, you fail, so I want to see some good action setting up on the smaller time frame chart that basically syncs up with the time frame on the larger swing chart.

Bourquin: If something is reaching an area where there's an important level, but it has already come a long way that day, then the chances are that it's going to bounce off of the daily breakout, rather than go through it, right?

Lund: Right. You have to remember that there are all sorts of participants who are watching charts in all different time frames. You've got your guys who are swing trading, you've got your intraday guys, you've got your scalpers, and you've got funds and people who are watching indicators or moving averages.

I find that when you can get a breakout that lines up with the greatest amount of those different factors—for example, if you get something that's hitting the intraday breakout, is on a daily breakout, and is also breaking out of the two hundred-day moving average—those can be some of the most powerful moves that you're going to find in the market.

Bourquin: I think a lot of traders, especially the new ones, have a difficult time with that balance, because they want things to confirm. They want a lot of confluence and a lot of things lining up, but I think they always have this question of, "How much is enough? Are two things enough? Three things?" How do you answer that question for yourself?

Lund: I usually look at the more macro of the setups, which is usually the swing chart, but I think you're right. I hate to make gambling and trading analogies, but I'm a poker player, and something that I've noticed in the last five, ten years—especially with the rise of Internet poker, before they shut it down—is that you would get a lot of young guys who just had no patience. They basically would be shoving all in when they didn't need to and could wait a little bit. The veteran guys who had small or mid-size stacks would just wait and wait, let people fold, and wait for better opportunities. I think it's the exact same thing in the market.

I think a lot of the newer traders get so wrapped up in the action, especially since the action is ginned up a lot by high-frequency trading. They don't have the patience to wait for stuff. I know it's a hackneyed term, but the fact of the matter is that you make most of your money by "sitting on your hands" in trading. I think there is just not enough of that with some new traders.

Bourquin: There's definitely something to that. There are so many good traders who are also excellent poker players. There has to be something to that, where one helps the other. I'm sure you've found that, too.

Lund: The little asterisk there about gambling and trading analogies is that poker probably requires more skill than any other gambling pursuit. Even though some wouldn't agree with that, it's not like you're going in there and playing roulette or something that is mostly based on chance. There is some skill, feel, and money management involved in playing poker. That is the one pursuit of gambling that does actually have some valid ties to trading.

Bourquin: Well, sure. There will always be different people at the final table, and it's often not the same guys who always show up there in the end.

Lund: The other analogy is that, if you have doctors at a poker table, they're usually really bad, and I find that the same thing is true in trading. Doctors who come into trading are generally really bad as well. Sorry, no offense to the doctors out there!

It's interesting, because one specialty or skill in one area doesn't necessarily translate to another. You always get the doctor who sits down at the table and thinks he can play poker because he's saving lives all day and is very educated, but he usually gets cleaned out. I think it's the same thing with trading. People come in with preconceived ideas about their skills and what they know, but the market just humbles them. That is another interesting parallel between poker and trading.

Bourquin: Your strategy seems relatively simple: you find things that are bouncing off a two hundred-day moving average or reaching an all-time high. When you say it, it sounds simple, like we can all do it. If that's the case, though, why do so many traders lose money? I've always been fascinated by the fact that when I talk to somebody about their trading strategy, I think I can do it myself. But when it comes to putting it into practice, people have a tough time. Why is that?

Lund: I think it's the same reason that people have trouble in all different areas of life. Ideas are a dime a dozen. I have a lot of ideas when it comes to trading. A lot of people who I work with in business have great ideas, too, but the people who can actually execute on those ideas and take them to fruition are few and far between. That's because it takes follow-through, focus, and dedication.

So many things happen throughout the course of a day when you're sitting there and trading. So many things threaten to take your attention away, whether it's a trading chat room or a news announcement. I think a lot of times people forget that trading is boring. You're sitting there and just repeating processes and patterns over and over again.

It's hard for people to do that over an extended period of time. It's not unlike gambling. Everybody knows how to play blackjack. You can even buy the cards that tell you exactly what you're supposed to do in any given situation, and if you do that correctly, you'll have somewhat of an edge over the house over time. But who does that? You don't want to sit there and play by the book. You want to have some fun, have some drinks, and talk to the guy next to you! But when you do all that stuff, it gets you off your game. There are so many ways that the exact same thing can happen in trading, which probably contributes to the fact that a lot of people can't be profitable in the long run.

Bourquin: Is there a recent trade or two that you could talk about that demonstrates how you trade?

Lund: Here's a trade that I did with Morgan Stanley recently.

If you drew a downtrend line to the start of 2011, you could see that Morgan Stanley was starting to come out of that downtrend. Then it bounced twice and made a double-bottom off of a support area. After it bounced and came up, it started to move sideways and consolidated—and it consolidated right below a resistance level that had been created from a pivot high.

A number of different factors were lining up. Morgan Stanley was coming out of and breaking a downtrend, it had a double-bottom, and then it formed a nice base below a resistance level. That pattern happens more often than you would think—and not just in daily charts, but in intraday charts, too. It was very easy to get a nice risk-reward ratio—maybe a 1:5 risk-reward ratio—off that trade, which ended up paying off.

Once again, trading is boring. It's not supposed to be like jumping out of a plane, and it's not supposed to be like laying in a hammock on a Sunday afternoon. It's neither super exciting nor super relaxing. It's supposed to be boring.

It's like washing your hair—you lather, rinse, repeat. In trading, you just find the same patterns over and over again.

Bourquin: Let me ask you about your profit target on that. Were you looking at a previous high, or how did you decide to get out?

Lund: When I was looking at the profit target on that, I think I had it around eighteen, and the reason I had it at eighteen was because it lined up with a pivot low before it double-topped. It also lined up with a congestion area.

Sometimes you look at a chart, and it's very obvious where overhead resistance is. Sometimes it's not so obvious and it's more of an art. I usually look at what the most obvious point is, and then I cheap it down a little bit. I always want to be a little more conservative, and I also tell people that there's nothing wrong with parceling out. When you get a nice strong break in a stock, the chances that it's going to go straight up to your target are pretty slim. If you need to take some profit off and book it to allow you to stay for the rest of the move, there's nothing wrong with that.

Bourquin: How many trades a week do you typically take?

Lund: Right now, I have a day job. I'm the vice president of strategic initiatives for a broker/dealer, so, unfortunately, I don't get to concentrate on the market as much as I would like. I'm usually trading maybe four, five times a week. When I was trading my own account and that was my only job, I was trading hundreds of times a week. I'm trading a lot less than I would like to right now, unfortunately.

Bourquin: How many positions are you comfortable handling at any one time?

Lund: Boy, I am not comfortable handling more than maybe two or three positions, and really, that is a function of the fact that I have attention-deficit hyperactivity disorder [ADHD]. I have been diagnosed that way, and I have been that way my whole life. If I have too much going on at one time, I just can't focus.

A lot of times, when people are trying to decide how they are going to trade, they have an image of themselves and how they think they should trade. They have an image of what trading is about, and a lot of the time, that image doesn't fit their personality at all. I think one of the keys to becoming a profitable trader over the long haul is to be perfectly honest with yourself, understand your strengths and weaknesses, and then trade in a style that complements those realities—not how you think you *should* be trading.

Trading the way that I do—limiting the number of positions I am in at any one time, only watching a certain amount of stocks, and doing it once a week—helps me deal with my ADHD and makes me a more profitable trader.

Bourquin: I think a lot of traders are also searching for what works for them. There is so much out there. There are different classes, there are different time frames, and there are a million indicators that people think are the Holy Grail—until they eventually find out that they are not. How did you come to this style of trading and settle upon it as something that works for you?

Lund: I read a post on a blog that I used to follow a long time ago by a blogger called Trader-X, and he talked about the concept of chasing success. He talked about how traders would start and say, "I am going to be a gap trader," and then they'd start doing gap trading a little bit. If it didn't work out for them the way they wanted, they'd say, "Forget it. I'm going to do swing trading."

In this way, many traders are constantly chasing this notion of success, instead of getting really good at one type of trading, or getting really good at one asset class, or narrowing their focus. For a long time, I did that, and I think a lot of people do that. I would change to the newest, hottest thing, and then, finally, as I got older and more mature, and had been around the block enough times, I realized that it's not about what's cool or what the newest thing is. It's about making money. That's all this is about.

Whatever way you can trade the markets that makes you money is the right way. If that's not what you're looking for—if you're looking to tell great stories about trading at your family reunion—then you're in it for the wrong reason.

Bourquin: Did you accidentally stumble upon the types of patterns that you look for, or how did you come to find them?

Lund: I learned the hard way. When I first started trading back in 1986, there was hardly any information out there about trading. I didn't even know what technical analysis was. Then, in the early nineties, I was on the Money Talk bulletin boards for Prodigy, and I got connected with some guys who knew a little bit about technical analysis. At that time, though, I still didn't know that much about it. It's been an evolution. I can't say that there was any illuminating moment that told me, "This is what I'm going to do." Over time, I learned what works best for me, and then I finally decided to stick with that.

Bourquin: Were you more profitable when you had the time to trade hundreds of times a week, or do you like not having the time to do it in that manner anymore?

Lund: It's funny. I actually make more money when I trade less. I had my own business for twenty years, and one of the nice things about having your own business is that you have the ability to trade if you want. I was at a desk, and I would trade. Day trading was not big back in the eighties, however, and anyway, because of my responsibilities with my company, I couldn't day trade. I was swing trading instead, but when I eventually sold my company, I said, "I am going to day trade. That's what I'm going to do. That's where it's at."

Looking back, I realized that I actually made more money when I was swing trading—and trading less—than I did when I was day trading. If there was a moment that I thought, "Maybe that's what I should do," that was it.

It reminds me of a chapter in a book that I read a long time ago. Ed Seykota was talking about how he would set up his trades during the day, and then that was it. He didn't have a computer on at his desk. He wasn't monitoring his trades. He knew what his stops were, and he was walking along the banks of Lake Tahoe, hanging out while his positions worked. Granted, it was a different time and a different way of trading, but that Zen-like approach, saying, "This is what I am going to set up. These are my risk parameters. I am going to put them in, and I am going to let the trade work." That really resonated with me.

Bourquin: A lot of people are using high-frequency trading as an excuse, if you will, for why they are not able to find good trades in today's markets. Is there validity to that, or no?

Lund: That's a really good question. I think you are right. I think a lot of people are using it as an excuse for why they're not profitable. There's no doubt that high-frequency trading is out there. You see it all the time. You just have to learn to adapt to it.

If you are going to trade patterns, you have to understand that high-frequency trading and algorithmic trading are going to distort those patterns to a point where you traditionally would have thought they were broken. Maybe you will see a cup with a handle, or maybe you will see a double-bottom, or maybe you will see a semi-triangle, and price will drop out of that pattern. In the past, you would say, "Okay, that's it. The pattern is broken." But then, miraculously, price will come back into that pattern and continue the way that you wanted.

There's a simple explanation for this. High-frequency trading is set up to go where the highest amount of orders are. It's set up to go where stop levels are, because the whole point is to get volume. But everyone knows where the stop levels are. Everyone can look at a chart. Everyone knows what price points are there.

I think high-frequency trading does have an impact, but I don't think it's anything that people can't adapt to if they are honest with themselves.

Bourquin: Did you ever do anything in your trading career that you felt really took you to the next level?

Lund: No, there really was no "Aha!" moment for me. This goes back to the question you asked earlier. When I decided that I was trading to make money and not to be cool or get in on the action, I stopped chasing different styles of trading.

I originally had this vision of myself as a true trader—a trader that can trade anything. In my mind, true traders can trade any equity class, they can trade short, and they can trade long. That was a trader to me. Now, I'm sure there are people out there who can do that. I have no doubt about that.

But that is a quixotic view of trading. I think that you should find what you are good at, find the areas that you know, and stick with those areas.

Coming to that realization helped me, but it wasn't an "Aha!" moment. It's just something that evolved over time.

Bourquin: If you see a symbol that you're not entirely familiar with, will you check if there is earnings or news out before you make a trading decision, or will you purely trade the chart?

Lund: No, I never look at fundamentals. The fundamentals play no part in my selection process. Around earnings season, I will look to see if something is coming up, but I never look at fundamentals. Price and volume are the only things I look at.

Bourquin: What about something like nonfarm payrolls or one of the other broad economic announcements that affect the overall market?

Lund: I don't follow that, but I should. In fact, just recently I was taking a trade in Lennar Corp., and I wasn't paying attention to the economic announcements. I was actually in a chat room, and somebody said that a report related to the housing market was going to be released in five minutes. I remember thinking to myself, "I should probably close this trade, even though the stock is going up," and, of course, I didn't.

The numbers came out, and they were bad. The stock reversed and stopped me out for a loss. Even after twenty-five years of trading, I still make that mistake, and I should probably check on macro factors more often than I do. I hate economics. I think it's so open to interpretation, and I don't even want to get into that interpretation game. I'm such a purist when it comes to price and volume. But if ignoring economic announcements actually harms me, I should be more aware of that.

Bourquin: What do you feel like you still need to improve upon as a trader? Maybe paying attention to economic announcements is your one thing?

Lund: I wish it were my only thing. The thing about trading is that there is so much that can go wrong at any given moment. It's like anything that you want to do consistently well in life. It's like being married. People think, "Hey, I've done all this planning. I went up to the altar, and said, 'I do.' That's it. I'm done. I'm married." But that's just the beginning of a lifelong process of always checking the pulse of that marriage, refining it, making sure you're on the same page, and working at it, just like you work on anything.

If you get complacent in your trading, so many things can change or go wrong. The problem with that is that one bad misstep can wipe out ten great moves. I have a lot of things that I always want to keep working on. I never want to get too complacent, and I never want to think that I've solved every problem, because that's when you put yourself in a really bad position.

Bourquin: You mentioned that your profitable Lennar trade became a negative one. Do trades like that make you start thinking about taking off half of your position at a certain point? Do you scale in or scale out of trades?

Lund: I do scale in and scale out of trades. With regards to the Lennar trade, first I thought I should close it. Then I said to myself, "I should take at least half off." But then, another evil part of me said, "Wait a minute. The stock's moving up. Maybe somebody knows something about this announcement. We're going to get a great move!" That's why I try to steer clear of fundamentals, because if I start playing that game, I'll just fake myself out.

I did not manage that trade how I should have, but generally, I will take partial profits—especially on really violent moves, like if a stock moves up really fast and spikes out of a resistance level. To me, those are the moves that often give up and end up turning around. Those are also a hallmark of attempts by high-frequency traders to run the stop level. The faster something spikes, the more inclined I am to take something off the table. Doing so gives me some room—or at least a profitable trade, if it comes back to breakeven.

Bourquin: Do you set an annual or monthly ROI percentage goal for yourself? Is there a flat dollar amount that you want to make in your account?

Lund: I've wrestled with that over the years, and there are two schools of thought. In the first school of thought, you get to a certain amount, and that's good. You don't want to push it, and so you can shut down your trading, or you can bank what you've got.

The other school of thought says that setting specific profit goals limits you. In other words, if you hit your profit goal and shut down your trading because you've made all the money you were expecting to for the day, month, or quarter, you may miss out on other trading opportunities.

The general rule that I follow is to never look at my P&L—at least not too closely. Going back to poker, I take a page from Phil Ivey, a great poker player. When he was asked how he deals with having $250,000 in the pot, he said something like, "You can't think of that money as a Ferrari. You can't even think of it in those terms, because if you change your perception of what you're doing, you'll change the way you're playing." I try to avoid looking at my P&L as much as I can. Obviously, I know where I stand, but I try not to focus on it.

When I've got a trade on, I never look at how much I am up or down dollarwise in that trade. I always look and see what the charts are saying, because the market doesn't care if you're up $100 or down $100. It will do whatever it wants to, based on those charts. I know what my P&L is, but I try not to focus on it, because, if I do, it'll throw me off my trading game.

Bourquin: Lately, I've been asked some questions about win/loss ratios, and the argument that always seems to crop up is, "Can I be right 30 percent of the time and, as long as I let my winners run and cut my losers quickly, still be okay?" What are your thoughts on that? Do you keep track of your winning and losing trades?

Lund: Yes, I absolutely believe in that. Even theoretically, limiting yourself to trades that have a good risk-reward ratio has to be a good thing. If you want to get down to the actual technicals of it, you can map it out where, if you're taking trades that have a 1:3 risk-reward ratio, you can be right only 30 percent of the time and still be profitable. I really believe in that.

I think it's very important from a psychological standpoint. You need to know where you're going to come out on a trade. If you know where you're going to come out and you're comfortable going into the trade and losing x amount of money, you're freed up to manage the trade in a more honest way. You're also less likely to do something that you wouldn't normally do.

Bourquin: Speaking of psychology, some would say that enduring losing trades 70 percent of the time is a tough way to make money because of what that does to you psychologically—never mind that you're doing well on 30 percent of your trades. What are your thoughts there?

Lund: That goes back to what I was talking about when I said that doctors are generally not good at poker or trading. Trading is one of the most counterintuitive things that you can do. Everything we've ever been taught goes against a proper trading mindset.

If you go to buy a new refrigerator at the store, you want to buy the refrigerator that is on sale. The cheaper it is, the better it is for you. But a refrigerator is a wasting asset. That's why your mindset works in that situation, because we're conditioned to think that cheaper is better.

A stock is not a wasting asset. If a stock is getting cheaper and cheaper, it means that nobody wants it. You want a stock that is getting more and more expensive.

People just can't accept it when you tell them that they're going to lose most of the time in trading. They go, "I don't understand that." It's funny, though, because they accept the same notion in baseball. If somebody hits .300 in baseball, they're a great player. But if someone bats 30 percent in trading, they feel like they are a failure.

It is possible to lose 70 percent of the time, but if you have good risk-reward ratios, you can lose that often or even more and still be profitable.

Bourquin: Let me ask you one more question about risk-reward ratios. What risk-reward ratio do you favor, and how do you determine what that ratio should be on any given trade?

Lund: I try to use a 1:3 risk-reward ratio, and here's the way I work: I'll look at a chart, and I'll say to myself, "Okay, here's where I'm going to enter the trade." I'll look at where my stop is going to be, and then I'll plot where I think my target is going to be. Then I'll say, "Okay, I'm willing to risk *x* amount of money on this trade."

Let's say I'm willing to risk $500 in a trade. I'll take the spread between my entry price and where I know I'll stop, and I'll divide that into the $500. Let's say I'm going to get into a stock at $100, but if it drops to $99.50, I'll get out. My spread, then, is 50 cents. Next, I'll divide 50 cents into the $500 that I'm willing to risk, which will size my position at one thousand shares. This way, I know for sure that if I hit my max stop, I'll lose my maximum dollar risk.

In this theoretical trade, I'm looking for a target of $1,500. I'm risking one times R, which is my risk of $500, and I'm looking for three times R, which is a reward of $1,500. Basically, I'm just reverse-engineering the size of my trades.

A lot of people arbitrarily pick a position size and say, "Ah, I'm going to go in with one thousand shares." That doesn't make any sense to me. You have to have a sizing methodology and a risk methodology that works with the chart and the patterns you're looking at.

Bourquin: In the final chapter of this book, "Twenty Habits of Wealthy Traders," I talk about that exact same thing. When I ask any good trader about their typical share size, they say, "Well, you've got to give me more information than that. You've got to tell me what I'm trading and how volatile it is. I don't do one thousand shares on everything."

Lund: Yes, and not to disparage anyone, but when you hear someone say, "Well, I traded one thousand shares," that's usually the mark of an amateur. It's usually the mark of someone who doesn't really understand risk-reward ratios in the market.

Michael Toma

*Professional risk manager **Michael Toma** actively trades US-based equity index and index futures markets, as well as the equity markets in mainland China. He also trades bond futures, which is an area that is often overlooked by short-term traders. In terms of his trading strategy, Toma uses a combination of technical analysis and stringent risk parameters to help him make consistently profitable trading decisions in the markets.*

Through speaking engagements and in his role as the vice president of operations at Pelagon Trading, Toma de-emphasizes the monetary aspect of trading, instead focusing on functions such as risk management, psychology, effective journaling, and data-driven analytics. His methods are sought-after by fund managers and other professionals who want to improve their trading performance, as well as by new traders who are in search of consistency and a more transparent approach to the markets. Toma has authored two books on trading and risk management and received the designation of Certified Risk Manager (CRM) in 2007.

Tim Bourquin: Mike, talk about the kind of trader you are and what you trade.

Michael Toma: For the most part, I'm an E-mini S&P futures [ES] trader, but I dabble in bond trading and bond futures, as well as in some other areas, like options and exchange-traded funds [ETFs].

Bourquin: Bond traders are rare. For whatever reason, you don't hear about a lot of short-term traders using bonds. Perhaps many just don't feel like they know that market well enough. What made you decide to trade the bond market?

Toma: I didn't know the bond market very well, either. I was at a Traders Expo and attended a bond seminar, and I thought that the setups were pretty good, and the trades looked clean. I require clean order flow and clean price action in any markets I trade, so I did some backtesting and subscribed to data feeds for bond futures after that. It's not my favorite market, and I'm still getting comfortable with it, but I track a lot of my trading activity, and the numbers are there. I just trade smaller lots as a result.

The ES often trade in small, choppy ranges, and when you have bond announcements about ten-year Treasury bills and Treasury notes, bond trading can rock. It kind of replaces some of the midday doldrums in ES trading for me.

Bourquin: There's some massive volume in bonds, and that's what the big boys are trading most of the time, so you've got a tremendous chance to get in and out quickly. Of course, massive volume and rapid-fire trades are not the first things many people think of when it comes to bonds, but you certainly can do that in the bond market.

Toma: Absolutely. One of the things you learn the hard way—as I did—is how the professionals trade: where they're going to be probing stops and where they're going to be looking at support and resistance.

Especially on announcement days, be very careful. Stay away and just monitor the market at first. Each market has its own style, and a lot of ES traders like that market because they understand its style and how it trades. Well, the bond market is unique in its own way, too. There's a learning curve, but now that I'm more comfortable with it, I would say that about 25 percent of my overall trading activity is on the ZB bond futures contract.

Bourquin: And are the setups you trade for bond futures the same as the ones you use when trading ES?

Toma: Yeah, for the most part. I use the same basic setups in both markets. I will adjust stops to get a little more wiggle room and risk/reward potential when trading ES, but I will widen my target as well.

Bourquin: What's the prototypical ES trade setup for you, and what characteristics do you like to see on the chart?

Toma: Well, I try to keep ten setups, and I think of those setups like horses in my stable. I monitor the market activity and my trade performance through all ten setups, and if they keep performing, I use them more frequently and at a higher contract level.

For those that don't, however, I either stop using them or move them off my list, potentially in favor of another setup that I may develop through my continuing research or elsewhere.

Since I started doing this about three years ago, my number one setup is one I call the "Secretariat," because it just continues to perform month after month. It's relatively simple, and I use it predominantly in the ES, but it can be used in bonds as well.

Basically, I use a nine-period exponential moving average [EMA] and a thirty-period weighted moving average [WMA] on a 1,224-tick chart. I have a couple of other indicators on it now, too, but when you're beginning to learn this setup, it's best to just monitor EMA and WMA and not clutter up the chart with other data or indicators.

I'm looking for a cross of the fast moving average, so I'll look for instances where the nine-period EMA crosses the thirty-period WMA on the upside, for example. That way, I'm going to be looking only for long-entry opportunities. Then, once it breaks out of that range, I'm expecting a pullback into that zone between the nine and the thirty and will aim to get in long and hopefully catch the resumption of that uptrend.

Bourquin: How did you figure out that this setup worked?

Toma: A lot of practice and a lot of backtesting. I'm a risk manager by trade, and while I consider myself to be a decent trader, I'm a really good risk manager. As a result of that, I'm very data driven. I do a lot of backtesting, I sample with different types of bar and tick charts, and I measure the ones that have the optimal return, given my level of risk.

I backtest everything rigorously, and for a setup to get on my top-ten list, it has to produce results in all different kinds of markets and work on both the long side and the short side. Then, even once it makes my list, I'll start trading that setup only one contract at a time.

Bourquin: Do you screen for your ten setups automatically using your trading software?

Toma: At this point, I can tell with just a quick glimpse when one of these setups is developing, but I also have alerts on my screen to show when the moving averages are crossing. That serves as the initial indication that a particular setup may be forming.

Bourquin: Mike, you've got ten setups, but if the Secretariat works best, why not just throw as much size as possible at that one and forget about all the others?

Toma: That's a great question, and the straight answer is because price action doesn't always allow for the setup to occur. Especially with the 1,224-tick charts I use, a lot of times a trend can just continue and never pull back to that "sweet spot," where I want to get in.

Now, I could just buy at the high and hope that it goes higher, but my whole mantra is not just to trade my setups, but also to get the best price. If I can't get it, then many times I'll just let it go.

I've passed on a lot of trades. There are probably more that I miss than I actually get, but when I do get them, I get a really good price. Even if it doesn't work and I get stopped out, my risk is limited because I got in at such a good price.

To summarize, the same setups don't always occur, especially on certain trend days—or even during specific times of the day. For example, I only target the Secretariat setup from the open [9:30 a.m. eastern time] until about 11:00 a.m. eastern time, and then from 2:45 p.m. eastern time to the close [4:00 p.m. eastern time] because those are the peak times for that setup.

Bourquin: I like the fact that you're "missing trades," only in the sense that you're not chasing them and are very strict about waiting for the required pullback before getting in.

Toma: That's one of my rules, and sometimes I look at it and wonder if it's a little too strict. It's easy to think, "Well, maybe I won't be getting in at the best price, but I'd be missing a lot by passing on it altogether."

Honestly, though, I have other setups that I can use, and I'm in a position now where I really don't want to take more than one trade at one time. I remember the last time we spoke, and we were talking about taking eight trades a day. Now I'm lucky if I can do four. I would say that 80 percent of my trades use only three of my ten setups.

Bourquin: Do you have each of the ten setups on a single chart, or do you use multiple charts that show a couple of setups on each one?

Toma: I have two or three charts on my main platform. I'll have my number one setup, the Secretariat, on one chart, because that's my bread and butter, and I don't want to miss that. My second setup is on another chart, and then I'll use one more chart with the other two or three setups that I'm constantly monitoring. I'll have alerts set up on those. I'm not really watching them closely at all times, but during non-peak hours, like the 10:00 a.m. to 2:00 p.m. eastern lunchtime hours, there are some other setups I'm looking at. When the time is right, I'll have those under the screen, and I'll blow them up and predominantly look at them while keeping an alert on my primary trade.

Bourquin: Let's talk about your second favorite setup. What's a good close second to the Secretariat?

Toma: I have a basic setup that relies only on the moving average convergence/divergence [MACD] indicator. Another one of my rules is that I must be on the proper side of the momentum, and I think the MACD is a really good way to do that.

I've actually taught my young nephew how to spot this setup and color coded it for him so that he can see when the MACD starts to reverse. I also showed him some basic rules and opened a little trading account for him, and the kid once had a week with seven wins and two losses and was up twelve points.

That made me think that traders as a whole, including myself, sometimes make this very, very difficult. Seeing it through his eyes, I came to understand that the kid has no fear. He looks at it as a game—he actually calls it "the game"—and he doesn't connect any monetary value to it. Maybe we all need to do that.

Bourquin: Sure. When you're paper trading, you're not dealing with real money, and you're free to trade like a kid, in a sense, because you're not worried about money. Some traders would say that they need the element of tension that real money brings, but most people would do much better if they didn't have to worry about that.

Toma: And that's very powerful, because 90 percent of the people who enter this business don't make money, but most of them would if they traded in a simulator. You can gain a psychological edge by taking the money aspect out of it. I look at a little eight-year-old kid doing it, and his biggest problem is that he hops up and leaves whenever SpongeBob comes on TV!

Personally, I don't put any profit and loss indicators on my screen. While that's still a challenge for me, I want to put myself in the state of mind where it's not about money; it's about implementing my trade plan.

Bourquin: A lot of successful traders talk about making the goal of their trading anything but money, but at the end of the day, we all know that it's about money. So, how do you set non-monetary goals for yourself?

Toma: My ultimate goal is just to follow my trade plan, so I have metrics that measure how well I do that. I'm pretty confident that my setups are going to be there and allow me to achieve my desired lifestyle, but it's a question of whether I implement my plan as efficiently as possible.

For example, I'll never say, "I want to make an average of three points a day." I did that at one point, but it doesn't really tell me anything. What if the market was able to give me fifteen points that day and I only took the three? Or, what if the market wasn't giving me anything and I got the three points, but I broke a rule to do so? I've learned to just have a good, solid plan that I'm comfortable with and focus solely on implementing that.

One of my key metrics is my average risk/reward ratio for all my trades throughout the month. While each one is different, I want it to be at least three-to-one on certain setups. If I find that, on average, my ratio was two-to-one, I need to look at what I did that month and modify something, because I will consider that a rule breaker, even if I've still made money in the process.

Maybe I'm a little neurotic about it, but I actually have penalties, and sometimes I have to go on simulation the next trading day if I've broken certain rules the day before. That's tough for me, because I'm a professional trader, but it helps create the discipline to not make that mistake again.

Bourquin: A lot of traders have a tough time deciding where to place stops and profit targets to achieve their desired risk/reward ratio. How do you determine those levels?

Toma: Well, my risk manager mentality means I'm really focusing on the risk, so I'm not too concerned about my profit target at first. I want to focus on how much I can afford to lose and, more importantly, how I'll know if I'm wrong about the trade.

In years past, I would set arbitrary stops, like six ticks or two points in the ES. However, because high volatility and algorithmic trading are so prevalent, that really didn't tell me that I was wrong. It only indicated that my maximum risk had been hit, so I needed to get out.

Here's one thing that may be contrary to public opinion: A lot of traders want to have two-to-one, three-to-one, or five-to-one risk/reward ratios. Well, that's great, but if I have a setup that gives me 70 percent, I don't mind taking one-to-one on that.

In the case of a setup that may only work 50 percent of the time, though, you'd want a two-, three-, or four-to-one risk/reward ratio.

Bourquin: Considering your Secretariat setup, how do you determine your stop levels? Is it a certain distance below a moving average line?

Toma: Yes, and in the past, I would have set it right below the thirty-period WMA. Now I want to give it more room, and especially on big trend days, I'll actually set a catastrophic stop of three, three-and-a-half points, depending on the day's average true range.

For the most part, though, my default is three points, and when a five-minute bar is broken below that, I'll know I'm wrong. On the other hand, if it's contained and just sticking within that area—even if it's two points and it doesn't look good—I'll know I'm not wrong yet. The six-tick stop players are all out already, and the trade hasn't gone bad.

Of course, I want to have something in there in case the next five-minute print is a ten-point bar caused by a big news announcement. So, the catastrophic stop is there for that reason. Once I start reaching those stop levels, I'll know I'm wrong, and I'll just close out and wait for the next opportunity.

Bourquin: Do you track the winning percentage of all of your setups?

Toma: Yes, I do. I actually have a grid, and I do a monthly report on each setup. I try to be accountable for everything and will even have other traders review it as part of that accountability.

I monitor those results, including the total point gain/loss, and I also have them broken down within five time periods throughout the regular trading day. That helps me find, for example, that a particular setup might be 64 percent accurate overall, but it is 76 percent accurate between 10:15 a.m. and noon. Then, after 1:30 p.m., it may be less than 50 percent accurate.

I have a big poster in my office highlighting the setups and time periods, and I'm always looking at it, so I know the bread-and-butter setups, historically. That gives me an edge. Like I said, I may not be the world's best trader, but I recognize edge, I recognize opportunity, and I know, historically, when my setups achieve optimum results.

Bourquin: It's interesting that you mentioned getting "an edge." I did a recent webinar with Corey Rosenbloom about just that. Does being able to match your setups with the optimum time of day create your edge, or is there more to it?

Toma: Corey's work is really good. He and I had coffee at a recent Traders Expo, and we were talking about our trading.

Like Corey, I also look at support and resistance when I do my research prior to the market open. I'll mark down certain pivot points, resistance levels, the previous day's highs and lows, and the overnight price action. These are the areas that I want to really focus on and be aware of whenever they're hit.

Say, for example, a Secretariat setup is developing right around an area that looked like prior support. That's sweet for me; it's what I wait for all day.

One of my rules is that I have to have confluence on each trade, and I'll use pivots or Fibonacci zones to get that confluence. I'm not a big Fib guy, but if it's going to match up with my other support levels, I will become one.

I do a lot of work with market profile, which isn't a favorite of many traders, primarily because it's a little difficult to understand, but also—and more importantly—because it usually doesn't come with a lot of the trading platforms out there. I subscribe to a service that gives me great levels, so I know when I'm wrong about a trade or where I can get in. All of those things help to give me a little extra edge.

Bourquin: The fan base among short-term traders may be growing, but I think that in the past, most people thought of market profile as an investing strategy. Now short-term traders are seeing that it works on their time frames as well.

Toma: I think of it as part of my overall development. In addition to my trading plan and my monthly assessments, I create a development plan every year. I write down the things that I want to learn and gain exposure to, and I'll look into them at seminars, expos, and on my own.

Market profile was one of those items on a past development plan. More recently, I'm trying to learn about other facets of the business at the same time that I'm learning some new strategies. With algorithmic trading now so prevalent, I'm learning more about that.

Bourquin: Can you recall something that came from your development plan that helped you reach that next level in your trading?

Toma: Sure. Developing my trade-tracking skills was very important, but the thing that has really brought me to the next level was learning to trade more like a tactician. I wanted to be like a robot. I found myself getting too involved in each setup and following every tick to the point where I'd be exhausted by the end of the day.

I had to make some changes to accommodate a more balanced lifestyle, and that became part of my development. When you get too emotionally involved, either you miss opportunities because you get scared, or you try to make up for prior losses and end up getting killed.

Being more robotic in trading my plan was a developmental goal of mine a couple of years ago, and I'm still working to improve at it. You never really perfect that. I'm really a plan-implementation specialist more than a trader, and if I can focus intently on just trading my plan, I know I'll be fine.

Bourquin: So many times I see people feverishly jumping between expo workshops like they're looking for the Holy Grail. You don't have that same frenetic pace. Would you agree that if those people would just focus on learning one thing at a time and putting it into practice, they would probably be better off?

Toma: Yes. I see it all the time. People come running up to me, asking if I can teach them a few setups, and I say, "Honestly, that's the easy part!" It's not about the setups; it's about building a lifestyle and building a business.

I think the biggest difference between amateur traders and those who trade successfully is the latter group's psychological edge. The most successful traders treat trading like a business. My best work is done when the markets aren't open. It's about preparedness and learning from others. I'm still learning, and I will be as long as I'm trading.

I feel for those people, because I used to be one of them. I was fortunate to have a mentor when I started out, and I owe so much to him. That got me on the right track, but if I would have left it at that, I never would have survived in this profession.

Bourquin: I always tell people attending a Traders Expo that, in addition to the speakers, some of the best traders in the country—or even the world—are in the hallways of the expo, walking around, just like us, which is awesome. I've picked up a ton of information over the years from talking to those people.

Mike, high-frequency trading [HFT] was an issue that we wanted to talk about. What adjustments have you made in response to HFT this year?

Toma: I was at a Traders Expo the first time that I heard someone mention algorithmic trading. I literally scribbled that on a piece of paper and didn't even know what it meant, but I knew I needed to look into it further.

I went to some local seminars in New York, and in talking to some quant traders, I found out that 70 percent of all market activity is driven by algorithmic program trading. The computers come in and probe an area below what retail traders consider support and then reverse back. That makes the retail guys get scared and cover their positions, and then the quant guys can ride the wave up.

In the past, I generally used arbitrary stops of two points or six ticks, which were usually below confluence support. So, for me to be stopped out, price had to break through what I considered to be multiple layers of support. With HFT, I found that price was being hit, reversing, and then going with the original direction more often.

As a result, I've had to adjust some of my stops. I've made them a little wider, but at the same time, I've had to learn how to piggyback on these quant trades. Sometimes it's difficult to detect when they're happening, but I'm using time and sales more to look at big block trades—especially at points of new highs or lows and areas where the average retail trader would have their stop.

Ironically, I just had one such trade that ran 10 points, although I was on it only for four. I need to keep looking at the way I handle those trades, but I could see the impact of HFT reflected in my numbers and had to be responsive.

Bourquin: So, you're now thinking like a quantitative trader, setting your stops further out so they're protected, and even trading on the side of the quants and buying their stops?

Toma: In my normal setups, I have moved my stops lower, so I've had to increase my target to maintain the same risk/reward ratio. I know very quickly if I'm on the wrong side of the trade. If I'm stopped out, I'll just move on to the next.

After some thorough backtesting, I added a new setup that capitalizes on this retail panic, and it is actually now my number three performer and the fastest-growing profit engine I have. It's tough to implement a new strategy like this, and now here I am, buying new lows. I never thought I would do that.

Bourquin: Can you describe that new setup and give an overview of how it works?

Toma: Sure. I'll use a breakout trade as an example. It doesn't happen all the time, but if, on an intraday basis, you have a high and a low, and the market comes down to test those lows, people would either buy at the lows or sell short once it broke the new lows.

A lot of times you'll see big blocks coming in until the new lows are hit, and then it will go down a few ticks before making a sudden reversal. I have my time and sales figures on the screen during those times, and while retail traders are there holding one or two short contracts, all of a sudden, it'll start to reverse.

When you see these big blocks of ES contracts—a hundred and up—coming in on the buy side, and now the market reverses a point or a point-and-a-half, the retail traders have their stops at six ticks or maybe two points, and once those start hitting, the algorithms will ride that wave. I try to jump on that, too.

Bourquin: Will you wait for those blocks to show up before you actually buy, or do you try and get in while the one- and two-contract orders are going through?

Toma: I'll actually see those blocks coming in, and the price may not jump immediately, but when you start seeing that reversal of about one point or a point-and-a-half, you have to know the average retail trader is going to start to panic. Once they do, they're going to start covering those shorts, and then you're just waiting and can ride that wave to your target once the panic sets in.

In a sense, it's taking advantage of the impulses of newer traders, but when it isn't going to work, you'll know right away and can get out quickly, so you don't have to risk a lot.

This setup required a psychological change, because I never thought like that. I was always an average retail trader, using three to five contracts, but now, with HFT, I have to think like the big boys. After talking to some of the quant traders and hedge fund guys about algorithmic trading, I realized that they're playing a totally different game, and the average retail trader is just a little fish in a very big pond.

Bourquin: You mentioned catching only four points of that ten-point move. Was four points your target, or did certain conditions make you exit that trade early?

Toma: Actually, one of my rules requires me to take smaller targets on my first trades each day, just to get some green in my account that I can play with for the rest of the day. If that were another type of setup or another time of day, I would've let it run. But since this was right near the open, I wanted to be more conservative.

The first half hour can be a little hectic, so I just took my profits and got out with no regrets. I traded my plan just as I wanted, and then I just moved on to the next one.

Twenty Habits of Wealthy Traders

In the course of interviewing hundreds of wealthy stock, option, and futures traders over the past year, I've had the privilege of hearing from some of the best independent traders in the world. I've asked them how they entered the trading business and how they learned how to make money consistently as a trader. I even asked how much money they make each year, and then hoped they wouldn't hang up on me or throw something heavy in my direction. None of them did, though only one has allowed me to actually publish the answer to that question in this book. Nearly all of them graciously answered my direct, probing, and sometimes very personal questions.

Not everyone was comfortable talking openly about their trading business and lifestyle. For some, the years they spent struggling with and studying the markets were difficult times, and they were unwilling to give a shortcut to the rest of the world by discussing their current trading methods. While I knew they were successful traders, they just weren't willing to transparently discuss their strategies. Though they agreed to be interviewed, their answers were short and guarded, and my relentless prying did little to crack their shell. I don't blame them. After years of highs and lows, in the markets and in their trading accounts, they had finally come across a strategy that worked for them and did not want to share it for fear that the method would become saturated by thousands of other traders.

Others, primarily the interviewees in this book, felt that there are truly no secrets that can't be learned by others. The most liquid markets, now global and bigger than ever, are too large for any one group of traders to affect in any meaningful way. Otherwise, eventually every trader would gravitate to the same moving averages, perhaps the 50- and 200-day moving averages, which would work as perfect support and resistance levels and enable them to make easy money trading off of those levels every time. We all know that is not the case.

Some of the traders I spoke with hold positions for a matter of minutes, making hundreds, even thousands of trades in a single day. Others hunt for one or two "big game" trades each month; trades that they are willing to hold for several weeks or even months until an ideal profit opportunity arises. All of them, without exception, have mastered the art of risk management, never allowing their losses to extend beyond predetermined levels. They weren't always that disciplined. Some told me stories of blown-up accounts, where they lost every penny before finally figuring out that discipline was the key to staying in the game.

Through those hundreds of interviews, some over the phone and some in person, I've chosen the top sixteen, resulting in the book you have been reading. Getting traders to open up about their strategies, backgrounds, struggles, and ultimate successes isn't easy. Traders are a curious bunch; sometimes they secretively guard their methods, and at other times they are open and transparent, understanding that there really are no secrets for making money as an independent trader. Hard work and discipline are the real keys to success as a short-term trader.

I also began noticing a pattern. After listening to them talk about how they make their living in the markets, I started hearing them say similar things about how they approach every trade. When traders who all make over $200,000 per year say the same things, I listen closely. As a trader myself, I too am looking for a nugget of wisdom that can help me make better decisions and, ultimately, more money.

I compiled a list of twenty habits that are common among almost every wealthy trader with whom I have spoken. Some will be familiar to you, others may be surprising. Either way, I hope you'll find at least one or two habits you can add to your own trading plan to make more money, more consistently, in whatever markets you trade.

Let's begin!

1. Wealthy traders are patient with winning trades and enormously impatient with losing trades

This first habit is straight out of Dennis Gartman's (TheGartmanLetter.com) trading playbook. Most traders become very anxious with winning trades because they don't want them to become losing trades. That's a good thing—until their impatience forces them to exit their winning position too early and leave money in the market. On the other hand, how many times have you said to yourself, "I'm going to let this losing trade go just a little bit longer and see if it turns around."? You've just been patient with a losing trade and impatient with your winner.

Wealthy traders flip this thought process around and do exactly the opposite. When they have a trade that is going well and is profitable, they remain patient and see how far it can really go. When they have a trade going against them, they immediately exit to limit the loss and begin looking for the next opportunity. If you've set a stop loss, never move it in hopes that your trade will turn around; it rarely will, and you will only increase your losses for the day. Start being patient with your winners and impatient with your losers. Doing so is the first step toward joining the minority ranks of wealthy traders.

2. Wealthy traders realize that making money is more important than being right

It is human nature to want to be correct in our assumptions and predictions about the market. We all want to believe we are interpreting market data properly and have made the right choice to go long or short the market. But wealthy traders rarely have a bias about the market prior to its open or entering a trade. Furthermore, in those cases when they do make the wrong trading decision and their trade becomes a loss, they will have no problem immediately making a trade in the other direction.

I have interviewed successful traders who form a bias in the morning and will only trade in the direction of that bias for the entire day, but they are rare. Instead of trying to force their opinion on the markets, determined to prove themselves correct, most wealthy traders will switch sides at a moment's notice if the market tells them it is time to do so—even if they were "sure" the market was going to go the other way that day. Being right is not important—growing their trading account and net worth is.

3. Wealthy traders view technical analysis as a picture of where traders are lining up to buy and sell

Many traders view moving averages, Fibonacci, and trend lines as exact indicators of where price is expected to turn and move in the opposite direction, but successful traders don't view technical analysis that way. Wealthy traders see charts as snapshots of where traders are lining up to buy or sell. Instead of seeing bars, lines, and clouds, wealthy traders see price points where traders have placed orders to enter and exit the market either as stop losses or entry points. The stock, option, or futures contract has no idea where it will find support or resistance. As experienced traders know, it is the market participants who determine these levels, and so successful traders will place their own orders around those levels to take advantage of the 95 percent of traders who lose money trading.

4. Before they enter every trade, wealthy traders know where they will exit for either a profit or loss

We've all heard that we should be using stops whenever we're trading to avoid large losses. However, very few traders actually know where they will place a stop and a profit target before they enter their trades. Wealthy traders leave nothing to chance and plan every trade in its entirety before they even enter the market.

Your written trading plan should include objective measures of where your stop loss should be placed as well as where you'll take profits. Not knowing, or simply guessing at, where these price points will be after you have entered a trade can lead to indecision or price targets outside of the average range of the security you are trading. Why set an arbitrary profit target of three points when the average range of that market is only two points?

Furthermore, wealthy traders set position sizes and stop losses that are almost always a function of their risk tolerance for any given trade. For example, if the maximum risk on any one trade is 2 percent of their trading account, they will calculate both the number of shares they will trade (based on the price of shares) and a reasonable stop loss before they place the trade. I rarely talk with a wealthy trader who says their position size is 1,000 shares. They usually tell me it depends entirely on what security they are trading. They take their maximum acceptable loss and work backward to find a stop loss and position size that matches that objective measure.

5. Wealthy traders approach trade number five with the same conviction as the previous four losing trades

We've all had that run of bad trades that shakes our confidence in the "edge" we think we have in the markets. Our setup appears again and instead of taking that fifth trade, we hesitate, not wanting to endure another losing trade.

Of course, that fifth trade ends up working beautifully, and not only would it have made up for our previous four losses, but it also would have put us net-positive for the day. If we truly believe our strategy is solid and the market has not indicated that something has changed, there's no reason to hesitate if the trade setup presents itself.

Even automated system traders will tell you that a run of losing trades that goes beyond the normal drawdown in backtests is normal. The key, of course, is knowing the difference between when your "edge" is no longer an "edge" and when you've simply had a statistical run of trades that just haven't worked out.

Wealthy traders are able to shrug off losing trades and enter the next trade with the same enthusiasm and confidence they had on the first trade. Teammates of Evan Longoria, an All-Star baseball player for the Tampa Bay Rays, often describe his batting success as his ability to forget about the previous bad swing or missed pitch and focus solely on the next pitch coming toward him. Similarly, wealthy traders have mastered the ability to forget about the previous trade and focus exclusively on the next opportunity.

Your trading plan should include some sort of consequence for a string of losing trades. For me personally, after four losing trades in a row, I force myself to trade a single share of stock until I feel confident in my trading decisions again. Yes, commissions will wipe out any profit on a single share of stock, but I would much rather pay a commission than take a large loss trying to force my will on the market.

6. Wealthy traders use "naked" charts

When I first began trading, I wanted to see confirmation from as many indicators as possible before entering a trade. I put so many lines, arcs, and levels on my charts that I could barely see the price bars beneath. As I matured as a trader, I began peeling off those indicators and eventually began to prefer charts with nothing more than price bars, volume, and pivot points that represented previous highs and lows. Nearly every wealthy trader I interview tells me that they watch one thing on their charts: price. By "naked" charts I mean those that are barren of indicators and show just price and perhaps volume at each price level.

At some point in every trader's career, they realize there is no magic indicator, no matter how hard they look for it. The only thing that matters is price—and supply and demand at that price. If you have an indicator you feel gives you greater insight into future price movement, excellent. Just know that too much faith in any one or combination of indicators is sure to fail at some point. Wealthy traders firmly believe in the phrase, "Price pays" and are able to trade with nothing but information on price and the demand in the market at that price.

7. Wealthy traders are comfortable making decisions with incomplete information

Many traders I speak with at events like the Traders Expo talk about getting to the point where trading is easier and comfortable. They yearn for the day when they are relaxed while trading and make money on a consistent basis. Unfortunately, I have to inform them that even the best traders are slightly uncomfortable sitting in that chair in front of their trading platform. While wealthy traders have become comfortable with that gnawing feeling we all get—that we are making decisions based on incomplete and imperfect data—it's likely you'll never be totally comfortable with your trading decisions because you'll never have enough information to know absolutely that you'll be on the right side of the market.

Wealthy traders have come to terms with this fact and have been able to make good trading decisions in spite of that uncomfortable feeling in the chair. They acknowledge it, and yet they are able to make clear decisions based on what they know and see. The day when trading is "easy" never comes, yet they are still able to acquire incredible wealth by trading the markets.

8. Wealthy traders stopped trying to pick tops and bottoms long ago

Most of the traders I talk to who are still struggling to find their "edge" in the markets are trying to pick tops and bottoms. Whether they are working with a one-minute chart or a daily chart, most traders are using every indicator and technical analysis tool they can find to spot those areas where price is going to reverse course and head in the other direction. Wealthy traders don't try to anticipate the top or bottom. They wait for it to happen and then capture the "meat," or the middle of the move, after it has started. The question they ask is, "Has the new direction been confirmed?" as opposed to most traders, who ask, "Is the trend ready to turn?"

Wealthy traders realize that the middle of the trend is where the money is made, so there's no need to capture every last tick or perfectly time the top or bottom. While most traders are afraid to buy all-time highs and sell all-time lows, wealthy traders know those are the best places to buy or sell. A trend is much more likely to continue than it is to reverse, so why are most traders trying to find that turning point instead of buying or selling the existing direction? Of course, this doesn't mean you don't protect yourself if the market does turn, but trying to capture that final upward tick before it heads lower is a fool's game. Wealthy traders don't do it, and neither should you.

9. Wealthy traders don't think of the market as "expensive" or "cheap"

Watch any business television channel for a while and you'll hear commentators refer to a stock or the oil market as looking "expensive" or "cheap" at given price levels. The vast majority of market participants will look at a stock and judge it to be "expensive" simply because it has had a long run to the upside. Twenty-five-cent call options that are far out of the money a week before expiration are "cheap" because the maximum you can lose is a quarter, right? Wealthy traders don't view price that way.

The only thing that matters to successful traders is this: is someone going to pay more or less for this stock five minutes from now, an hour from now, or a day from now, depending on their time frame? Google stock that is priced at $650 isn't expensive if someone is willing to pay $651 for it in thirty minutes. Likewise, penny stocks are great because you can buy a lot of shares in a small account, but is $2.00 really a good buy if tomorrow they are only worth $1.50?

Successful short-term traders who make their living buying and selling only care about being able to profit on a given security during its holding period. Leave the arguments about whether $150 oil is ridiculously overvalued in the context of the current political climate for the long-term investors and talking heads on TV. If I believe someone will be willing to buy oil futures at $505 in two hours, I'll buy $500 oil all day long.

There is no "cheap" or "expensive" in the eyes of a wealthy trader.

10. Wealthy traders are aggressive with size when they are doing well, and modest when they are not

Dennis Gartman is famous for telling traders, "Do more of what is working and less of what is not." It seems simplistic, but you'd be surprised how many traders try to make up for losses by simply doubling their share size while using the exact same strategy that resulted in their losses in the first place. They also fail to capitalize immediately on fast-gaining positions and instead anxiously sell their positions just when the wealthy trader would be doubling his or her position. Once again, the inexperienced trader does the exact opposite of what a wealthy trader would do.

Wealthy traders are masters of piling on huge size when they are trading well and feel like they are interpreting market data properly. They are also experts at dramatically reducing position size when they are not faring well in the markets. Instead of attempting to make up for losses by adding size, they quickly scale back to tiny positions until they are "reading" the market with more confidence.

Almost every wealthy trader I have interviewed has told me that just one or two trades a month make their month. Some have said that one or two trades a year make their year. Imagine the patience it must take to wait for those special trades every month or year. Wealthy traders possess that patience.

They are quick to recognize those "make-my-month" trades and quickly scale in with extra size once their initial positions show profits. They trade normal position size and make some, then lose some. But when those one or two trades come along that they feel very strongly about, they scale in big and with enormous confidence. They take "letting their winners run" to the extreme and are able to see that "great trade" materialize before their eyes.

This doesn't mean they throw their risk parameters out the window. On the contrary, their risk tolerance remains as disciplined as ever. But they realize that not taking advantage of the opportunity at hand can also cost them money. Knowing when those trades come along is a matter of experience and confidence in their trading system.

11. Wealthy traders realize the market will be open again tomorrow

One thing that always surprises me about new traders is that they often give themselves more grief for missing a trade than for taking a loss on a trade. It's absurd, really. They are more upset when their trading account remains flat than they are when it has decreased because they were in a trade that didn't work out as planned.

Wealthy traders understand that their job is not to be actively trading at all times, regardless of the market environment. Instead, their job is to wait for the *right* trades to come along and actively manage their positions during the *right* market environment. I see this a lot with traders who have quit their regular jobs to become full-time traders. If they sat in front of their monitors all day at any other job, they'd be branded as lazy or unproductive, and would probably get fired. Therefore, it's reasonable to think that if your job is trading, you must be trading at all times, right? Wrong. And experienced traders are fine "sitting on their hands" until the right trade presents itself.

It's easy to get caught up in the mindset that a certain trade is a once-in-a-lifetime opportunity that you can't afford to miss because there will never be another chance to capitalize on it. That's simply incorrect. There will always be another chance to buy an Apple at $110 or short a Netflix at $275. Perhaps the opportunity won't be in those stocks specifically, but the market will offer you another chance at a money-making trade. Relax and get ready for the next trade; it will happen. Don't beat yourself up when you miss what you think was a terrific trade. Rejoice in the fact that your trading account is stable and you didn't lose money forcing a trade that wasn't a winner. Another opportunity is just around the corner.

12. Wealthy traders *never* add to a losing position

This one really shouldn't need any explanation at all, but I will back it up with further commentary anyway.

If there is one thing that decimates trading accounts more than anything else, it's adding to losing positions or letting trades go beyond their stop losses. Wealthy traders do not add to a losing trade, period. They will often add to winning positions, however. Many traders do the exact opposite in order to "make up" for a losing trade they "just know" is going to turn around. Don't fall into this trap. Add to winners and be ruthlessly impatient with your losers (See Habit #1).

The only exception to this rule—and I hate to even mention it for fear it will give you an excuse to break the rule—is when experienced traders with *very large* accounts have a specific plan to build an enormous position for a longer-term trade in a particular security. Only then might they need to "leg in" to a position to get the full size in place even when their first entry is losing. And they will only do so if it has not hit their stop loss, of course.

For 99 percent of all retail traders, if you never add to a losing position, you will avoid the pitfall that has sent more full-time, at-home traders back to their day jobs than any other mistake. Remember Dennis Gartman's advice: "Do more of what is working ..." (only add to winners), "... and less of what is not" (never add to losers.)

13. Wealthy traders judge their trading success on anything but money

We are all in this game to make money and hopefully become wealthy doing what we love. Wealthy traders didn't get that way by trading for fun. Money is the end game and anyone who says otherwise is a fool. However, money corrupts our decision-making process because it is impossible to remove our emotions and desires for riches from the process of trading.

Wealthy traders know this and make anything other than money the goal of their trading. For example, one wealthy trader I spoke with judged his success by his ability to refrain from breaking a single one of his ten written rules, some of which may be in these twenty habits! He knew that if he didn't break his rules and made adherence to his rules the goal of each trading day, the money would simply follow as a by-product of strict discipline.

Traders who set a goal for themselves of making $100, $500, or $1,000 per day in the market are destined to overtrade and force bad trades in an effort to achieve that desire. Some days the markets just aren't willing to give you that profit. Your specific trading strategy just may not yield your daily goal every day, and you'll end up taking on more risk the following days to make up for it. That never works.

Instead, set goals for yourself that, if followed strictly, will result in dollars earned. Whatever the goal, no matter whether it is spotting a particular pattern while it is developing or getting solid entry prices for your trades, make it anything but money and the profits will come to you as a result.

14. Wealthy traders read about mobs, riots, and human psychology

There are hundreds of terrific trading books out there. (*Bloomberg Visual Guide to Candlestick Charting*, by Michael C. Thomsett [Bloomberg Press, 2012], is one that I'm reading at the moment.) Wealthy traders read them too and some may even write one themselves. But many of the wealthy traders I talked with realized early on in their trading careers that the markets are driven by human greed, fear, and panic—the same emotions that drive rioters to overturn cars and break store windows.

There are several excellent trading books that aren't actually about trading at all but nevertheless will give you insight into what drives human behavior in a variety of situations. One my favorites is *The Wisdom of Crowds*, by James Surowiecki (Doubleday, 2004). Another is *The Art of Strategy*, by Avinash Dixit and Barry Nalebuff (W. W. Norton & Company, 2008). And finally, a third book I recommend is *Markets, Mobs, and Mayhem*, by Robert Menschel (Wiley, 2002).

Books that address the basic premises of human nature will give you a new perspective on how supply and demand in any market move prices—and price is king. Some traders even insist that price, and only price, is what matters. News, technical analysis, and depth of market screens only serve to distract us from the only thing that truly matters to the markets: price action.

Whether you believe that or not, educate yourself on crowd mentality and you'll better understand how to profit from the madness of the markets. It's the secret trick that wealthy traders use to drain the accounts of less experienced traders by taking the other side of their trades.

15. Wealthy traders see themselves as market makers

They may not be "market makers" in the strictest sense of the term, but wealthy traders do one thing well that all official market makers do: they provide liquidity to the markets. In other words, they find ways to profit in the market by providing trading volume with their positions. This is a nuanced point and a bit confusing to understand, so let me use a few hypothetical examples to illustrate this point.

Let's say goat milk is the hot commodity at the grocery store. The local financial news network has stories from the grocery store about how goat milk is the most popular item being sold, and food blogs are all talking about the latest price movement in goat milk. You decide you want to be a part of the goat milk craze and head down to your local store. You make your way to the back of the store, open the refrigerator door, and grab two gallons of goat milk. You return to the front of the store and get in line with everyone else who has their carts loaded with goat milk, signifying that you are a newbie trader along with everyone else in line.

The wealthy trader hears about the goat milk craze and also takes a trip to the supermarket. But instead of heading to the refrigerator to buy goat's milk along with everyone else, he goes straight to the checkout line and taps the store employee on the shoulder. "Go ahead and take a break, I'll handle the register for a while." The wealthy trader then steps in to facilitate the goat's milk transactions and makes a market in goat's milk, profiting each time.

Do you see the difference? How about one more example.

In the United States, every year around the winter holiday season, there is a hot toy that every child wants. Parents go to extreme lengths to find and purchase the toy for their children, paying double or triple the normal price just to get the bright, shiny object for their loved ones. Not the wealthy trader.

The wealthy trader will go find two or three of the popular toys and negotiate with the seller to get the best price for the item. Instead of giving the toy to her children, she proceeds straight to eBay and lists the toy with a 50 percent markup from what she paid for it. She makes a market for that toy and provides liquidity to the parents desperate to buy it.

Wealthy traders have only a very slightly different outlook when it comes to trading, yet their unique perspective makes a huge difference in how they approach the markets and look for money-making trades.

Think like a market maker, not just a trader—wealthy traders do and so should you.

16. Wealthy traders practice reading the right side of a chart, not the left

It's easy to read the left side of the chart. Even a brand-new trader can spot the "head-and-shoulders" candlestick pattern that happened last month or last year. We can all quickly pick out the "bear flag" or "bull pennant" pattern long after it has occurred.

The trick is seeing those patterns as they are happening. The money is made trading that pattern while it is still developing, not two weeks later. Positioning yourself to profit from chart patterns is only possible if you become an expert at reading the right side of a chart—the part that isn't there yet.

I'm not saying that wealthy traders can predict the future. On the contrary, they see the same exact data you and I see. The difference is that wealthy traders are able to visualize the next bar and the next after that—before it prints on the chart. They see the chart patterns as they are forming and are able to position themselves in a trade ahead of a pattern's completion, and make money before everyone else catches on and dives into the markets.

Being able to spot chart patterns as they are developing in real time takes experience. You've got to watch charts develop for months, sometimes years, in the same security until you become familiar with the behavior of that security and can tell when a pattern is forming. You can achieve this level of acumen by visualizing where the next bar will print before it actually appears on the chart. Surprisingly, the more you do it for a specific stock, ETF, or index future, the better you will become at spotting chart patterns before your fellow market participants.

Make an effort to practice reading the right side of the chart, not the left. You can be the best left-side chart reader on the planet and it won't make you a penny. The right side of the chart is where all the money is waiting for you.

17. Wealthy traders have an "edge" in the market

In the movie *City Slickers*, Jack Palance's character, Curly, tells Billy Crystal's character, Mitch, that the secret to life is "one thing." When Mitch asks what it is, Curly says, "That's what you gotta figure out." Every wealthy trader has discovered what that "one thing" is for their own account. It's their "edge" in the markets. Without some sort of objective edge in the market, you are simply guessing, and guessing on your trades is not a long-term strategy. It may work occasionally and for short periods of time, but if you want to make trading a lifelong career, you must develop an edge.

What exactly is an edge? It is anything that you feel gives you a greater-than-50-percent chance of determining the future direction of price. If you ask 100 wealthy traders what their edge is, you will get 100 different answers. Most traders are constantly searching for the one "Holy Grail" trading strategy or system. And while the "Holy Grail" trading system does exist, it's not a one-size-fits-all approach to the markets. It's whatever you find works for you over time to give you a greater-than-50-percent chance of entering a winning trade every day.

One trader's edge may come from combining areas of support and resistance, represented by previous highs and lows on a chart. Another trader might get a leg up in the markets by combining the "Williams %R" indicator with trend lines drawn on weekly or monthly price charts. The point is, your "edge" is going to be unique to you because you have to be able to spot the best environment to apply your strategy to the market—and that's unique to everyone.

Some traders thrive in periods of high volatility, where earnings surprises rip a market up and down within a matter of hours. Other traders excel in slow and steady large-cap index ETFs, where the normal range per day is a few points. You have to find your "one thing" and capitalize on it with as much size as you can within your risk tolerance.

Without an edge, you are doomed to failure as a guessing trader.

18. Wealthy traders determine position size based on risk, not round numbers

I once asked a very wealthy trader how many shares of stock he bought at a time. He looked me straight in the eyes and said, "That's the dumbest question I've ever heard." After he saw the look on my face, he laughed and explained why. What he meant was that the question about position sizing was like asking wine connoisseurs what kind of wine they like. They will tell you that it depends entirely on what is being served for dinner. The question is incomplete and cannot be answered without more information.

Are you trading Google stock at $650 per share or Dean Foods stock at $13? Only then can wealthy traders tell you what their position size would be. This is because their position sizing is based entirely on their risk management parameters. They decide how much they are willing to risk in the trade and the volatility of the instrument, and then work their way backward to come up with the number of shares they will buy or sell.

The average trading range for higher-priced stocks is likely to be far larger than it is for a lower-priced stock. Therefore, the position size for a higher-priced stock will likely be much lower because the trader will have to endure more "wobble" in that stock. One thousand shares of Google is likely to have a much different volatility than one thousand shares of Dean Foods. Of course, you could place a $0.25 stop loss on your Google trade, but unless the trade immediately goes in your favor and never looks back, you'll likely be stopped out every time before the trade has time to work. Google is simply too volatile a stock to have a $0.25 stop on a regular basis.

Instead of automatically trading 500 shares every time they place a trade, wealthy traders calculate the amount of risk they are willing to take on and the average trading range of the instrument, and then they determine the position size based on those two factors. A nice round number sounds great in theory, but it can cause you to take on much more risk than you are able to absorb, or less than you should, thereby limiting your profits.

Experienced traders will likely have more complex formulas, but here's a simple starting formula you can use for position sizing: take the maximum percentage of your account that you are willing to risk, and divide it by the stop loss that will give the trade time to work.

Let's use nice, even numbers as an example. If your trading account is $10,000 and you are risking a maximum of 2 percent of your account on any single trade, your maximum loss would be $200. If your entry price is $10 and your stop loss is $9, you are risking $1 per share. Now, to use the position sizing formula, the number of shares we can purchase is equal to our maximum loss ($200) divided by our stop loss size ($1). You can therefore purchase 200 shares.

If the stock is less volatile and you feel you can tighten the stop to $0.50 without getting washed out before the trade has time to work, you could purchase 400 shares ($200 divided by $0.50). In either case, if the stock reaches our stop loss and we have to exit the trade, we know we're not going to lose more than 2 percent of our total trading account.

This may be an over-simplification for experienced traders with complex strategies, but for nearly all retail traders, it is an objective way to ensure that you are never taking on too much risk in any single trade. Wealthy traders do it and so should you.

You can find an online position-sizing calculator at http://oak.ucc.nau.edu/del/stockcalcs/sizer.aspx.

19. Wealthy traders buy strong markets and sell weak markets

Many traders have an obsession with finding turning points in the market. You'll hear traders on Twitter and on message boards constantly talking about "trading reversals" and finding "tops" and "bottoms." Yet print out a chart of any stock, ETF, index, or futures contract and grab a pencil. Humor me with this little experiment. Draw a vertical line just before and just after major reversals of direction, either up or down. Now, how much of that chart is made up of reversals and how much of it is made up of a one-directional trend? I'll bet that the majority of the chart—at least 80 percent—is in the area between the reversals and where the market is trending in one direction. So why do most traders try to make money in 20 percent of the chart? Wouldn't you rather try trading in the 80 percent of the chart that is trending in one direction?

Wealthy traders stopped trying to pick tops and bottoms long ago and instead focus on the 80 percent of the chart that make up the trends. If you find that more than 20 percent of a given chart consists of reversals or you can't even decide where to draw your vertical lines, you probably shouldn't be trading that instrument. Look for an easier chart to trade.

Wealthy traders stick to buying strong uptrends and selling strong downtrends. If you're struggling to make money as a trader, I'd suggest doing one thing: buy 52-week highs and sell short 52-week lows. I can assure you that those are probably much higher-probability trades than you are taking now. Stop looking for reversals at new highs and just trade along with the trend (using your proper position sizing according to your risk tolerance, of course) until that trend changes.

If wealthy traders are buying strong stocks and selling weak ones, why aren't you?

20. Wealthy traders play the reaction, not the news

You've seen it time and time again. A company beats earnings estimates heartily and shareholders are rewarded by a sudden move to the downside. Perhaps the good news wasn't good enough. Perhaps it had a nice run-up in earnings in anticipation of the good news and now traders are taking profits. Whatever the reason, it is extremely difficult to predict what the actual reaction to any news will be on a stock until the market shows you what it wants to do.

Wealthy traders know that trying to predict movement of any instrument based on the news affecting it is exceedingly difficult. However, trading the reaction to that news after the initial move is made is an effective strategy when combined with simple technical analysis.

Also, the initial reaction to any news is almost always an overreaction that fades in strength once the market snaps back. This may be one of the only times wealthy traders hunt for that turn, top, or bottom on a short-term trade.

Conclusion

Hopefully at least one or two of these habits of wealthy traders will resonate with you and you'll add them to your own trading rules. Make all of them habits of your own and you are much more likely to join the ranks of elite traders who make a nice living on their own terms in the market.

These are just a few of the habits that wealthy traders follow. I'm sure you can think of a few to add to this list. Traders who follow these and make them habits of their own give themselves the best chance of becoming wealthy themselves. Disregard them, and your path to success will be much longer and the value of your trading account will be much smaller.

Index

U

V

W, X, Y, Z

Printed in Great Britain
by Amazon

AMINAH'S WORLD

An activity book and
children's guide
about artist
Aminah Brenda Lynn
Robinson

BY CAROLE MILLER GENSHAFT

CMOA Columbus Museum of Art

COLUMBUS, OHIO

When she was just three years old, Brenda Lynn Robinson knew she wanted to be an artist. Even though her parents didn't call themselves "artists," they were. Brenda's father taught her how to make paper pulp from scraps, stomp out the water, dry the sheets in the sun, and sew the pages together to make books. Her mother taught her to do needlework and make colorful tablecloths by sewing hundreds of buttons on pieces of cloth.

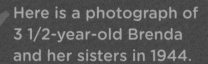

Here is a photograph of 3 1/2-year-old Brenda and her sisters in 1944.

Find Brenda and her younger sister Sharon and her older sister Sue.

Brenda painted this <u>self-portrait</u> when she was 10 years old.

This is one of many drawings the young artist made with <u>charcoal</u> and <u>pastel</u>. The dog was her prize for winning a Thanksgiving turkey-drawing contest sponsored by a local TV station.

Find the sketchpad Brenda always carried with her and her perky pet dog named Charcoal.

Brenda with her parents and sisters. She is seated on the step between her dad and mom.

Brenda lived with her family in Columbus, Ohio, in a newly built apartment complex called Poindexter Village. Everyone knew each other there and the adults helped raise all the children. Everyone was "family."

This is a photograph of Poindexter Village in the 1940s—probably when the neighborhood kids were in school!

Compare the black-and-white photograph of Poindexter Village with Brenda's painting of the same scene inside these pages.

THE PENETRATION GAME

One of the most important things Brenda learned from her father was how to do "penetrations." Her father taught her to "penetrate" a scene of a person or place by looking at it carefully to notice every detail. You can play this game with a family member or friend to test your skills of observation.

1. Close your eyes and describe what you see to your friend.

2. Open your eyes, and with your friend, look for things you missed.

3. Close your eyes again and say what you see now.

4. Keep trying until you cannot find anything to add.

Now let your friend try to test his or her skills of observation!

Brenda saw this girl with an umbrella on the street one day, and carefully observed every detail about her using the penetration method. When she returned home, she drew this portrait.

The artist used fine lines to create shading and add depth to the drawing. This technique is called <u>cross-hatching</u>.

MAKIN' SWEETSOAP IN THA

©1995 Aminah BRENDA LYNN ROBINSON   FolkLife in PoinDEXTER V

Every six months or so, Brenda's family made their own soap from bacon grease. They bought lilac or rose oil at the drugstore to make it smell sweet. They poured the mixture into a big tin pan, let it harden, and then cut it into pieces.

Brenda is sitting on her front stoop in a red dress in this painting.

Q:

What activity do you like doing with your family?

After Brenda graduated from high school, she went to the Columbus Art School (now the Columbus College of Art and Design). She also worked at the Columbus Public Library, which was located nearby.

Brenda used city directories and maps she found at the library to gather information about the old neighborhoods she had heard stories about from her elders. She combined this research with her own memories to create "Memory Maps" like the one inside these pages.

In 1974, Brenda and her son Sydney moved into the house that would become the artist's beloved home and studio for the rest of her life.

Brenda built some of her own furniture for the house, including this chair, which she entitled *Gift of Love*. She assembled this chair with wood and leather scraps she carved. She added hogmawg figures of her family. <u>Hogmawg</u> is a clay-like material Brenda made from mud, sticks, leaves, and glue.

Brenda carved crosses into the legs of the chair because the Christian religion was important to her. She also embedded music boxes to provide the comforting sound of gospel music.

Look for the crosses she carved on the legs of the chair.

EVERY DAY LIFE & HISTORY OF AFRO-AMERIKANS FEATURING COLUMBUS, OHIO

Q: What do you think she kept in the box on the side of the chair?

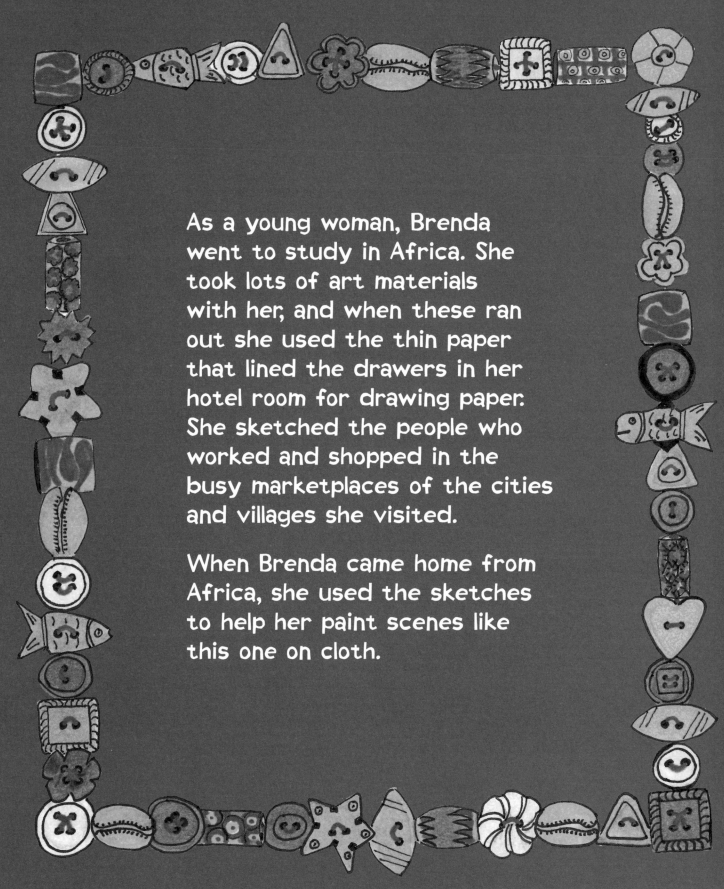

As a young woman, Brenda went to study in Africa. She took lots of art materials with her, and when these ran out she used the thin paper that lined the drawers in her hotel room for drawing paper. She sketched the people who worked and shopped in the busy marketplaces of the cities and villages she visited.

When Brenda came home from Africa, she used the sketches to help her paint scenes like this one on cloth.

Can you find someone holding a baby?
Taking a nap?
Driving a donkey cart?

During a trip to Egypt, a holy man gave Brenda the name "Aminah." The name means "trustworthy" in both <u>Arabic</u> and <u>Swahili</u>. She added it to the names her parents had given her to become Aminah Brenda Lynn Robinson.

Aminah Brenda Lynn Robinson

Q: Do you know what your name means and why it was given to you?

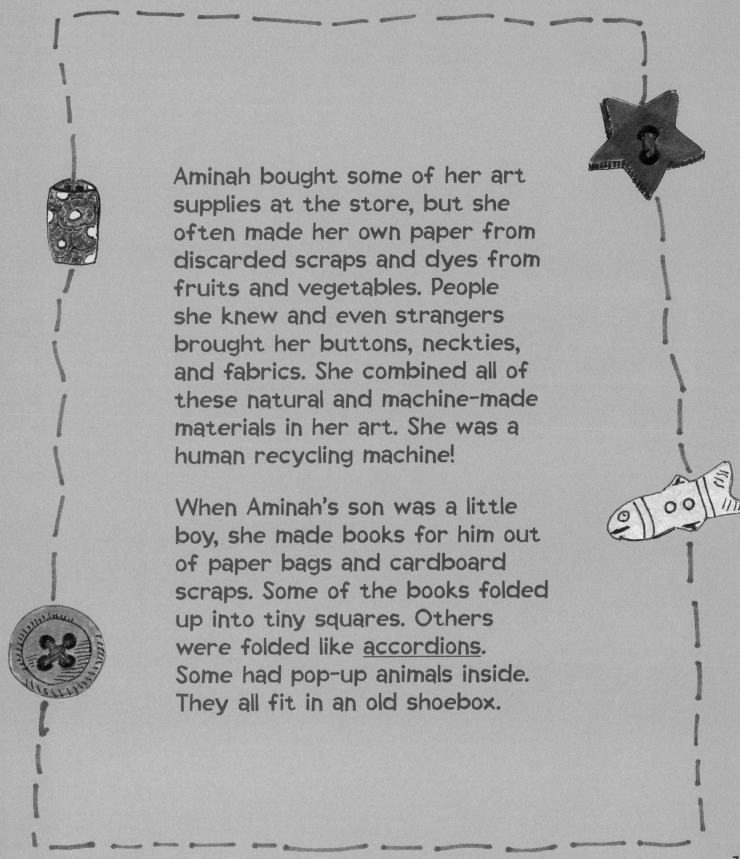

Aminah bought some of her art supplies at the store, but she often made her own paper from discarded scraps and dyes from fruits and vegetables. People she knew and even strangers brought her buttons, neckties, and fabrics. She combined all of these natural and machine-made materials in her art. She was a human recycling machine!

When Aminah's son was a little boy, she made books for him out of paper bags and cardboard scraps. Some of the books folded up into tiny squares. Others were folded like <u>accordions</u>. Some had pop-up animals inside. They all fit in an old shoebox.

31

AMINAH 1997

5-10

Book Edition 8

6-10

AMINAH
1997

Edition 8 6/10 page 1997 aminah robinson

Folk artist Elijah Pierce lived near Aminah and was a good friend of hers. Mr. Pierce worked as a barber in a shop around the corner from the art school Aminah attended and the Columbus Museum of Art, which she often visited. Mr. Pierce carved animals, Biblical stories, and folktales from wood in between cutting his customers' hair.

Aminah created this RagGonNon about Mr. Pierce's barber shop. "RagGonNon" is Aminah's word for a work of art that goes on and on, has layers of meaning, and is made from a variety of materials. Aminah believed a RagGonNon is never finished because each person who sees it has something to add to it.

Turn the page to see a detail of this RagGonNon.

Find a photograph of Elijah Pierce.

Search for Mr. Pierce giving someone a haircut. (Hint: Look for his yellow scissors.)

Search for the wind-up key to one of the music box workings Aminah embedded in this RagGonNon. (Hint: It is on red fabric in the upper-right-hand part of the RagGonNon.)

Find an American flag.

Aminah's work was inspired by the African concept of <u>Sankofa,</u> the need to remember and honor the past in order to move forward. Aminah's ancestors, like those of so many African Americans, were kidnapped in Africa and forced into slavery in the Americas.

 Look for the following natural and machine-made objects in this sculpture:

In this sculpture, Aminah honors the brave individuals in Columbus, Ohio, who helped escaped slaves on their journey to freedom in Canada in the 1800s. Those who helped escaped slaves seek freedom were known as <u>abolitionists</u> and were part of a system known as the <u>Underground Railroad</u>.

This sculpture is made with <u>hogmawg</u> and ordinary objects Aminah found and collected.

BUTTONS | CLOTHESPINS | BOTTLE CAPS | STICKS CLOTH SCRAPS | STRING | HOGMAWG

UNWRITTEN LOVE LETTERS

Much of Aminah's art reflects her strong belief in equal rights for all people, regardless of the color of their skin, nationality, or religion. She participated in the <u>Civil Rights</u> March on Washington in 1963 and later recorded her memory of hearing <u>Dr. Martin Luther King, Jr.</u> deliver his "I Have a Dream" speech.

Aminah carefully unfolded an envelope she received in the mail and used it as a surface for illustrating her memory of Dr. King and the March. She called this envelope art form "<u>Unwritten Love Letters</u>" and used it to memorialize many events and individuals.

FIGHTER FOR WOMEN'S RIGHTS SOJOURNER TRUTH

This *Unwritten Love Letter* celebrates the life of Sojourner Truth, an <u>abolitionist</u> and women's rights activist.

Aminah made this *Unwritten Love Letter* about one of her favorite writers, Alice Walker.

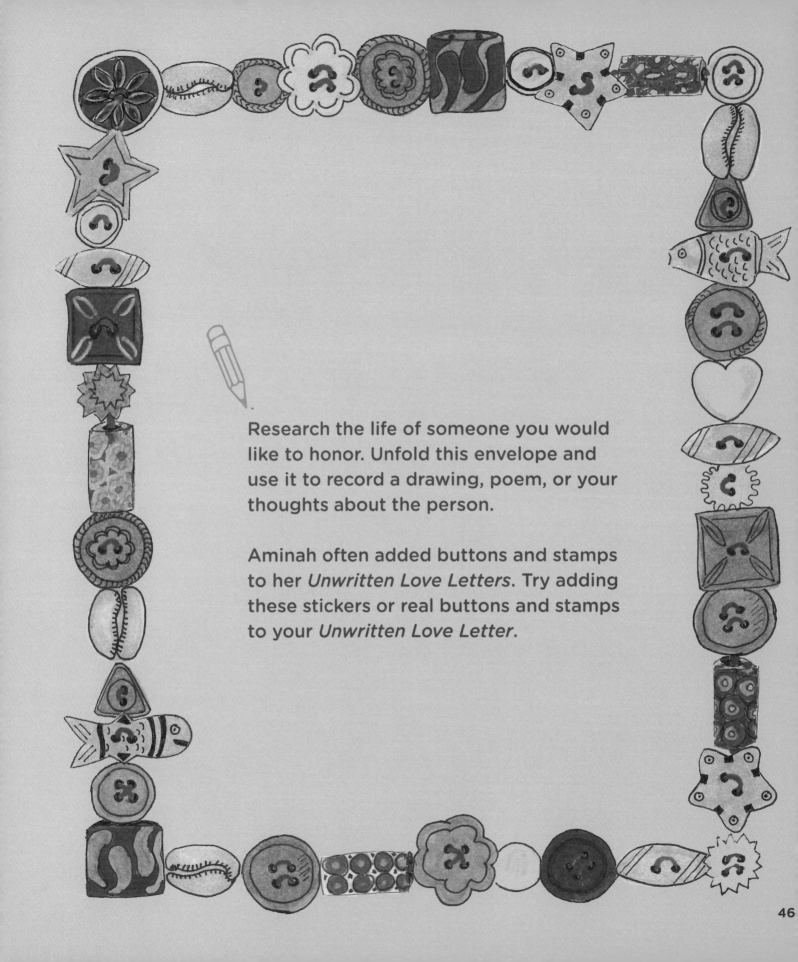

Research the life of someone you would like to honor. Unfold this envelope and use it to record a drawing, poem, or your thoughts about the person.

Aminah often added buttons and stamps to her *Unwritten Love Letters*. Try adding these stickers or real buttons and stamps to your *Unwritten Love Letter*.

Aminah loved to listen to African American <u>gospel music</u>. She associated these songs with the strong women who tried to keep their families together during slavery. She drew <u>portraits</u> like this one to <u>symbolize</u> the songs.

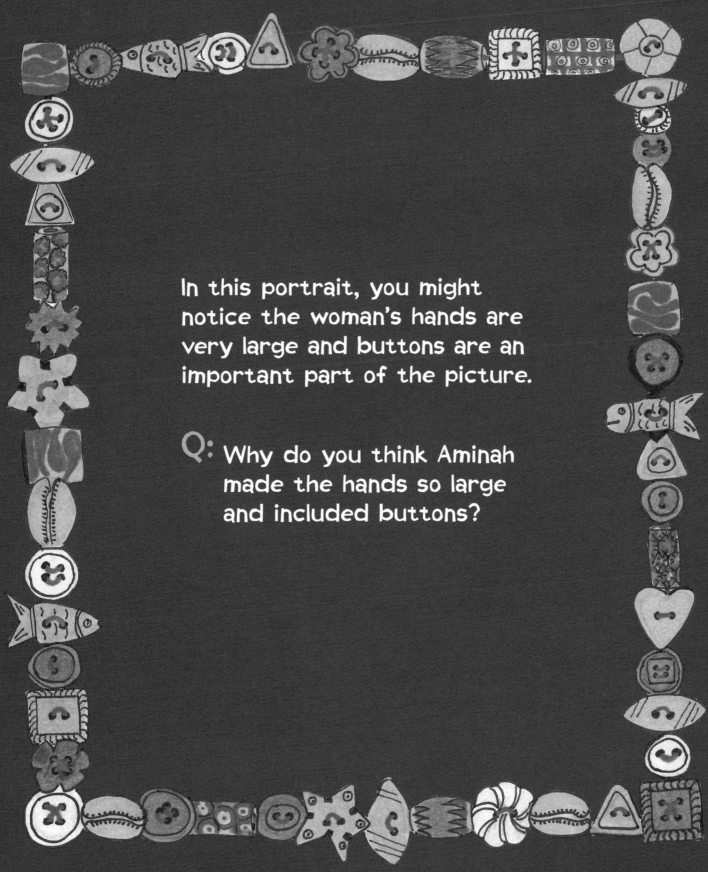

In this portrait, you might notice the woman's hands are very large and buttons are an important part of the picture.

Q: Why do you think Aminah made the hands so large and included buttons?

PRESIDENTIAL SUITE

In 2008, Aminah began working on a series about Barack Obama, who had just been elected the 44th President of the United States. This <u>collage</u> is a celebration of the Obama family as they walk in the Rose Garden at the White House. To make this collage, Aminah glued fabric and paper to her painting.

Button-beaded Folded Manuscript page
© 2007-2010 aminah Brenda L. Robinson

Find President Obama, First Lady Michelle Obama and her mother, daughters Malia and Sasha, and First Dog Bo.

Try making a collage about your family. First draw a picture of your family on paper. Cut out shapes and pictures from fabrics, magazines, and computer printouts and attach them to your picture with glue.

Bo, walking the First Family through the Rose Garden...

Book of Revelations: The Presidential Family and Community Suite

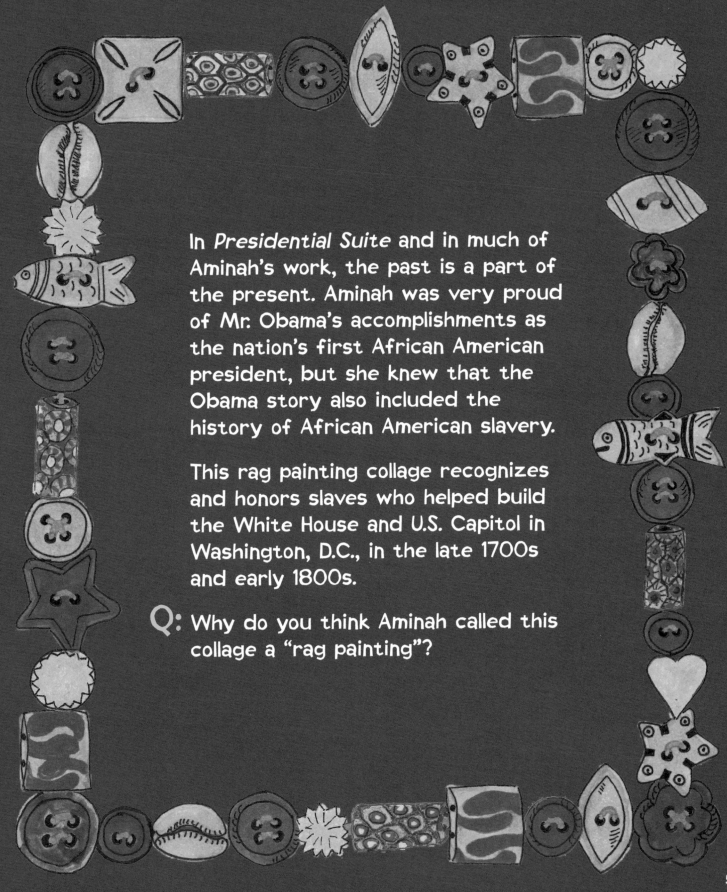

In *Presidential Suite* and in much of Aminah's work, the past is a part of the present. Aminah was very proud of Mr. Obama's accomplishments as the nation's first African American president, but she knew that the Obama story also included the history of African American slavery.

This rag painting collage recognizes and honors slaves who helped build the White House and U.S. Capitol in Washington, D.C., in the late 1700s and early 1800s.

Q: Why do you think Aminah called this collage a "rag painting"?

WING FOR OUR ANCESTORS
THE SLAVES WHO LABORED AND BUILT THE
NATION'S CAPITAL IN WASHINGTON D.C.
1793 — DURING THE CIVIL WAR

Aminah found information for much of her work in books and newspapers, but even more important to her were the conversations and art lessons she had with her Uncle Alvin and other elders.

You can learn from your elders, too!

Select an older relative to interview. Ask questions about his or her life and note the answers on the blank pages that follow. Here are some questions you might want to ask:

Where and when were you born?

What is your earliest memory?

What was your favorite toy and why?

What did you like most and least about school?

What words of advice do you have for young people?

Take the information you gather and create a drawing, poem, or story that you can share with others.

Until her death in 2015 at the age of 75, Aminah's goal was to remember, document, and honor the past through her art. Her message is for all of us to do the same in whatever creative form we choose and be sure to PASS IT ON!

GLOSSARY

Abolitionists
People who helped slaves seek freedom.

Accordion
Musical wind instrument having device with folds or bends; (adjective) having folds or bends.

Arabic
Language spoken throughout the Middle East and in much of North Africa.

Charcoal
Black crayon made of compressed, burned wood; also the name of Aminah's childhood dog.

Civil Rights
Rights of personal liberty guaranteed to U.S. citizens by the 13th and 14th amendments to the Constitution and by acts of Congress.

Collage
Two-dimensional art form made by gluing pieces of paper, cloth, wood, or other materials to a flat surface.

Cross-hatching
A series of lines that create shading in a drawing.

Folk artist
An artist who received no formal art training in school but learned to make art through traditions handed down from generation to generation.

Gospel music
A form of religious music that originated in the churches of black populations in the southern United States. Containing elements of jazz and blues, it often takes the form of a call and response between the preacher and the congregation.

Hogmawg
Aminah's term for a mixture of leaves, sticks, mud, clay and lime used in both two- and three-dimensional work.

Martin Luther King, Jr.
(1929–1968) was a Baptist minister and activist who was a leader in the Civil Rights Movement. He delivered a stirring "I Have a Dream" speech about freedom for all at the March on Washington, D.C., August 28, 1963, at the Lincoln Memorial.

Pastel
Crayon or stick made of powdered pigments (plant or animal substances of color).

Penetration
Observation of a scene, event, or person with great concentration and attention to every detail.

Portrait
Painting, drawing, or photograph of a person.

Rag painting
Type of art in which fabric scraps are attached to a drawing or painting like a collage.

RagGonNon
Aminah's term for a complex work of art that has many layers and often takes years to create.

Sankofa
African concept of understanding the past in order to move forward; the need to look back before advancing.

Self-portrait
Portrait of an artist created by the artist.

Soothsayer
Person supposedly able to foresee the future.

Swahili
Language spoken in much of East Africa.

Symbolize
To use something that stands for something else.

Underground Railroad
Network of secret routes and safe houses established in the United States during the early-to mid-19th century, and used by African American slaves to escape into free states and Canada with the aid of abolitionists who were sympathetic to their cause.

All art is by Aminah Brenda Lynn Robinson, American, 1940–2015, unless otherwise indicated.

FRONT COVER
Sunday Afternoon Art Lessons with Uncle Alvin, detail, 1983, paint on cloth, 67 x 37½ in. Collection of John D. Kennedy

PAGE 2
Unknown photographer, Aminah, Age 10, Columbus Museum of Art, Ohio: Estate of Aminah Brenda Lynn Robinson

PAGE 2
Unknown photographer, Aminah and her sisters, Columbus Museum of Art, Ohio: Estate of Aminah Brenda Lynn Robinson

PAGE 3
Untitled (Self-portrait), 1950, Watercolor on paper. Columbus Museum of Art, Ohio: Estate of Aminah Brenda Lynn Robinson

PAGE 4
Untitled (Self-portrait walking with dog and sketchbook), 1950. Charcoal and pastel on paper, 13 x 10 in. Columbus Museum of Art, Ohio: Gift of the Artist. 2014.050.007

PAGE 5
Unknown photographer, Robinson family at track meet, 1951, Columbus Museum of Art, Ohio: Estate of Aminah Brenda Lynn Robinson

PAGE 5
Chi Cho (Dog), charcoal on paper, 1950

PAGE 6-7
Unknown photographer, Poindexter Village, 1940s

PAGE 8-11
Sidewalks of Poindexter Village, 1999, watercolor on heavy paper, 30 x 109½ in. Columbus Museum of Art, Ohio: Estate of the Artist

PAGE 13
Poindexter Girl with Umbrella, 1971. Pen and ink and pastel on Pellon™ fabric, 37¾ x 25 in. Columbus Museum of Art, Ohio: Gift of the Artist. 2011.006.005

PAGE 14-15
Makin' Sweet Soap in the Backyard, 1995. Paint on cloth, 55 x 75 in. Private collection

PAGE 16 & 18-21
Mt. Vernon Avenue, South Side of the Street (Memory Map, Page Three), 1900–1957, and detail, 1989–92. RagGonNon: Paint on cloth with thread and buttons, 40 x 216 in. Columbus Museum of Art, Ohio: Gift of the Artist. 2009.035.005

PAGE 24
Carole Genshaft, Aminah in front of her home, 2006, Digital image

PAGE 25
Gift of Love, and detail, 1974–2002, Wood, hogmawg, mud, leather, music boxes, and found objects, 61 x 35 x 556 in. Columbus Museum of Art, Ohio: Gift of the Artist. 2008.2002

PAGE 27
Streets of Dakar, Senegal, 1980. Paint on cloth, 101 x 95 in. Columbus Museum of Art, Ohio: Gift of the Artist. 2014.050.040

PAGE 28
Kojo Kamau, American, 1940–2016. *Brenda Lynn Robinson demonstrating spinning*, detail, 1979. Gelatin silver print, 15¼ x 12⅛ in. Columbus Museum of Art, Ohio: Gift of Roy Gottlieb, DDS. 2015.035.008

PAGE 29
The Eyes of the People are the Spirit of Afrika, 1980. Pen and ink, graphite, and colored pencils with thread and beads on homemade paper, 15½ x 27 in. Private collection

PAGE 31
Sydney's Memorial, detail, 1967–2002, Button, beaded RagGonNon Music Box Pop-Up BoOk: Cloth, paper and paint, music boxes, and found objects, 33½ x 486 x 17½ in. Columbus Museum of Art: Estate of Aminah Brenda Lynn Robinson.

PAGE 32-33
Untitled (Costume Designs for Symphonic Poem), 1997. Woodcut, 28¹¹⁄₁₆ x 22⁷⁄₁₆ in. Columbus Museum of Art: Museum Purchase with funds donated by friends and colleagues of Dennison W. Griffth in honor of his distinguished service to the museum. 1998.010.005 and .006.

PAGE 38
Kojo Kamau, American, 1940–2016, *Elijah Pierce, The Woodcarver*, 1974, Gelatin silver print. Columbus Museum of Art, Ohio, Museum Purchase, Alfred L. Wilson Fund of the Columbus Foundation. 1989.008

PAGE 39 & 40-41
A Holy Place, and detail, 1984–93, Mixed media, 17 x 67½ in. Columbus Museum of Art, Ohio: Gift of the Artist in memory of her son Sydney Edward Robinson, 1967–94. 1993.005

PAGE 42-43
John T. Ward Transporting Fugitives in Columbus, Ohio, to Freedom, 1800s, 1982. Wood, hogmawg, and found objects, 24¼ x 63 x 30 in. Columbus Museum of Art, Ohio: Gift of JP Morgan Chase. 2007.016

PAGE 44
Unwritten Love Letter: March on Washington, 1989. Pen, ink, and pastel on hand-dyed envelope, 9⁹⁄₁₆ x 16⅜ in. Private collection

PAGE 45
Unwritten Love Letter: Sojourner Truth, 1988, Mixed media on hand-dyed envelope, Private collection

PAGE 45
Unwritten Love Letter: Alice Walker, 1989, Mixed media on hand-dyed envelope, Columbus Museum of Art, Ohio: estate of the Artist

PAGE 48
The Teachings (cover book illustration), 1992, pen, ink, and found objects on paper, 26 x 20 in. Columbus Museum of Art, Ohio: Gift of the Artist. 2014.050.024

PAGE 50-51
Presidential Suite: Bo Walking First Family Through the Rose Garden, 2007-10, Mixed media on heavy stock. Columbus Museum of Art, Ohio: Estate of the Artist

PAGE 53
Presidential Suite: Wing of Our Ancestor, 2007-10, Mixed media on heavy stock, 19 x 121 in. Columbus Museum of Art, Ohio: Estate of the Artist

PAGE 54
Sunday Afternoon Art Lessons with Uncle Alvin, 1983, Paint on cloth, 67 x 37½ in. Collection of John D. Kennedy

PAGE 55
Aminah, 2015, photograph courtesy of Hammond Harkins Galleries

BACK COVER
A Holy Place, detail, 1984-93, Mixed media, 17 x 67½ in. Columbus Museum of Art, Ohio: Gift of the Artist in memory of her son Sydney Edward Robinson, 1967-94. 1993.005

Published by
Columbus Museum of Art
480 East Broad Street
Columbus, Ohio, 43215

www.columbusmuseum.org

Designed by Erica Anderson
Printed by Galison/Mudpuppy

LCCN: 2017037313
ISBN: 978-0-918881-35-9

Library of Congress Cataloging-in-Publication Data

Names: Genshaft, Carole Miller, author.
Title: Aminah's world : an activity book and children's guide about artist
  Aminah Brenda Lynn Robinson / by Carole Miller Genshaft.
Description: Columbus, Ohio : Columbus Museum of Art, 2017. | Audience: Ages
  7-12. | Audience: Grades 4 to 6.
Identifiers: LCCN 2017037313 | ISBN 9780918881359 (hardcover)
Subjects: LCSH: Robinson, Aminah Brenda Lynn--Juvenile literature. | Creative
  activities and seat work.
Classification: LCC N6537.R5738 G46 2017 | DDC 371.3--dc23
LC record available at https://lccn.loc.gov/2017037313

Carole M. Genshaft is Curator-at-Large at the Columbus Museum of Art, where she has organized many exhibitions about the life and work of Aminah Brenda Lynn Robinson. Dr. Genshaft has been with the museum since 1984 and was Director of Education from 1996 until 2006. During that time, she developed the museum's first major interactive exhibition, *Eye Spy: Adventures in Art*. She received her undergraduate degree in art history from Syracuse University, a master's degree in library science from Case Western Reserve University, and her doctorate in art education from The Ohio State University.

Acknowledgments

Many thanks to Aminah Brenda Lynn Robinson for the many conversations during her lifetime that serve as the basis for this book. My appreciation to Columbus Museum of Art Executive Director Nannette V. Maciejunes for her encouragement and support and to the following readers who provided valued feedback: Eleanor Moss Berman, Jaden Dunn, Eli Genshaft, Lindsay Genshaft, Sophie Genshaft Bryan Moss, Tate Pedersen, Nicole Rome, Mitch Slevc, Toni Smith, and Carol Wilkerson. Special thanks to designer Erica Anderson for her devotion to this project. Thanks to the Ohio Arts Council, the Greater Columbus Arts Council, Nationwide Foundation, and the William C. and Naoma W. Denison, Frederic W. and Elizabeth E. Heimberger, Paul-Henri Bourguignon and Erika Bourguignon Fund for Visual Art, and Bette Wallach funds of The Columbus Foundation for their ongoing support of the Columbus Museum of Art.

References:

Symphonic Poem: The Art of Aminah Brenda Lynn Robinson (Columbus Museum of Art in association with Harry N. Abrams, Inc., Publishers, 2002)

Gilman, A. and Tannenbaum, B., *The Ragmud Collection: Books by Aminah Robinson* (Toledo Museum of Art, 2010)

To view more work by Aminah, visit:

www.columbusmuseum.org

www.aminahsworld.org